MOTOR TRUCKS OF AMERICA

First Edition
by James A. Wren and Genevieve J. Wren for
Motor Vehicle Manufacturers Association
of the United States, Inc.

The University of Michigan Press
Ann Arbor

Published in the United States of America by
The University of Michigan Press and simultaneously
in Rexdale, Canada, by John Wiley & Sons Canada, Limited
Manufactured in the United States of America

Library of Congress Cataloging in Publication Data

Wren, James A   1928–
    Motor trucks of America.

    Includes index.
    1. Motor-trucks, American—History.   I. Wren,
Genevieve J., 1928–   joint author.   II. Motor
Vehicle Manufacturers Association of the United States.
III. Title.
TL230.W73   388.34′4′0973   79-13986
ISBN 0-472-06313-8

Preface

Today the United States truck industry stands as a most significant contributor to America's economy, growth, and prosperity. Every facet of American life is touched by the versatile load-hauling utility of the truck. The industry employs over 14 million Americans and hauls three out of every four tons of our country's goods. Be it the needs of farming, business, construction, government, medicine, or just fun and travel, the truck serves those needs.

Although the story of the automobile is widely known, not as well known is the parallel development of the motor truck industry. That amazing success story is chronicled in the following pages.

In less than a hundred years, our trucking industry evolved into the world's industrial leader. Trucking played a vital role in transforming an agrarian land with few roads into the most progressive country on earth.

Each year's major milestones attempt to capture some of the industry's color, excitement, and economic impact. Statistical highlights showing facts and figures and brief biographical sketches of the outstanding truck pioneers are gathered in separate sections. The roll call lists hundreds of American trucks that have appeared through the years.

Few realize that the truck's beginning preceded the automobile. Motorized truck hauling began in the United States around 1890. In those pioneer years, hundreds of intent backyard mechanics were building motor vehicles including trucks.

Earlier accounts, however, detail two previous centuries of sputtering, steam-power-wheeled hauling attempts throughout the world.

In America in 1805, Oliver Evans produced what we now call *an amphibious truck.* It was a dredging barge on steam-powered wheels which also moved goods on the Philadelphia waterfront. In France in 1769, army engineer Nicholas Cugot harnessed steampower to drive a wheeled tractor to haul guns and cannon. It traveled only three miles per hour and had no steering or brakes, but it was capable of moving without animal muscle. And steam-powered carriages were in operation on England's roads during the first half of the nineteenth century.

Historians tend to trace the U.S. trucking industry's start to 1903 in New York when trucks were first tested and proved worthy to replace horse and wagon for carrying capacity, speed, and economy. Those test results stimulated motor truck use, and the manufacture of trucks sky-rocketed. Within five years, over 4,000 trucks were transporting goods of every type. Before another decade passed, production totaled 100,000 units. By 1920, production figures grew to over 1 million trucks. In 1978, almost 4 million trucks were sold in that single year and over 30 million trucks were registered.

Few of us realize how intimately our everyday living depends on the trucking industry. Trucks carry almost everything we eat, wear, or use. They are indispensible in building our homes. They carry emergency medical and fire fighting equipment. Thousands are used in specialized construction services, such as logging, mining, and oil drilling.

Motor truck history is as vast as it is diverse. The following chronological history can only provide highlights. We welcome information about events that may have been omitted and should be added to subsequent revisions, lest they be lost to history forever.

James Wren

Genevieve Wren

Acknowledgments

One of the pleasures in writing a book is that it provides an opportunity to publicly thank numerous friends and associates. Their valued insight, guidance, and encouragement as well as criticism made the project possible and enjoyable.

We are indebted first and foremost to friends and associates at the Motor Vehicle Manufacturers Association: Dr. William McLean was an early and earnest supporter. It was his urging and staunch effort that got the wheels rolling initially. Peter Griskivich endorsed the project and provided encouragement throughout. His critical reading of the manuscript and his comments are gratefully acknowledged. Lou Bridenstine gave his support at a crucial time and kept the project alive. Gena Falkowska was a tremendous help with the original draft, as were Karen Prymak, Dan Kirchner, and Ed Surant. Otto Merte lent his photographic expertise in capturing some of the critical pictorial highlights. Bernice Huffman assisted in obtaining historic MVMA photographs. Margaret Martin's and the late Jerry Boron's knowledge of truck history kept us in line when we started to stray. Fred Chapman offered valuable constructive assistance. Al Rothenberg obtained several key photographs. Jacques Evers offered his expertise with the statistical data. Bernice Baker compiled the statistical information in the Highlights. Jim Rose and Doris Maiert gave excellent production assistance. Chuck Witzke provided current photographs and photographic suggestions.

A number of automotive experts and individuals also contributed valued assistance. Space limitations prevent listing all participants, but we would be remiss if we did not at least thank the following individuals: John Conde, Curator of Transportation at the Henry Ford Museum, provided a number of excellent photographs as well as his encouragement and constructive criticism. Jim Bradley, Curator of the National Automotive History Collection at the Detroit Public Library, graciously gave his assistance and generous access to the historic and photographic collections files. Dr. Robert Lusk inspired our research in truck history and recognized the need for telling its story. George Hanley of GM added valuable comments. George Damman concurred with our pioneer selections. Jim Bibb and Jim Wagner critiqued with their constructive comments. Paul O. Sichert, Assistant to the Chairman, The Budd Company, provided biographical information on Edward Budd. Dana Corporation graciously gave biographical material on Charles Dana.

Photographs used in the book were primarily from the MVMA files and Otto Merte reproductions. However, several key historic photographs were contributed by Cummins Engine Company, Public Information Manager Ann C. Smith; Ford Archives, Henry Ford Museum, David Crippen; Fruehauf Corporation, Linda A. deRutter; Heil Company, Director of Advertising and Public Relations Paul D. Miller; Oshkosh Motor Truck, and Strick Corporation.

We also gratefully acknowledge the time and assistance provided by the public relations staffs of the MVMA member companies:

American Motors Corporation
Chevrolet Motor Division of General Motors
Chrysler Corporation
Duplex Truck Division of the Nolan Company
Ford Motor Company
Freightliner Corporation
GMC Truck and Coach Division of General Motors
International Harvester Company
Paccar, Incorporated
Walter Motor Truck Company
White Motor Corporation

Finally, our sincere thanks are extended to all the past and present writers who have recorded the colorful highlights of a vast and diverse industry. Our research included a number of excellent automotive reference works, including books, periodicals, technical papers, and advertising brochures. Early reference periodicals of primary importance were *Commercial Vehicle, Horseless Age,* and *Motor Truck.* We were fortunate that excellent trade journals such as *Commercial Car Journal, Fleet Owner,* and *Power Wagon/Trucking Business* have had long and continuous publication runs.

This chronicle is dedicated to the memory of: William L. Powlison who compiled the original AMA chronology; Christy Borth who was responsible for reviving and revising the original; Herbert Berggruen who had a great sense of history; Karen Decker who would have been pleased that her nurturing of the historic items was worthwhile after all.

Contents

Milestones

Before the Horseless Carriage
The concept of using engines on wheels to haul huge loads intrigued men for centuries. They tinkered with new power sources and toyed with their potentials—despite endless failures—until their persistence brought the dawning of a new age of energy.

As this age dawned, truck development began to parallel that of the automobile although it remained somewhat in the background.

Development was spurred by an avalanche of ideas for motor vehicles that swept across America. This flow of creative energy came shortly after the Europeans harnessed gasoline to wheels in the mid-eighties and, as one writer explained it, "kindled the flame of invention . . . that has burned with ever-increasing vigor up to the present."

As the promise of increased prosperity and an easier way of life through powered wagons became visible, the public's attitude changed: derision changed to lively interest. And the labor-saving, time-saving potentials of motorized wagons for economy and wealth began to excite industrial, commercial, and public interests alike.

The Eighteen Nineties

1895

Motorized Wheels Begin to Turn

The dawn of motorized transportation turned into an explosive happening around 1895 in America.

In that horse-and-buggy year, among burgeoning ranks of inventors from hundreds of home workshops in America, ingenious ideas began to evolve: moving wheels with steam, electricity, or gasoline. The inventors' goals were both practical and utilitarian: They wanted to lighten and speed up the endless work of moving goods, hauling crops, spreading lime, filling silos, or transporting people. The growing needs of our country demanded access to sparsely populated areas and cities that railroads and horse and buggies could not offer.

By September 1, 1895, the United States patent office overflowed with more than 500 applications for patents on vehicle motors alone. Between July and November of that year, no fewer than 300 types of motor vehicles were under construction—some destined to succeed and many to fail. This outpouring of American ingenuity offered an avalanche of enlightening ways to power, control, strengthen, and manufacture horseless vehicles.

Both electricity and steam initially gave gasoline engines stiff competition. But in 1895, electricity was elite for its magic cleanliness and silence.

Two early pioneers in electrical engineering, Henry Morris and Pedro Salom of Philadelphia, combined determination with inventiveness to become authorities in producing electric batteries and commercial vehicles. In an important *Times-Herald Contest* of 1895, their electric vehicle won a gold medal for superior craftsmanship in "absolute safety, elegance of design, cleanliness, simplicity of construction and control, economy of power, operation, and cost, ease of handling, and absence of noise, odor, heat, or vibration." When interviewed by *Motorcycle Maker and Dealer*, the conscientious pioneers said "the most practical application for our vehicle is for service as delivery wagons and cab carriages . . . and for their great magnitude in business possiblilites." They estimated construction costs at $600 to $800 for utility delivery wagons and

$1,200 to $1,500 for pleasure carriages. Their electric vehicles could attain a speed of 20 miles per hour on good roads and travel fifty to 100 miles on one charge, depending on speed and grades. The batteries in the winning vehicle weighed 160 pounds each. The motor weight was 300 pounds, for a total weight of 1,650 pounds—considerably lighter than their earlier experimental vehicle which had weighed 4,250 pounds. Their experimental delivery wagons had run several hundred miles over city streets and boulevards without mishap. Henry Timken, of Timken roller-bearing-axle-and-suspension fame, was one of the judges for their winning vehicle.

A cornerstone in vehicular progress, the *Chicago Times-Herald's* 52 1/2 mile race was run on a bitterly cold Thanksgiving Day. It was run on difficult, slushy wintery roads under adverse racing conditions so extreme that the entrants were challenged to the extreme. The race was won by J. Frank Duryea in a Duryea motor wagon, averaging 7 1/2 miles per hour.

George Westinghouse, inventor of air brakes for railway steam engines in Pittsburgh, Pennsylvania, began work on a gas engine for "the driving of dynamos" with economy and efficiency.

Production rights to produce the famous European Daimler gasoline motor vehicles in America were acquired by New York piano manufacturer, William Steinway. He built a factory, the Daimler Motor Company, at Steinway, Long Island, to produce 2 to 3 1/2 horsepower motor vehicles for commercial purposes.

Another piano manufacturer, George Schleicher of Stamford, Connecticut, constructed a motorized business wagon, featuring corrugated, stamped steel wheels. It was a heavy vehicle, its large rear wheels alone weighing 100 pounds each.

Using an internal gear drive with a 2-horsepower Daimler motor, Richard Steward of Pocantico Hills, New York, built an experimental commercial business vehicle.

Significant to delivery-and-passenger service was the use of two *gasoline* tricycles of two horsepower capacity for a mail route in California between Ukiah and Harris at an average speed of twelve miles per hour—a rapid pace for the poor country roads of that day. The gasoline-powered tricycles were also capable of carrying passengers.

A patent covering the major features of a gasoline automobile was granted to George B. Selden for a basic road vehicle. The United

States patent 549160 was initially applied for sixteen years earlier in 1879. Features of special significance were: an internal combustion engine of the 2-cycle type using hydrocarbon fuel, and a clutch or disconnecting device between the engine and the propelling wheels. Eventually, most manufacturers paid royalty fees for each vehicle manufactured that used Selden's concept. It later became one of the most famous patent suits in American history.

1896

Experimentation and Adaptation

Inspired by success and confident that their experiments in new energy could ease the burdens of hauling goods and expedite moving people, enlighted inventors increased their efforts.

In most instances, early entrepreneurs were self-taught, with an instinctive ability to handle tools and create machinery. Few pioneers had formal engineering training.

A self-propelled steam wagon for hauling furniture was ordered by a department store—Shepard and Company—in Providence, Rhode Island. This vehicle was energized with a steam boiler built with a 6-horsepower engine located under the wagon bed. Drive was by means of a side chain.

Two electric delivery wagons were built by the American Electric Vehicle Company of Chicago for Charles A. Stevens Brothers, a silk house in Chicago, Illinois. The manufacturer claimed that its forty-four storage batteries weighed only thirteen pounds each.

In 1896, Morris and Salom, pioneer electrical engineers and winners of gold medals for the craftsmanship of their vehicle in the *Times-Herald* Race of 1895, founded the Electric Carriage and Wagon Company to manufacture Hansom cabs. Fleets of their electric Hansom cabs were operating in Philadelphia by 1896 and in New York City the next year. These silent cabs were the first horseless carriages seen in operation by large numbers of the general public. They were an instant success.

A 10-horsepower kerosene motor was adapted to a buckboard for carrying excursion parties to resorts in the Portland area. It was built by C. S. Fairfield of Portland, Missouri.

The Langert Company of Philadelphia filed an entry for its gasoline delivery wagon in the Cosmopolitan Memorial Day Race in New York City.

1895   George B. Selden sitting in a model built to the specifications of his famous patent—America's first gasoline motor-vehicle patent. Designed to haul goods as well as carry passengers, it had front-wheel drive with a transverse engine.

1897   Electric delivery wagon built for Stevens and Brothers Silk House by the American Electric Company, both of Chicago, Illinois.

1897 Clean and elegant electric cabs were an immediate success on New York's Fifth Avenue.

1897   Hansom electric cabs were the first horseless carriages seen by the public when Morris and Salom started carriage cab services in New York and Philadelphia.

1898 The Best Automobile Train was used for hauling lumber and ore in California. The traction engine weighed 13 1/2 tons and could pull loads as heavy as 75 tons on the four trailers at speeds of 3 to 4 miles per hour.

1898 The first gasoline-powered truck manufactured by Winton. Eight others were built during the year.

1897

Electric Cabs Lead the Way

In 1897, electricity, with its quiet magiclike force, changed America's way of living. It provided the power for a surge of Hansom cabs in the cities, and quickly increased the number of transport wagons engaged by merchants.

Clean, quiet, odor-free elegance and easy operation were electricity's prime appeals. Electricity was ideal for short distances where cities already had roads. It was seriously considered as the solution to our nation's growing transportation needs if only battery weight could be lightened and range increased. Neither was an electric vehicle's unique potential for enhancing a dynamic company image overlooked by merchants. But delivery movement beyond the cities continued to be limited for reasons: our nation still lacked country roads, although trucks later helped produce those roads.

Electricity enjoyed almost instant success in the cities. After a mere four months of operation, electric Hansom service introduced to New York's Fifth Avenue on March 27, 1897, had carried 4,765 passengers and compiled 14,459 miles by twelve Hansom cabs in use. This was reported by its manufacturer, the Electric Carriage and Wagon Company of Philadelphia, founded by electrical pioneers Morris and Salom the previous year.

Two electric delivery wagons for silk merchants Charles A. Stevens and Brothers, which had been built the previous year by Morris and Salom's American Electric Vehicle Company of Chicago, were so successful that four more wagons of the same style were on order. Removal of a small control lever at the seat, normally used for reverse, prevented the theft of the vehicles.

Canada's first motor vehicle was an electric with lines similar to a Hansom cab, constructed in Toronto for F. B. Featherstonbaugh. Mounted on three pneumatic bicycle tires, the vehicle featured foot-operated brakes and a flexible transparent celluloid shield which could close the front of the vehicle.

Pittsburgh Motor Vehicle Company was incorporated October 2 with Louis S. Clarke as president. Its first vehicle was a motorized tricycle Model I.

Rudolph Diesel's invention of a Rational Heat Motor was described in *Zeitschrift des Vereines Deutscher Ingenieure,* July 10, 17, and 24, 1897.

1898

Gasoline Truck Debuts

Before the end of the century, America's first gasoline truck was in use. Despite an early start, truck development lagged far behind autos.

Winton Motor Vehicle Company of Cleveland introduced a gasoline-powered commercial delivery wagon. It had pneumatic tires, wire-spoked wheels, and a single cylinder horizontal engine. Eight more were being constructed, each weighing 1,325 pounds.

A 2-cylinder gasoline engine delivery wagon was introduced by Duryea Motor Company. It weighed 750 pounds. The company advertised that the two cylinders were independent of each other so that one could operate without the other if necessary. A deodorized gasoline was used to "obviate all odor in the exhaust."

Consolidated Ice Company of New York asked bids for converting 1,000 wagons to power-driven vehicles for ice delivery. A contract stipulation was that the power "must necessarily be free from heat and smell, for the heat would melt the ice and the odor would be absorbed by the ice."

An electric delivery wagon built on a framework of tubular steel was offered by Riker Electric Company of Brooklyn, New York. Batteries were arranged in crates so that the number of crates used was varied according to weight and capacity of the vehicle. It was claimed that distances from twenty-five to thirty miles at a nine-mile rate could be obtained on one charge of batteries. The storage battery had forty-eight cells, 100-ampere-hour capacity at 5-hour discharge rate, weighed 1,000 pounds, and occupied space under the front seat.

Gorham Manufacturing Company, silversmiths, purchased two Riker electric delivery wagons built to their own design.

Riker also designed an electric delivery wagon for the well-known dry goods house of B. Altman and Company of New York.

An experimental *Auto Buggy* was built by E. A. Johnston, an engineer with McCormick Harvester. The passenger-utility vehicle was operated on streets of Chicago as the prototype for International Harvester's *Auto Buggy*.

Pittsburgh Motor Company announced that, by substituting a suitable box for the seat, its phaeton model could be converted into a delivery vehicle.

A central plant facility was established by the Electric Vehicle Company at 1684 Broadway in New York City for the care and maintenance of the company's 100 electric Hansom cabs used in New York.

A motor vehicle liability insurance policy was issued to Dr. Truman Martin of Buffalo, New York. Coverage was from $5,000 to $10,000.

Henry Timken developed the Timken tapered roller bearings.

Best Manufacturing of San Leandro, California, built the first truck trailer.

A crude oil-burning tractor was designed to haul two trailer wagons at four to eight miles an hour.

1899

Motor Truck Industry Begins

The century ended on a winning note with the motor truck well on its way! Government interests joined merchants in purchasing and road-testing the new power that man's ingenuity offered. Hope to ease the drudgery of hauling goods was at hand. A new economy was starting to roll!

Experiments in collecting mail with motor vehicles were conducted in Buffalo, Cleveland, and Washington by the United States Post Office.

The U.S. Army purchased Woods's electric vehicles for assignments in general transportation.

Electric delivery wagons were put to use by large retail stores in New York and Boston.

Columbia Automobile Company introduced an electric emergency wagon built to accommodate a crew of four or five men. It was equipped with fire extinguishers, extension ladder, stretcher, lanterns, and a complete kit of linemen's tools and apparatus. The vehicle weighed 4,500 pounds and had a range of eighteen miles at a speed of ten miles per hour.

Fischer Equipment Company of Chicago delivered two heavy electric delivery wagons to the U.S. Signal Corps. The wagons had a range of thirty miles at an average speed of twelve miles per hour. The vehicles were fitted with attachments so horses could be used if necessary.

A police patrol wagon designed by Frank Fowler Loomis of Akron, Ohio, was put in service by the Akron police department in June 1899. The electric vehicle weighed 5,500 pounds and was powered by two 6-horsepower motors. Three brakes were provided. It had three speeds and could travel up to sixteen miles per hour.

Andrew Riker established a new plant for the Riker Electric Company at Elizabeth, New Jersey, to produce a full line of electric commercial delivery wagons and passenger vehicles. Riker's first big electric truck was proclaimed as the world's largest, a midget by today's standards. The truck platform measured fourteen feet long, six feet wide. When loaded, the truck carried six tons, the batteries accounting for 1 1/2 tons. Two 10-horsepower electric motors were geared directly to the rear wheels. Speed was five miles per hour when fully loaded. One charge of its batteries gave it a twenty mile radius of operation at an average cost of 3/4 cents per mile.

Pittsburgh Motor Vehicle Company made its first truck, and on August 28 adopted the name The Autocar Company.

One hundred Winton gasoline-powered delivery wagons were ordered by the Dr. Pierce Medical Company of Buffalo. List price was $1,200 each so that the total order represented $120,000. The wagons were to be used solely to distribute advertising circulars.

An electric cab in Boston demonstrated its capabilities by pulling a 17-ton load for nearly one mile.

Duryea Manufacturing Company, Peoria, Illinois, introduced a light delivery wagon powered by a 3-cylinder square gasoline engine. Cylinder and bores were 4 1/2 × 4 1/2 inches. A single lever in the center of the seat started, steered, changed speeds and stopped the wagon. Gross vehicle weight was 800 pounds.

Martin Payne, a wagonmaker of Troy, New York, applied gasoline motors to two delivery wagons for local merchants.

B. Altman and Company of New York ordered twelve gasoline trucks to add to their fleet of electric trucks.

A stable for renting, selling, and repairing motor vehicles was established by W. T. McCullough of Boston.

The American Motor Company of New York City opened a garage with "competent mechanics always on hand to make repairs when necessary."

Motor vehicle and driver licensing started in Chicago. Driver's fee was $3 for the first year and $1 for renewals.

Chicago authorized a Board of Examiners of Operators of Automobiles to ascertain the qualifications of persons seeking licenses.

Goodyear Tire and Rubber Company announced the sale of its solid rubber tire manufacturing facilities to concentrate on the manufacture of the newly patented pneumatic tires which featured a cushion of air in their membranes of rubber for a softer ride on rough roads.

The Nineteen Hundreds

1900

First New York Auto Show

As the century began, the culmination of close to a decade of developmental work on motor vehicles in the United States assembled for presentation to the public at the First National Auto Show of the Automobile Club of America held in New York City.

The show was held November 3 through 10 in Madison Square Garden, where thirty-five manufacturers of motor vehicles displayed over 200 vehicles and demonstrated others on an oval track in an amphitheatre.

On the roof of the building, the Mobile Company erected a 200-foot incline to demonstrate climbing ability of its vehicles and the skill of Joseph McDuffe who negotiated several turns and grades up to 35 percent.

The most prominent display of commercial vehicles was by Riker Electric which displayed, in addition to a "golf break," an electric street-railway repair wagon, a 20-passenger bus, a patrol wagon, and a delivery truck.

Some radical inventions were: Gasoline engines placed in the front of the vehicle under the hood for the first time by American makers; engine crankshafts positioned lengthwise in Columbia and Daimler delivery wagons; Rambler and Winton crankshafts positioned crosswise; round steering wheels, float-feed carburetors, and governors on ignitions.

Trucks were used to transport some of the vehicles to the auto show.

Five electric delivery wagons staged a quick-stop contest at the New York Auto Show. Driving 100 feet, the drivers stopped as quickly as possible. Stopping distances varied from 6 to 23 feet, and their times varied from 5 4/5 to 8 3/5 seconds.

The National Association of Automobile Manufacturers was formed.

People's Automobile Company of Cleveland introduced a 1-cylinder, gasoline-powered bus, the *Pioneer*. Transmission was by gears and chain.

Mack introduced its *first* vehicle—a gasoline-powered (4-cylinder-opposed-engine), 20-passenger bus which served for eight years as a bus. It was then converted to a truck and ran for nine more years.

Woods built an electric truck for piano delivery.

A **6-cylinder** gasoline engine vehicle was built by Max Grabowsky of Detroit and sold to the American Garment Company.

The Detroit Automobile Company provided a gasoline-powered delivery wagon for mail delivery tests in Detroit.

The White brothers introduced their first truck, a steam-powered light delivery truck.

Phoenix Motor Vehicle and Engine Company introduced a 2-cylinder gasoline engine delivery wagon with a capacity of 1,200 pounds.

Magnus Hendrickson built his first motor truck. It had wooden spoke wheels with steel bands for tires.

Four-wheel drive and a hydraulic clutch were featured by the Cunningham steam truck.

Municipal legislation grew as officials attempted to control the speed of motor vehicles. The majority of municipalities favored a six-mile-per-hour limit.

Many municipal park commissioners required motor vehicle users to display "license numbers in figures not less than two inches in height; and on the lamps of each vehicle, license numbers in figures not less than one inch in height."

The First International Automobile Exhibition and Tournament was held in Chicago. The reliability, flexibility, and simplicity of controlling a Chicago Gasoline Delivery Wagon was demonstrated by driving it up a grade of thirty degrees.

New York City acquired a motor-driven ambulance.

The New York Journal used six Electric Vehicle Wagons for newspaper delivery. Not to be outdone, the *New York World* ordered seven Woods Electric Wagons.

In Detroit, Henry Ford's newly established Detroit Auto Company completed its first commercial vehicle van: a gasoline-powered *Delivery Wagon.* It was sold to a Detroit shoe firm, Newcomb, Endicott and Company. Extensive use of aluminum contributed to a light vehicle for its time. Sporting an enclosed delivery top, its selling price was $1,000.

1901

Speed Limits Set as Traffic Grows

With America's appetite whetted toward speed to shorten travel time, legislation passed by the General Assembly of Connecticut ironically regulated the speed of motor vehicles to twelve miles per hour within city limits and fifteen miles per hour outside city limits.

Some cities like Saginaw, Michigan, restricted the speed of automobiles to six miles per hour, yet allowed bicycles to travel up to ten miles per hour.

New York began licensing motor vehicles at $1 per car. The revenue amounted to $950.

Electric Vehicle Company, owner of the Selden patent, threatened suits against automobile manufacturers not licensed by the firm.

Joseph W. Jones sold a vehicle speed-recording device actuated by a small friction wheel coming in contact with a flanged ring attached to a wheel. The cost: $15, including gearing.

Electric carriages met all Baltimore and Ohio trains upon their arrival in New York, Philadelphia, Washington, and Chicago. Information on rates, vehicles, and routes were distributed to passengers as the trains approached those cities.

Several railroads purchased gasoline commercial vehicles for short hauls and for service where no rail lines existed.

Three Hub-Motor electric buses were placed in operation in Chicago. The vehicles were manufactured by the Westinghouse Company, which had acquired rights to the patents of H. L. Irwin and Charles Berg. The buses seated twenty passengers inside the bus and twenty outside.

Delivery vehicles increased in size and, consequently, steering became difficult. This led owners to ask manufacturers to provide some method of power steering.

Milwaukee Automobile Company produced a steam truck, capable of hauling a 4,000-pound load. A light steam delivery wagon was also available.

The St. Louis Motor Carriage wagon was used by the Jesse French Piano and Organ Company for hauling. The delivery wagon weighed 3,600 pounds with a wagon bed of 12 × 5 feet.

The Baldwin Steam Delivery Wagon was introduced.

The Sturgis truck, manufactured in Los Angeles, featured a gasoline tank under the seat, a fuel pump and a 100-gallon water

tank under the platform with a circulating pump.
The White brothers built a 5-ton steam truck.
Autocar built its first shaft-driven automobile.
Heil Company began developing vehicle bodies in Milwaukee, Wisconsin.
Most manufacturers provided means for locking gasoline throttles, ignition switches, or other parts of vehicles to combat an auto theft problem.
Demand for anti-freeze solutions increased as motor vehicles were used in winter. There was also demand for heaters.
Service stations opened in eastern cities.
Overloading caused tire problems and the industry looked to dual wheels as a solution.
Sheet-metal bodies were used by several makers.
New three-wheel delivery vehicles were introduced by Duryea and Osborne.
The steering wheel had virtually ousted the tiller steering system.
A gasoline storage facility for direct service to motor vehicles became available at a storage and repair station in New York City. The bulk gasoline tank was outside the building for safety and connected to the basement by pipe. Gasoline could be dispensed by a self-measuring device, eliminating all handling and pouring of the inflammable fluid.

1902

Drivers and Maintenance Major Problems

Thirty-nine leading fleet operators in New York City were interviewed by the *Horseless Age* to determine "successful or unsuccessful commercial operation of automobile delivery wagons." Most users found their commercial delivery vehicles successful, doing more work than horses, although they cost more, and they served as a good advertisement on city streets. But a consensus revealed that: Commercial motor vehicles were still in the experimental stage; they had to be adapted to individual needs; operating personnel were a problem and would continue to be for some time until men were properly trained to drive vehicles and make minor repairs and adjustments en route; users had to have their own service stations to ensure best quality of maintenance and to keep costs down.

Most truck manufacturers offered free demonstrations to prospective buyers and provided demonstration drivers with the vehicles during delivery of merchandise.

Merchants found that the delivery of C.O.D. parcels posed a problem: drivers were kept waiting while purchasers tried on the merchandise for size or fit. The manufacturers were unable to keep drivers in winter because there were no heaters in the trucks.

Commerical motor vehicle users expressed interest in having manufacturers develop truck tractors with some detachable trailer combination. Principal advantage for this type of vehicle was to reduce idle time of the power unit while a trailer was being loaded and unloaded.

Max Grabowsky organized the Rapid Motor Company to build 1-cylinder gasoline-powered trucks. (In later years his company became a part of General Motors.)

International Harvester was organized through the merger of the McCormick Company, Deering, Plano, Milwaukee, plus Warder, Bushnell, and Glessner.

Fischer Company of Hoboken, New Jersey, developed "combination electric" vehicles which used electricity generated by a gasoline engine for propulsion.

The Locomobile became the first American gasoline car with a 4-cylinder, water-cooled, front-mounted engine.

Louis S. Clarke, of Autocar Company, designed porcelain spark plug insulation, and patented the double-reduction principle in rear axle construction.

Performance data compiled by a leading New York City department store gave the following performance data on its gasoline delivery wagon: During April, their vehicle traveled 1,431 miles, made 1,184 stops, consumed 142 1/4 gallons of gasoline. It did the work of six horses and two wagons, at a saving of $216 per month.

The Electric Vehicle Company was given the right by a court decision to make and use Sterling Elliott's steering knuckle.

In Indiana, the first Studebakers were built. They were electric passenger cars and trucks.

Packard was granted a patent on November 4 for a gearshift "H" slot, which later became standard for American automobiles.

Handbooks and instruction manuals were given out by automobile and parts manufacturers.

1903
Knox a Broadway Hit

On Broadway, May 20 and 21, in a contest of *commercial* vehicles, test trials were held before merchants to determine which trucks were dependable enough to replace horse and wagon for commercial purposes. With the press in full force and judges scrutinizing miniscule operating and cost details, eight manufacturers fielded eleven vehicles of which four were "heavies" running on steam. Included were six steam, four gasoline, one electric.

Five categories were tested: economy, reliability, durability, speed, and carrying capacity. The first day's competition was a nonstop speed run through the city, including the upward incline of a steep hill. The second day required 10 to 100 stops to simulate an ordinary business day's stops—a much truer test of their commercial abilities.

Most vehicles overheated. Knox became a "star." The success of the Knox air-cooled gasoline model over the steam trucks greatly boosted confidence in gasoline models. It provided the stimulus that thrust gasoline trucks ahead of steam and electric as a replacement for horse and wagon.

John Wanamaker, R. H. Macy and Company, and other leading department stores opened sales rooms for motor vehicles, passenger cars, and commercial vehicles.

The Peerless Company adopted a pressed-steel frame construction— one of the major technical improvements during the year. Three other manufacturers used the frame construction shortly afterwards.

Mack Brothers' "Manhattan" sight-seeing bus toured Brooklyn's Prospect Park. It was powered by a vertical 4-cylinder L-head gasoline engine with 60 horsepower.

Anheuser-Busch Brewing Company of St. Louis, Missouri, purchased twenty 5-ton trucks, based on the success of its two vehicles tested the previous year.

The Ford Motor Company was incorporated with a capitalization of $150,000 in stock, $100,000 issued, and $28,000 paid in cash. Henry Ford held 255 shares of the capital stock of the company, and was elected vice-president late in the year.

The Association of Licensed Automobile Manufacturers was organized to operate under the Selden patent of 1895 which featured the internal combustion engine using hydrocarbon fuel. Litigation was initiated against several manufacturers, one of which was Ford Motor Company, for infringement of the patent.

A power steering arrangement was used in a heavy-duty Columbia Electric motor truck. A separate electric motor furnished the power.

A power take-off was perfected by B. A. Gramm.

Other improvements in the year included: Automotive ignition "auxiliary spark gap"; air-cooled engines; pressed-steel frames with channel sections; antifriction bearings.

A honeycomb radiator was exhibited by Whitelock Coil Pipe Company of Hartford, Connecticut.

The Hoffman Automobile and Manufacturing Company of Cleveland, Ohio, announced its "general utility car" with a long body and wheel base. It was to be used for three purposes: a two-passenger car, a four-passenger car, or a small delivery car.

Fleet shop: The U.S. Express Company established complete automotive service in Columbus, Ohio, for all vehicles rather than restricting service to its own.

LaFrance merged with International Fire Engine, adopting a new name: The American LaFrance Fire Engine Company.

Clarence Spicer started making universal joints for the industry.

1904

Motor Trucks Outperform Horses

A test run conducted by an express company showed motor trucks made more deliveries in better time, went farther, and occupied less ground space than horses.

Pneumatic tires were used on passenger cars and very light trucks. The big trucks—up to 10-ton capacity—still used solid tires.

The use of dual wheels on a driving axle became a more general practice for medium-weight delivery wagons.

The Cudahy Packing, Anheuser-Busch Brewers, the U.S. Express, and the U.S. Post Office were but a few of the growing number of sizeable "fleet" operations.

Ford began production on a new commercial vehicle for the 1905 season, the model E delivery wagon with 2-cylinder engine which sold for $950.

1900 The first gasoline filling stations were portable.

1905 Cadillac offered a model F delivery truck with a 76-inch wheelbase. Priced at $950, it was available in maroon with black trimming.

21

1900   First electric ambulance in New York City.

1900   The first two White trucks, both light steamers, were built in 1900 and delivered to the Denver Dry Goods Company in 1901.

1903 Power steering was used on this Columbia 5-ton electric truck. A separate electric motor assisted the driver in turning the front wheels.

1904 Deliveries by horse versus truck were tested by the American Express Company. The results proved the truck's superiority and immediately affected scores of businesses.

1904 Rambler delivery wagon built by the Jeffery Company.

1904 Sturdy Oldsmobile truck sporting pneumatic tires moved the mail.

1905   The Manhattan—first bus built by the famous Mack Brothers.

1904   The first Diamond-T truck was introduced this year.

1905 The first Ford delivery car advertised reliability, durability, simplicity, and economy as its prime requisites. Based on the Ford model-C chassis, the car was equipped with posthorn, side oil lamps, and a tool box.

Ford Motor Company opened its first branch (on Jefferson Avenue, Detroit).

The first White bus appeared.

Max Grabowsky incorporated Rapid Motor Truck and built a factory in Pontiac, Michigan, to build gasoline-powered motor trucks.

Carl Graham Fisher and James A. Allison organized the Prest-O-Lite Company to perfect a safe method of using acetylene gas for automobile headlights.

Speed limits reached up to ten and twelve miles per hour.

Weed tire chains were introduced.

Oldsmobile offered a light delivery car.

A government study revealed that dirt surfaces covered most of our country's two million miles of roads.

The YMCA started a school for vehicle mechanics in Detroit.

The International Brotherhood of Teamsters was formed.

The shifting of sliding gears received much attention by many manufacturers in advertising. The Rodgers Company of Columbus stated in its *Imperial* literature: "Beyond question there is no slipping, it is absolutely positive." Marble Swift stated: "Two years' experience makes it safe for us to say now that five dollars will cover repairs on our transmission gear for five years." Despite manufacturers' claims, the inexperienced truck driver was ever audible in his clashing of gears.

Models such as the Moyea used double disc drives, doing away with transmission gears altogether.

This is the first year truck registrations were counted separately from automobile registrations. Trucks totaled 700, most were electric with steam vehicles running a close second.

1904   total production: 700.

1905

Famous Makes Join the Ranks

This year gave birth to many famous name makes in the truck industry: The Diamond-T Company was organized by C. A. Tilt; Dart began its long history as a custom truck builder; International Harvester introduced its high wheel model truck. Motor trucks were also introduced by established automobile makers, such as Packard, Oldsmobile, Maxwell, and Mitchell.

Nine electric and seven gasoline commercial cars were displayed at the New York Automobile Show.

The demand for commercial automobiles was strong. Many firms were building pleasure vehicles, but trucks were in short supply.

The Society of Automobile Engineers (SAE) was formed.

A universal complaint by most truck owners was that excessive oil dripped from their motor vehicles. The problem was more than a mere nuisance. In Washington, D.C., motor-vehicle operators whose vehicles dripped oil on the streets were taken to police court, fined five dollars, and warned that heavier fines would be levied if the offense was repeated.

Other states required licenses for all vehicles and would arrest and fine motorists even though they were out-of-state visitors.

In New York City two chauffeurs were arrested for speeding and sentenced to five days in jail.

A bill was introduced in the 59th Congress to regulate—by states—the operation of automobiles and *other* motor vehicles. The bill died in committee, but was the first attempt by the federal government to regulate motor vehicles.

The Sierra Railroad of California started a service using automobiles with flanged wheels on their tracks. The vehicles were under orders from the train dispatcher's office. Each vehicle could carry three passengers and was hired at the rate of a full train fare for each passenger plus a five dollar fee for the chauffeur's expenses.

Some states which required registration for motor vehicles exempted nonresidents from other states or municipalities. However, other states required registrations or limited the number of days nonresidents could drive their vehicles in the state. Missouri had one of the most notorious automotive laws. It required a license for each county in which the car was driven.

Knox manufactured an air-cooled model with a rated capacity of 6,000 pounds. Plans were also announced for a twenty-eight-passenger sight-seeing bus.

Many large firms ordered a quantity of motor trucks at one time rather than singly as had been the practice earlier.

Many "horse" fleets, by this time, included more than one truck. Using trucks successfully were department stores, municipalities, flour millers, hardware dealers, public utilities, express companies, and breweries.

Maxwell entered the truck field when it introduced a 3,000 pound model with a double-opposed 18-horsepower engine.

Newstadt Automobile Supply Company of St. Louis, Missouri, built a gasoline hose wagon for the Torrent Hose Company of Ithaca, New York.

Rollin White was awarded a gold medal at the St. Louis World's Fair for conspicuous, inventive skill in developing a steam truck.

Bus operations were started on New York's Fifth Avenue.

Truck use continued to grow and fleet operations increased. Anheuser-Busch Brewing Company of St. Louis, Missouri, boasted a fleet of thirty-five vehicles and intended to order more.

Brewers were some of the best customers of the truck industry, and one of the early industries to use motor trucks extensively.

Cadillac delivery wagons were used by rival newspapers in Harrisburg, Pennsylvania. They claimed average running costs of less than $3 a day.

Packard introduced several 2-cylinder trucks designed to carry a 3,000-pound load. One, a platform model, was 15 feet 4 inches long. The other enclosed model was 11 feet long, 5 feet wide, and 6 feet high.

A Fifth Avenue electric coach built by the General Electric Company and J. B. Brill Company featured a combination gasoline-electric system. A unique feature was an electric attachment that automatically showed a red sign in daylight hours and a red light at night whenever the vehicle stopped.

Diamond-T Motor Car Company of Chicago was formed.

The average wage for a truck driver in New York City was $20 a week as compared to the wagon drivers who earned $14 a week.

Mack advertised an automatic starter containing a "power spring, which imparts a number of revolutions to the engine without relieving the compression. The engine re-energizes the spring and disconnects it, ready for future use. The engine can still be started by hand, if so desired."

Census Bureau reported that electric heavy delivery wagons outnumbered the gasoline type by 109 to 55. Gasoline light delivery wagons outnumbered electrics 140 to 109. Average prices were: gasoline light delivery wagon, $1,542; electric light delivery, $2,161; gasoline heavy delivery, $3,072; electric heavy delivery, $4,201.

Commercial vehicle production increased to 750 units.

1906

Rough Roads Dictate Design

With many roads merely mud-channeled, stone-studded dirt paths, the deplorable condition of rough roads in America was a dominant factor in the design of early motor trucks. Structural strength and durability, along with ride and suspension equipment, were the foremost vehicle features. These were used to cope with the deep ruts and treacherous stones which could easily wreck a motorized vehicle, especially with weather changes. The component parts had to be big—to be big, they had to be heavy!

A tendency toward smaller load-capacity trucks developed as a solution to conquering road hazards.

Equalizer and supplementary spiral spring-and-cushion devices were used in conjunction with leaf springs to relieve tire stress and lessen vibration.

Twin tires on rear wheels were used by Hewitt.

The four-wheel drive and four-wheel steer electric truck by Couple Gear Freight Wheel was capable of moving directly sideways in the street, without first maneuvering forward or backward.

The Hewitt light delivery wagon had a sliding body which moved rearward about two feet on the frame to provide access to the motor. The engine was mounted on a separate frame for easy removal.

The Atlas truck—manufactured by Knox Motor Truck Company—also showed an unusual design: The water-cooled motor and transmission mechanism were grouped just in front of the rear axle on a coil-spring-suspended channel frame.

The Knox delivery wagon featured a separate, special angle steel frame for the engine to permit torsional movement without altering alignment of engine and transmission.

The White Company was incorporated as separate from The White Sewing Machine Company.

Engine governors were recommended to reduce speeding. Recording devices, such as the Monitor recorder, exhibited by Baldwin Chain and Manufacturing Company, made a permanent record of every stop, start, and speed in a day's run.

Fewer truck manufacturers made all the parts they used. Parts and component unit manufacturers produced parts of equally good or better quality, at better prices, and in greater quantity. Examples were, pressed steel frames, drop-forged axles, radiators, ignition devices, universal joints, brakes, ad infinitum.

Joseph Horne Company of Pittsburgh placed a competent mechanic with several assistants in charge of the fleet. The mechanics supervised repair jobs and instructed prospective drivers.

The diversified use of electric trucks was shown by New York Edison for thawing water mains, cleaning arc lamps, transport of men and equipment, lamp renewal, and tree trimming.

Most business fleets used both electric vehicles (for short hauls) and gasoline vehicles.

An electric street sprinkler was produced by Electric Vehicle Company for Hartford, Connecticut.

Gasoline trucks were admitted to New York docks and wharves, after investigation proved they did not endanger property or imperil insurance.

Autocar Equipment Company's 3-ton truck was fitted with a glass front running from the towboard to the top. Sand boxes were also fitted at the top of the rear wheels and operated by valves from the driver's seat to provide traction on ice and snow.

Biddle Murray's 3-ton model had a twenty-six-gallon gasoline tank with a four-gallon reserve equipment for emergencies.

Premier offered an air-cooled, 4-cylinder, transversely mounted engine on its delivery model.

The motor on the 3-ton model Hewitt was enclosed in a steel case which could be locked.

A distinct feature of Studebaker electric freight wagons was the location of a battery under the center of the frame. Its battery compartment was built integral with the frame.

Thermo siphon engine cooling was favored by commercial car users. Several makes used belt-driven fans for cooling systems.

The Giroux Consolidated Mines Company of Los Angeles, California, used a Thomas light truck with an armor-plated body to transport gold.

Magnus Hendrickson invented hollow-spoke wheels (which are still in use on most heavy duty trucks).

The 2-ton Pope gasoline truck featured a 3-speed transmission. Each speed was controlled by a magnetic clutch.

A caravan of White trucks was organized in Los Angeles by Walter

C. White and rushed to San Francisco to aid in relief operations following the catastrophic earthquake in that city. Help and supplies were rushed to victims of the stricken city.

New Jersey and Ohio were the first states to classify vehicles according to horse power.

Commercial vehicle production increased to 800 units.

1907

The Gasoline Age Arrives

For the first time, at the Grand Central Palace Auto Show in New York, commercial vehicles were shown on the first floor rather than a basement or an obscure corner of the exhibit hall.

The commercial vehicle section proved to be one of the centers of interest and for business transactions.

The show also was indicative of the trend in truck manufacturing as the majority of makes shown were gasoline powered. There were now more than four times as many manufacturers of gasoline trucks as there were of electric and steam-powered trucks. Although the electric truck was still favored for heavy hauling, gasoline power was closing ground rapidly.

Fleet operators requested that manufacturers develop interchangeable power plants to ease maintenance problems.

C. G. Strang of Brooklyn established a household moving van service with two 3-ton trucks and one 5-ton truck.

International Harvester Company built its first automotive vehicle in January, 1907, in Chicago: a 2-cylinder air-cooled engine powered the high-wheeled "Auto Wagon" designed for hauling farm produce. The truck plant was moved to Akron, Ohio, in October, 1907.

The Thomas Wagon, built in Vernon, New York, had an open-bed box body which was easily removable for repairs or inspection of the gas motor and chassis. The truck had a load capacity of three tons, wheelbase of 180 inches had a tread of 56 inches.

Loveless Transfer Company in Warren, Ohio, mounted a special closed bus body on a Packard truck chassis. A 4-cylinder gas engine was mounted above the front axle under the driver's seat.

A Reliance 3-ton truck was driven from Detroit to Chicago with a 2-ton load and four passengers in a demonstration coinciding with the Chicago Auto Show. The trip of 304 miles over frozen roads took thirty-three hours and forty-nine minutes of actual driving time, using fifty-eight gallons of gasoline at only thirteen cents a gallon.

National Cash Register Company in Dayton constructed a large brick garage to accommodate its growing fleet of six salesmen's cars, and four large trucks. The company employed three drivers for gasoline cars, four drivers for the electric trucks, a general maintenance manager, and two electricians. The drivers of the gasoline trucks repaired their own vehicles.

Autocar introduced a 2-ton truck with a shaft-driven axle and high maneuverability. Mud aprons were used under the engine.

The mechanical branch of Association of Licensed Auto Manufacturers developed spark plug construction standards.

Firestone introduced a demountable rim.

The Coppock 1-ton truck featured a 2-cylinder, 2-cycle engine mounted under the driver's seat with dual mufflers and transmission brakes.

The Sternberg Manufacturing Company was formed in West Allis, Wisconsin, to build trucks.

The city of Milwaukee, Wisconsin, used three Johnson Service Steam Wagons for mail collection.

Euclid as well as Sternberg entered the truck field.

E. R. Thomas Company introduced a taxicab with taximeter.

R. H. Macy and Company in New York City added fifteen electric delivery wagons to its fleet of delivery trucks. In 1903, Macy had originally purchased fifteen Columbia electric wagons.

The Torbensen truck featured a double-opposed, air-cooled engine mounted on a subframe pivoted on the main frame.

The Heil Company built a huge tank trailer of riveted construction with a 200-gallon fuel hauling capacity.

The Alden Sampson road train consisted of a tractor with a 4-cylinder engine and three trailers. The tractor and trailers each had six wheels, the center wheels were electrically driven from the tractor engine, which was geared to a direct current dynamo.

The first Commercial Vehicle Show in America was held in the Armory in Chicago, November 30 through December 7.

The Auto Transit Company in Philadelphia introduced a number of double-decker electric minibuses.

1907 production: 1,000 trucks.

1908

Traffic Jams Invite Regulation

Traffic congestion was such a problem in major cities that regulation was mandatory. Some New York City regulations were adopted. Traffic police directed traffic. Wagon and truck traffic was moved to right lanes, fast traffic to left lanes; limited parking and one-way streets were established; standard hand signals were established to indicate direction.

Autocar entered the commercial vehicle field with its type XVIII Autocar: 85-inch wheelbase, speeds from two to twenty-five miles per hour, and 2,000-pound pay load. A special feature was a double reduction gear on the rear axle. The company discontinued passenger car production to concentrate on 1 1/2-ton trucks of 97-inch wheelbase, with engines under the seats.

General Motors was organized and acquired the Rapid Motor Vehicle Company, maker of one of the first gasoline-powered commercial vehicles to appear in America, the Rapid motor truck. This year, GM also acquired the Reliance Motor Company in Owosso, Michigan.

Otto Zachow and William Besserdich of Clintonville, Wisconsin, developed a number of successful four-wheel-drive motor vehicles.

A Duplex four-wheel-drive truck had its first run, tested by Dolson Automobile Company.

Overland (Willys) trucks were introduced.

International Motor Car Company of Philadelphia built a front-drive motor truck.

The Commercial Car Manufacturers Association was formed with G. M. Weeks as president and Walter Wardrop as manager.

Among developments of the year: Marmon V-4 engine, self-sealing innertube tread design on tires, electric dynamometer, sleeve-valve engine, silent timing chains, baked enamel finishes.

Henry Ford designed his Model-T car, which was used extensively as a commercial vehicle and on farms.

Other noteworthy improvements of the year were: carburetor and manifold design reached new heights; one-piece manifold introduced; body design and construction considered vocational needs; control levers and foot pedals improved; fewer gadgets mounted on dash; body frames, especially for heavy-duty trucks, trussed for greater rigidity.

1906   Early Maxwell truck used to deliver an automobile.

1906   Popular with sightseeing tourists in New York City, these "rubber-neck" wagons provided visitors with their first ride in the new-fangled electric horseless carriage.

1907   First International Harvester high wheeler wagon with woodframe and hard rubber tires.

1908   Early GM cab-over-engine truck when right-hand drive and hard rubber tires were still in use.

1908   The Duplex Power Car—first road test demonstrated the practicality of 4-wheel drive.

1909   Reliance truck with Rapidmotor Company written on the body served to herald the joining of the two companies under the General Motors banner.

1909   Duplex model-A hauling truck.

1909 Early road-building attempts were almost futile. It took the truck to build our nation's roads and literally lift America out of the mud.

1909 First mile of concrete highway in U.S. was laid in Detroit on Woodward between Six and Seven Mile roads.

International Harvester developed overhead chain-drive camshafts for use with prototype vehicles.
Production increased over 1907 to 1500 trucks.

1909

Motor Truck Fleets Grow

The motor truck fleet concept continued to grow, as successful companies with trucks began to purchase additional models.

Not all experiences were successful. Many companies placed the vehicles in the hands of untrained drivers with no mechanical skills. The combination of reckless driving, poor roads, and inadequate maintenance soon ruined the vehicles. Companies such as the Smith and Sons Grocery in Detroit purchased fleets of trucks but seldom used them, selling them within a few months. Fortunately, this was overshadowed by growing success of numerous fleets.

Truck production gained momentum in pace with this growing demand. Production in 1909 doubled over the preceding year.

The Anheuser-Busch Brewing Association continued to maintain a large fleet of motor wagons. For the past five years, the company had operated a fleet of forty to fifty vehicles. This year the total number was over fifty with twenty trucks of 5-ton capacity. Maintenance was stressed.

The H. C. Piercy Company, a delivery firm for eighty New York merchandising houses, ordered twenty-five Studebaker electric delivery trucks to replace 300 horses and 200 wagons.

Numerous taxi companies were organized, primarily in larger cities.

The Aeolian Company, a New York piano and organ manufacturer, announced that, after four years of testing, the firm would use motor vehicles exclusively for delivery. Eight Studebaker electric and three Sauer gasoline trucks were ordered.

The New York *Herald* and the *Evening Telegraph* purchased a fleet of Renault trucks to distribute newspapers.

Max Grabowsky's Rapid Motor Vehicle Company joined General Motors.

Motor mail service started in New York City. The Motor Delivery Company used fourteen electric motor trucks provided by General Vehicle Company for the service. The schedule called for 162 weekly trips and 577 miles daily. Mail service had been operating successfully in Milwaukee for the past two years and in Detroit and Indianapolis for shorter periods.

Marshall Field and Company established a motor truck service between Chicago and its western suburbs.

Judge Hough of the U.S. Circuit Court for the Southern District of New York held that the Selden patent was valid and covered the modern gasoline automobile.

The Hackett Motor Car Company of New York was typical of growing interurban businesses. Starting in 1907 with only one truck, the company expanded to ten trucks within 2 1/2 years. It serviced a 17 1/2-mile route. The trucks were all Mack Manhattans: seven 5-ton trucks, two 3-ton trucks, and one 2-ton truck.

The Adams Express Company had fourteen Packard trucks.

Gas-electric trucks increased in number. Typical of the "mixed system drive" was the Couple Gear Freight Wheel truck, with electric drive powered by an internal combustion engine. The engine drove a generator to provide current for electric motors in each wheel.

The Randolph 4-ton truck had two large radiators in side panels under the driver's seat. Water was circulated by a large centrifugal pump.

An increasing number of motor vehicles were sold to fire departments for pumping engines. The movement paralleled the growing use of motorized police patrol wagons and ambulances.

New York City introduced a Knox combination hose-carrying and turret pipe fire truck. The truck was a regular 5-ton commercial model fitted with a steel-sided body and wood-covered slate floor. The turret pipe issued a 3-inch stream of water. Hoses were connected to a new high-pressure water system in the city.

The Manly hydraulic transmission was introduced by Manly Drive Company. An engine-driven pump sent oil to two oil motors which drove rear wheels through chains and sprockets. The oil flow could be reversed for backward motion.

Two Franklin light motor trucks driving side-by-side hauled a 2-ton box measuring 15 × 8 feet.

An automobile stage line was operated from Fairbanks, Alaska, to the mining camps 100 miles north. The motor vehicles used were White Steamers.

The Sternberg truck demonstrated a motor truck's ability to negotiate snow-covered roads with a full load. Starting from its home base in Milwaukee, the Sternberg traveled over 100 miles to Chicago on snow covered, deeply rutted, frozen roads. The trip took seven hours and forty minutes, used twelve gallons of gasoline, and two quarts of oil.

At the New York Show, 91 percent of the engines were of the 4-cycle type; 64 percent were 4 cylinder; 36 percent, 2 cylinder. Most had chain drive. Vehicles above one ton had solid tires, and all vehicles had two sets of brakes.

The use of pneumatic tires on trucks—until now considered impractical—grew. Use on vehicles up to 1 1/2 tons was noted.

The first rural mile of concrete pavement in the United States opened July 4 outside Detroit, Michigan. The pavement was constructed on Woodward Avenue (now U.S. 10) between Six Mile and Seven Mile roads, at a cost of $13,534.59.

The Ford Roadster model, which retailed at $385, was the basis for many trucks. For an additional $385, numerous companies, such as Form-A-Truck, furnished an assembly consisting of half-a-frame, two solid tire wheels on a solid axle, sprockets, and chain. The owner removed the turtle-back of the roadster, slipped the truck frame over it, pulled the housing up to the underside of the frame, installed the two sprockets to serve as a jack shaft, attached the chain and his Ford truck was ready for business.

Hewitt built a 10-ton 4-cylinder truck with planetary transmission and a case-hardened crankshaft.

Gramm trucks featured overdrive transmissions.

Kelsey-Hayes Company was founded.

Duplex Power Car Company became the new truck nameplate which replaced Dolson Automobile Company.

A number of devices and accessories were exhibited at the shows. The most outstanding was a whistle warning device to indicate when gasoline tanks were filled. A. R. Mosler and Company displayed a novel signaling device—a combination of stop light, slow signal, and arrows for turn signals.

A new feature was a steering wheel with a corrugated underside for a better grip.

Production in 1909 totaled: 3,297 trucks.

The Tens

1910

Ease of Maintenance a Must

The commercial vehicle appealed to business interests primarily as a time-and-labor-saving device to increase earnings. Consequently, radical changes and designs were not as evident in trucks as in the passenger cars.

There were innovations, but the major emphasis was to keep trucks in constant use. Ease of maintenance, sturdiness, and dependability therefore dominated truck interest.

Autocar offered a school for driving, repair, and maintenance for buyers' drivers to help sell vehicles. Prospective buyers feared placing valuable equipment in inexperienced hands.

This was the first year the truck industry had its own show.

The American Locomotive 4-ton model located its 4-cylinder engine under the driver's seat on a subframe to allow quick removal of the engine. The radiator and gasoline tank were mounted on flexible springs for easy removal.

The Autocar truck featured a hinged seat and hood that could be raised above the fuel tank to expose the engine. The engine was mounted with the transmission and could be removed as a unit or separately.

A factory maintenance contract was offered by Rapid. Trucks could be garaged and maintained for $20 to $35.

Four Wheel Drive Auto Company, Clintonville, Wisconsin, began manufacturing four-wheel-drive vehicles.

Reo announced its Speed Wagon, a low-priced light delivery truck.

The Grabowsky Power Wagon arranged its power plant on a front steel frame that slid onto the chassis frame, so that engine and transmission could be drawn forward for inspection, repair or, if desired, be completely removed and quickly replaced by another engine. The front end of the frame was hinged.

Hewitt gas trucks offered an optional fuel system; trucks could run on alcohol for use on piers or wherever gasoline was forbidden.

The Alden-Sampson truck enclosed drive chains in oil-tight steel cases. A differential interlock enabled both wheels to lock together if one lost traction or if the chain broke.

The White Company introduced its first gasoline truck, a 3-ton model.

The Merchant delivery wagon had a special engine cradle flexibly mounted on a frame support attached by six bolts. The 2-cylinder, water-cooled engine could be removed in thirty minutes.

The engine of the Templeton-DuBrie truck was a 2-cycle, 2-cylinder, water-cooled 20-horsepower model. The cylinders were cast en bloc and the bores had two diameters: the explosion chamber was 4 1/2 inches, the compression chamber was 6 inches.

The Couple Gear Company converted a horse-drawn ambulance into a gas-electric model for the American Society for the Prevention of Cruelty to Animals.

Street commissioners in Boston permitted operation of a Couple Gear truck and trailer. Each could haul five tons. The permit was for thirty days, pending a demonstration.

The Willys 800-pound gasoline motor wagon featured a pedal-controlled planetary change-speed mechanism.

Mack adopted the Bulldog crest trademark.

A Studebaker electric was designed to haul automobiles, carriages, or wagons. The body platform was built on a slight incline with a tail gate or ramp section on the end. A special electric hoist under the driver's seat pulled the car abroad.

The first 100 percent truck fleet was created as Gimbels changed its delivery system to 88 motor vehicles in conjunction with the opening of a new store on Sixth Avenue in New York City.

Motor moving van service increased in New York. City dwellers moved to permanent country homes in spring and back to the city in fall.

Gasoline was delivered by truck in New York.

Heavy steam trucks were no longer being produced.

Franklin and Motorette offered light delivery trucks.

Central Oil Company built what may have been the first drive-in gasoline station in Detroit.

The Fischer gas-electric 1902 model was said to be the largest truck still in daily service. It carried nearly nine tons.

G. A. Schact produced a complete line of trucks, from a 1,000-pound delivery unit to a 3-ton chain-drive chassis.

The American Standard truck featured four-wheel drive, a two-cycle engine, and chain drive to front and rear axle, both of which were turned by a fifth wheel.

International Harvester changed the name of its Auto Wagon to International.

John Wanamaker stores in New York and Philadelphia used special removable inner bodies or crates on rollers on their 3-ton Packard trucks. The cargo could be loaded in the store and then onto the trucks. Wanamaker claimed this kept their trucks on the road rather than waiting at the loading docks.

Mack produced a truck for hauling milk.

American LaFrance introduced its fire engine.

Federal Motor of Detroit introduced a 1 1/2-ton truck with a 4-cylinder continental engine.

1910   production doubled over last year: 6,000 units

1911
Selden Patent's End Stimulates Industry

This year marked a turning point in industry, *especially for gasoline motor trucks,* as involvement with the Selden patent ended!

The U.S. Circuit Court of Appeals in New York held that, although the Selden patent of 1895 was valid, it was not being infringed on by manufacturers, thus ending the payment of royalties that had disrupted the early industry. The Selden patent had been in litigation eight years, since 1903.

The Selden patent covered vehicles with Brayton 2-cycle internal combustion engines using hydrocarbon fuel, plus a clutch or disconnecting device between the engines and propelling wheels. Most vehicles used the 4-cycle Otto engines.

Even though the Selden patent had only one year more to run, to be free of royalty payment and license restrictions was a boon to vehicle manufacturers.

While production had doubled in several of the preceding four years, just one year of royalty-free production was significant to the industry. Design and engineering changes that year were indicative of new enthusiasm, producing a newsworthy year for motor truck developments.

The first National Truck Show in Madison Square Garden featured 286 exhibitors, 27 of whom showed gasoline trucks; 7 displayed electric trucks. Eighteen were motorcycle exhibits.

The first transcontinental motor truck trip was made by a Sauer truck. The tour started March 4 from Denver, drove to Los

Angeles and then to San Francisco. The truck was shipped by rail to Pueblo, Colorado, to begin the trip to New York June 12 under its own power.

General Motors Truck Company was formed in Pontiac, Michigan, consolidating Rapid Motor and Reliance Truck companies.

General Motors Trucks made its debut by announcing it would manufacture electric trucks.

An electric self-starter was invented by Charles Kettering of the Dayton Engineering Laboratories Company (DELCO). His *Delco* device to replace hand cranking was watched by truck interests who had been experimenting with similar devices, using compressed air, electric, explosive gas, and numerous energy sources.

International Motors was formed by consolidating Mack, Sauer, and Hewitt companies.

Studebaker switched to gasoline and dropped electric vehicles.

Pierce Arrow began making 5-ton trucks.

Center lines were painted on highways in Michigan's Wayne County.

The Society of Automotive Engineers persisted in its efforts toward standardization. Eventually, standardization provided the means to make United States automotive industry production world renowned.

SAE recommended standard dimensions for solid tires.

Unit power plants with quick removable features grew in popularity.

For easy lumber loading, the Reliance truck used special floating rollers and rear lever control.

Knox offered a dump truck for coal delivery with a hoist operated either by hand or motor. Side and rear panels allowed it to be converted to a two-ton to seven-ton stake truck.

Remington and LaFrance heavy-duty truck used a Manly hydraulic transmission.

Pope Hartford Truck featured a gear-driven cooling pump and double belt-driven cooling fans.

The Walter Auto Company of New Jersey switched from manufacturing cars to heavy-duty trucks. It was renamed the Walter Motor Company.

Lauth-Juergens built its first tilt-cab model truck.

White added a gasoline-powered taxi to its line of vehicles.

Large truck installations had trouble obtaining and holding efficient drivers.

Atlantic City, New Jersey, had exclusive motor truck mail service. **For each** pleasure horse, it was estimated that nine others were used for work. With approximately 400,000 pleasure cars already in use, the need and potential for commercial vehicles was obvious.

Diamond-T concentrated on motor trucks and discontinued passenger cars.

Trucks got into snow removal. A 7-ton Mack dump truck with snow plow attachment made news as it cleaned up New York streets after a snow storm.

Five hundred trucks were viewed in Philadelphia's commercial car parade.

With truck breakdowns on bad roads a major problem, Autocar Service Department established a "Relief Service on Wheels" for immediate repair service, available day or night. Each of the company's three branches outfitted maintenance and repair wagons with tools, spare axles, heavy duty vices, and devices to pull a truck out of a ditch.

C. W. Jones, of speedometer fame, sold an instrument to register all vehicle movements, so owners could tally the speeds, the times the vehicles were in actual service, times stopped, and the like, to coordinate routing.

A fleet of seven Packard gasoline patrol wagons was introduced by the Detroit Police Department. The trucks replaced thirty-six horses and ten wagons.

Gimbels used a fleet of 100 Studebaker electric delivery vehicles.

The *Chicago Evening American* sponsored a nine-day reliability run from Detroit to Chicago and back. The 756-mile distance was successfully completed by twenty-five of the twenty-six entries. The trucks were fully loaded.

Estimates placed over 20,000 commercial vehicles in use in the United States. New York City alone had 2,500.

Production climbed sharply again: 10,681 trucks and buses.

1912

The Motor Truck Comes of Age

Although 1912 is sacrosanct in automotive history as the year that Kettering's electric starter was applied to Cadillac automobiles, the year also brought a somewhat subtle and new approach to motor trucks by the press and even the manufacturers. Emphasis on innovations and design complemented continued interest in the accessibility of engines and transmissions. A new interest in truck engineering and styling gained momentum.

Perhaps the growing activities in trucks by prestige automobile manufacturers, such as Pierce-Arrow, Marmon, Locomobile, Lozier, and Packard, influenced the new interest. In any event, truck innovations were off and running and, in some cases, even predated use in automobiles.

A number of higher priced trucks were equipped with air brakes. The Sauer 6 1/2-ton model was typical. Compressed air and gas, electric, and explosive gas were used for starting purposes.

Commer truck was equipped with a specially designed automatic shifting transmission.

Eckhard truck used auxiliary coil springs with a torsion rod connecting the front and rear axles, a brass water pipe, two clutches, two differential locks, and a 6-cylinder engine.

Locomobile entered the commercial car field with a 5-ton truck called the American. Accessibility of engine and other components were emphasized. The driver's seat tilted back while floor plates and side members were removed. The radiator was mounted on rubber blocks for easy removal.

Four Wheel Drive Company produced its first four-wheel-drive truck and test drove it for the army.

A. O. Smith, a producer of pressed steel, entered the truck field with a 3-ton model featuring removable components. The transmission, drive shaft, differential and rear axle were covered by a single-cast steel housing.

The Lozier cab was hinged so it could be tilted back for access to the engine, mounted on a spring-suspended subframe.

Use of auxiliary springs found wide application. The function was to absorb the shock of the body on the running gear.

Willys used a 3/4 floating rear axle in 1913 models and a one-unit transmission and differential.

Marmon entered the commercial car field with a 1,500-pound delivery truck. Noteworthy was the removal of the gas tank from under the right seat to the outside of the seat panel. A transaxle was also featured.

Dispatch Truck offered a 1,000-pound model with twin disc friction-drive transmission, which eliminated clutch, gearset, and differential. The Dispatch truck also had a starter button on the dash.

GV Electric Truck had sliding doors and sliding steps.

Autocar and Mack featured an automatic clutch release which worked with the emergency brake to prevent damage to the gears.

The foot accelerator appeared on models in many forms.

Stedgeman offered an optional adjustable brake and clutch pedal. The adjustment could be made on the shaft at the factory or it could be made at a later time.

The Schmidt, Best, and Commer trucks provided a gear-shift lever under the wheel on the steering post.

Brockway Motor Company was organized to build trucks by George A. Brockway, famous carriage builder.

The driver received some attention as truck models appeared with the roof extended over the driver and passenger seat. Packard offered such a model.

Blair Truck offered a three-point suspension system hinging the engine subframe to the main frame so the engine was flexible in any position.

General Motors Truck manufactured a complete line of electric trucks with batteries moved from amidships to a front-end location above the frame.

General Motors' famous GMC nameplate made its first highway appearance.

Adams hood was hinged at the back.

Lansden Electric used pedals for both service and emergency brakes. The controller was continuous torque type, fully enclosed, and gear-operated by a handle, left of the steering column.

The Adams truck radiator was mounted behind the engine. Its cooling fan was in the flywheel and a filling cap was fitted on each side of the radiator.

Front Drive Motor Company of Hoboken, New Jersey, built its first Christie tractor for New York's fire department. It replaced horse-drawn fire wagons.

Folding starting cranks appeared on many vehicles.

Moon Buggy Company of St. Louis built a 3,000-pound chain-drive delivery car in three models. A Continental motor, pressure cooling, and pressure lubrication systems were featured.

1910 International Harvester delivery model.

1910 First Federal Motor Truck Company's stake model was powered by a 4-cylinder engine with a governed speed of 15 miles per hour and sold for $1,800.

1910 The Buick light truck with a 2-cylinder engine under the seat was used for fast special delivery of journals in New York City.

1910 International Harvester's first bookmobile truck brought the library to the countryside.

1910   Mud-rutted   roads   were   a   major   truck   problem.

1910   Public utility work truck.

1910 Packard police wagon.

1911 The New York Fire Department introduced a high-pressure hose on the Gramm fire truck.

1911 The first National Truck Show was held at Madison Square Garden in New York City. It opened to the public on January 16 and featured 28 gasoline and 7 electric trucks among 286 exhibitors.

1912 National Truck Show.

1911　The motor truck's advertising potential was evident as illustrated by a Brooklyn baking company's delivery model.

1912   Walter truck offered leaf-spring front suspension with air hydraulic shock absorbers.

1911   The Sauer on the nation's first transcontinental motor truck trip from California to New York.

1912   GMC chain-drive model-H with 3 1/2-ton body was used for moving and storage work. Note the right-hand steering and engine under the seat.

1912   The first truck built by Brockway, designed for durability and heavy hauling.

Crow Elkhart featured a removable rack between the top and bottom of an enclosed body for parcel storage. Its hinged seat section could be raised to allow long bundles, such as rolls of carpet, to be stored the length of the body.

National Association of Automobile Manufacturers adopted a ninety-day warranty for new trucks. The commercial vehicle committee also recommended that a plate cautioning against overloading be conspicuously mounted.

A 3-ton cargo of soap was delivered in a transcontinental run from Philadelphia to Petaluma, California. A 3 1/2-ton Alco delivered the goods in fifty-five days, 4,145 miles.

The world's largest pneumatic tires—38 × 8 inches—were manufactured by the United States Tire Company for a Mais high speed ladder truck for fire fighting.

Willys-Overland purchased the controlling interest in Gramm Motor Company.

Decatur Truck was reorganized under the name of Grand Rapids Motor Truck Company.

Pitt Motor Car Company succeeded Lion Motor Truck Company.

Gramm-Bernstein Truck Company was formed.

Duquesne Motor Car Company formed to build motor trucks.

Stewart Motor Corporation was formed to enter the truck field.

Krebs Commercial Motor Car Company was established by former officers of the Elmore Company in Clyde, Ohio, which had been purchased by General Motors.

United States Motors reorganized.

Budd Manufacturing Company was organized in Philadelphia.

Pierce-Arrow ordered an all-steel, one-piece brewery body from Fale and Kilburr body manufacturers.

Selden Truck Sales Company sold trucks on a deferred pay plan.

A commercial vehicle survey revealed that few motor trucks actually replaced the horse and wagon. In many cases, they extended business by moving the horse and wagon to lighter loads. Motor trucks carried the heavier loads, extending the life of the horse.

In Chicago, motor buses charged 10¢ a ride while horse-drawn buses charged 50¢. The Chicago Motor Transport Company found profit so good, that it soon ordered eight more White buses.

The Interstate Commerce Commission ruled in the case of Auto Vehicle Company versus Chicago–Milwaukee–St. Paul Railroad: metal motor vehicle parts shipped in carload lots from Milwaukee to Louisiana should be rated fourth class rather than first class rate charged by the railroad.

The Great Eagle ambulance and Knox fire truck offered 6-cylinder engines.

A commercial vehicle parade was held in Philadelphia. More than 500 vehicles participated.

The Lozier 5-ton truck made its debut at the Detroit Automobile Show. The Commerce model made by Chalmers was also introduced.

Production boomed to double output: 22,000 trucks and buses.

1913

Gas Soars to 18¢ a Gallon

A steady gain in industry showed 300 manufacturers producing electric-and-gasoline vehicles in the United States. Trucks most demanded were in the 2,000-to-6,000 pound ranges.

Right-hand steering wheels were used on most trucks, but a big change-over to left-hand steering was near.

Chain-drive dominated the final-drive arrangement in 1913, although a growing number of trucks were starting to use other drives, such as bevel gear with the shaft drive, a worm gear with the shaft drive (an overhead or underhung worm), or a final-gear drive, either internal or external.

Three-speed transmissions were the most popular among manufacturers and were usually placed amidships. Transmissions by four manufacturers were placed on the rear axle.

Rollers were fitted into the rear position of some truck bodies for loading or unloading cumbersome items, an arrangement especially helpful to lumber firms and building contractors.

Custom design—or the encouragement of individual owner preferences—emerged in 1913 as a dynamic new engineering concept that boosted sales. Prospective customers were welcomed to join in planning designs or specifications to fit their hauling jobs. As buyer satisfaction increased, so did production. Consequently, a wide array of specialized trucks began a new upswing in production.

The versatility of a steel body came into its own. Its strength, durability, and suitability for a variety of industries were big factors in its success.

Commercial Truck Company built an electric motor truck for Philadelphia Electric Company to transport telephone poles, some 90 feet long. The 6-ton truck had four-wheel drive and 30-mile range. A separate electric motor controlled pole loading and un-loading.

Thomas B. Jeffery Company introduced the four-wheel-drive Quad 1-ton truck which sold for $1,325. Over 5,500 were produced the first year.

To serve the army, Thomas B. Jeffery, Kenosha, Wisconsin, built a truck to meet U.S. army specifications. The truck had four-wheel drive, four-wheel steering, four-wheel brakes, 120-inch wheelbase, and a 1 1/2 tonnage.

Hendrickson Motor Truck of Chicago was organized.

Duplex Power Car Company reorganized in Charlotte, Michigan, to manufacture four-wheel drive motor trucks.

Standardization of parts, self-starters, and enclosed driving chains was evident at the New York Show.

Innovative trends appeared when mechanical parts were built below the chassis, so that any type of body could be attached.

An enclosed, silent chain of the inverted-tooth type became popular in heavy-duty, electric trucks. The motor was suspended behind the differential casing with the chain transmitting motor power to the differential. The final drive was through a double roller chain.

Large-capacity truck bodies concentrated on providing adequate loading space and reliable security. In contrast, light retail delivery models preferred distinctiveness, color, and keen appearance.

Truck bodies began taking a sportive look of glamour with color-cued tones, informative advertising, and identifying logos.

A survey showed that breweries were the biggest users of trucks.

Standard Oil announced a new fuel for trucks called *Motor Spirit.* The new fuel (made from fuel oil residues of crude oil after gasoline, kerosene, lubricating oils, etc. were distilled from the crude under high pressure and heat) cost 3 cents less a gallon than gasoline, and gave a 25 percent increase in efficiency, according to company officials. The only drawback was a strong fuel odor.

A scarcity of gasoline—with prices soaring to 18 cents a gallon—stimulated a determined search for new fuels.

Gasene, developed by the Cornplanters Refining Company, was proposed, as was the use of peat.

Ford Motor tested a gas carburetor that mixed city gas with air. The carburetor was devised by the Detroit City Gas Company.

Leland James designed a small freight truck in Salt Lake City, Utah, and formed a company to deliver sand and gravel.

Carburetors were heated by exhaust gas.

Bendix drive for electric starters was shown for the first time.

Pierce-Arrow put headlamps on the fenders.

A fuel-economy test run for trucks was sponsored by the *Washington Post.* The four-day demonstration of eighteen trucks was won by a Vulcan Truck which carried one ton for one mile at the rate of 1.22 cents.

The National Association of Automobile Manufacturers adopted a standard new "caution plate" for commercial motor vehicles. Measuring 9 × 3 inches, the caution plate read: "CAUTION— overloading or overspeeding will void your warranty."

Sixty-eight motor truck manufacturers fitted their vehicles with speed governors to limit speeds.

To demonstrate its hydraulic drive, an American LaFrance 4 1/2-ton truck pulled a load of 52 tons in New York City.

The Boston Truck Show featured forty-eight gas trucks, six electric, but only one steam truck, the Stanley.

Motor trucks helped rescue stranded flood victims in the midwest. One hundred truck makes were supplied by various manufacturers within a 200-mile radius of Dayton.

A severe "driver crisis" based on inexperience or meager driving skills persisted as one of the trucking industry's most critical problems. Compounding the problem, drivers lacking mechanical knowledge of their vehicles created high maintenance costs.

United States Postal Transfer Service ordered eighty ALCO trucks for hauling mail at a cost of $225,000.

The use of small electric trucks for city delivery was said to be on the increase. This year there were eighteen makes and eighty-six models.

The U.S. Army Engineers crossed Alaska in a White 1,500-pound model. The 826-mile trip took twenty-two days, a new mapping route to interior Alaskan towns saved a month in delivery.

Gulf Oil Company was the first United States petroleum firm to distribute free road maps.

Expressly designed for dumping purposes, the Couple Gear Company created a special electric, low-body, four-wheel drive-and-steer truck. The body was forty inches from the ground; the cab twenty-eight inches.

A 288-mile contest for trucks with a test route winding through high mountains and low valleys of Maryland and Pennsylvania was sponsored by the *Washington Post*. The International Harvester High Wheeler turned in a perfect score to capture a Silver Cup Award.

Production continued to increase: 23,500 trucks and buses.

1914

War in Europe Creates Truck Demand

War in Europe increased the demand for motor trucks. More than 1,000 units were ordered by France—the major purchaser—followed by England. Over half (600 units) were ordered from White.

The war was responsible for several states levying what was termed a "war tax" on vehicle registrations and driver license applications.

The use of trailers continued to grow, despite truck manufacturers' negative attitudes and complaints regarding lack-of-power for uphill hauls.

Six-cylinder engines were offered on the Great Eagle model and the Gramm 5-ton model.

Worm-driven rear axle and double-reduction gear use increased.

The August C. Fruehauf Company, a growing blacksmith shop in Detroit, built a semitrailer for the Sibley Lumber Company.

Henry Ford announced a $5 minimum daily wage for nonsalary employees over the age of twenty-two and eight-hour days with profit sharing.

Ford Model-T chassis was used by numerous truck manufacturers to build trucks.

Pacific Motor Truck Company ordered 104 trucks at 5-ton capacities.

Macy and Company announced that Massachusetts Institute of Technology would begin an extensive study of the Macy delivery system to determine the best method of operation in the 2,500 square mile area. The 400-vehicle fleet operated at a cost of $1 million a year.

Public Service Express, Incorporated, of New York City announced the purchase of fifty Stegeman trucks for use in a cooperative delivery service by twelve department stores. The joint express company owned and operated the trucks and maintained a repair shop and garage.

A blizzard struck New York City, heaping fifteen inches of snow and demonstrating again the advantage of trucks over horses in winter weather. Truck users such as Gimbels and Wanamakers reported delivery business as usual although at a slower pace. As a rule, the trucks could do a full day's work, while horses could work only half a day every other day.

Many manufacturers attached instruction plates to the dashes of their vehicles to alert drivers of oiling and lubrication procedures.

The Famous Mack AC "Bulldog" model was introduced.

The Rambler Quad was renamed the Jeffrey Quad, available as a 2 tonner and powered by a 21.4 horsepower engine.

The Denby Motor Truck Company was organized.

The Pull-More Truck Company featured a detachable power unit on its front-wheel-drive truck. A tilt cab was contemplated.

The National Automobile Chamber of Commerce joined forces with the spring manufacturers to appeal against truck overloading.

The following manufacturers reported expansion: Atterbury, Blair, Bowling Green, Couple Gear Duplex, Four Wheel Drive, General Vehicle, Kelly-Springfield, Knox, Koehler, LeMoon, Lippard, Motor Kart, Nelson, and Stewart.

The Merchants and Evans Company offered a front-drive tractor, the Devon, and an inner-supporting trailer with a fifth wheel.

The first STOP sign used to control traffic was in Detroit.

Total production for the year 1914: 24,900 trucks.

1915

Orders Skyrocket: Trucks Become Vital

The European war continued to demonstrate the importance of motor trucks. Demand skyrocketed. More trucks were shipped in one month than the total shipped in 1913.

The intensity of the war illustrated the advantages of four-wheel-drive trucks in rough terrain, thus great emphasis was placed on those models.

Gasoline prices increased to 20 cents a gallon.

The First National Automobile Manufacturer's Association convention of truck manufacturers was held in Detroit. Objectives were to develop standards for speed ratings, body-weight allowances, frame width and lengths, warranty forms, and caution plates.

Raises, profit-sharing, insurance benefits, bonuses, and several pension plans were offered to workers by the prospering automotive industry.

Transit strikes resulted in a wave of 5-cent jitney entrepreneurs and private car owners who offered short hauls at low prices.

Four-cylinder engines, three-speed gear boxes, and pneumatic tires on trucks under 1,500 pounds dominated the truck show.

The Garford Motor Truck debuted in Ohio.

Packard introduced six worm-drive trucks.

Standard entered the small truck field with a 2-ton model.

Niles Car and Manufacturing Company announced plans to build general delivery trucks.

Sternberg changed its name to Sterling Motor Truck Company.

Touraine changed its name to Vim Motor Truck Company.

Gerlinger Manufacturing Company was established in Portland, Oregon, to build trucks for the lumber industry.

Yellowstone National Park was opened to tourists.

The Liberty Bell of Philadelphia was transported from Pennsylvania to the Panama-Pacific Exposition by a White truck.

Jeffery used metal wheels on its truck models.

C. H. Martin developed his rocking fifth wheel, an important semitrailer-tractor development.

Southern California spent $7 million for road construction. Half was spent in Los Angeles County where 404 miles of asphalt streets ranked it the "number one state" in road development.

GMC introduced Truck Model 49, with a 2-horsepower, 2-ton capacity, dual chain-drive, 4-cylinder engine—its first model with the driver's seat on the left side. The new model introduced the windshield as standard equipment and featured solid hard rubber tires and oil lamps on the front and rear.

Total production for 1915: 74,000 trucks.

1916

Rising Prices Demand Efficiency Measures

The war in Europe was felt by the American people as shortages and rising prices rivaled each other. Wholesale gasoline rose to 24 cents a gallon in New York, raising the vehicle owners' prices to 26 to 31 cents a gallon. Only a year earlier, drivers winced when prices soared to 14 or 17 cents a gallon.

Increasing costs of materials and labor—coupled with rising war production demands—found most manufacturers concentrating on efficiency systems to offset or equalize rising costs.

The Federal Trade Commission investigated the high prices of gasoline.

The Republic Motor Truck Company adopted a bonus system for factory employees.

During a transit strike in New York City, simple soap boxes were improvised as passenger seats on truck bodies—and business continued as usual.

Trucks in the 2- to 3-ton range were the most popular. Electric starting and electric lighting were now offered as standard equipment by thirty-eight manufacturers. The use of electric starters on trucks was limited mostly to light delivery vehicles.

Pump or pressure cooling systems dominated 80 percent of the truck field. Only 20 percent used thermo-syphon cooling systems, while air-cooled trucks had faded in popularity.

The Hotchkiss drive, that is, taking an axle torque-and-thrust through the vehicle springs, was used by most trucks.

Cast steel wheels were popular.

The government called for bids on fifty-four truck chassis for army operations in Mexico against Pancho Villa.

Motorbus manufacturing increased. That increase signaled an end to the short-lived jitney-bus era.

An overland trip by a GMC truck from Seattle to New York City carried a full load for a total mileage of 3,710 in thirty days. The load was a ton of Carnation evaporated milk.

A truck altitude record was set by two Jeffrey Quad Trucks which hauled heavy ore up the Andes Mountains in South America, 15,000 feet above the level of the Pacific Ocean or 2 1/2 miles high. One 75-mile mountain run involved road grades up to 20 percent, with temperatures dropping as low as zero degrees Fahrenheit.

1913   The GMC electric truck had hard rubber tires and chain drive. The 2-ton model was the latest word in highway hauling.

1913   Willys utility truck with pneumatic tires in front and hard rubber tires in the rear. (*Courtesy John Conde Collection, Bloomfield Hills, Michigan*)

1914 The first Fruehauf innovation, converted from a 1911 model-T Ford chassis. (*Courtesy Henry Ford Museum, Dearborn, Michigan*)

1913 Lauth-Juergens model-J 5-ton tilt cab. It cost $4,500.

1914 The short-lived cyclecar craze offered the American public small, low-priced, light-weight vehicles. More than 50 manufacturers offered a variety of small delivery and passenger cars, such as these two Mercury vehicles.

1915 Traction strikes in several large cities started a movement to use jitney buses. The small-bus trend swept the country with vehicles such as this International Auto Wagon which offered rides for a nickel.

1914 Wilcox Motor Car Company built this unusual right-drive tank truck for the Marshall Oil Company.

1915 The Jeffery Quad with versatile 4-wheel drive and steering tractive capabilities. (*Courtesy John Conde Collection, Bloomfield Hills, Michigan*)

1915 Packard 2-ton truck with body by Seaman Company. (*Courtesy John Conde Collection, Bloomfield Hills, Michigan*)

1916 This was the last year for model-T truck conversions such as this one by Proctor-Keefe. In 1917 Ford began production of a 1-ton truck chassis. (*Courtesy National Automotive History Collection, Detroit Public Library*)

1916 Despite snow, business as usual in this Nash Quad. (*Courtesy John Conde Collection, Bloomfield Hills, Michigan*)

Diamond-T, long a supplier of cars and trucks to Chicago and neighboring areas, widened its sales capabilities throughout the United States.

A proposed merger of Willys-Overland, Hudson, Chalmers, and Kish was abandoned.

Charles W. Nash, the retiring president of General Motors Company, purchased the Thomas B. Jeffery Company for about $9 million with Lee, Higgenson, and Company.

Locomobile Trucks changed its name to Riker, differentiating between passenger cars and trucks.

The National United Service Company acquired Arbenz Car Company.

The White Motor Company was incorporated as a manufacturing organization and The White Company became its sales subsidiary.

Buick discontinued its 1,500-pound delivery truck.

Mais discontinued the manufacture of trucks.

Vulcan trucks were discontinued.

The Cadillac Motor Car Company sued the Cadillac Auto Truck Company and asked that the latter be restrained from using the name Cadillac.

The United Motors Corporation was formed by merging: The Pearlman Rim Corporation, The New Departure Manufacturing Company, The Hyatt Roller Bearing Company, The Delco Company, and Remy Electric Accessory Company.

Wichita Falls Motor Trucks used natural gas in fuel tests.

The Dey Electric Corporation announced plans to build a low-priced utility car.

No fewer than nineteen body manufacturers built stock model bodies for Ford vehicles.

A need for improved highways became critical. America's tremendous increase in vehicle production created a vital need for truck highways, plus an entire highway network to connect the country's industrial centers. Yet the growth of highways was agonizingly slow. The program involved awakening the public to realize the numerous transportation and economic advantages.

Fortunately, the inevitability of a national highway network was seen. Definite plans for its development started July 11, 1916, when the Federal Aid Road Act apportioned funds to states, based on one-third of their *area* ratio, one-third on their *population* ratio, and one-third on their ratio of rural delivery routes. Congress provided $5 million to improve rural delivery routes, then added $270 million in the next four years.

A rash of unfair truck taxes appeared in many U.S. cities as a result of road damage. Many taxes were based on weight alone and failed to consider speed, the number of wheels which supported the load, the type of tires used, or the like.

Overland trips to deliver new trucks were organized by dealers because of a threatened railroad strike.

San Francisco announced a nonskid pavement which used crushed rock mixed with asphalt for better traction.

New York's legislature directed the commissioner of highways, the superintendent of public works, and the state engineer to prepare a classification for registering motor vehicles used as trucks and buses, based on highway wear and tear by such vehicles.

Maxwell entered the commercial vehicle field with a 1-ton model, priced at $775.

Studebaker introduced a 1/2-ton station body with removable seats.

GMC truck production was up to 4,000 units per year, ranging from 1 1/4-ton to 5-ton capacity.

Fuel tanks on the Hoover truck were located on the right side of the chassis under the floor with a filler cap and gauge directly in front of the driver. The system was a Carter Vacuum Feed.

Rotary disc spreaders were used on trucks to spread sand in slippery weather. The device was connected by a chain to the drive shaft and clamped to the rear for easy removal. Sand was spread thirty feet to the side.

Krebs trucks offered a governor to limit top speed and provide automatic throttle control. The driver merely set a desired speed that was automatically maintained even on up-and-down grades.

Moreland trucks were equipped with a gasifier which could use a California distillate, a low-gravity fuel cheaper than gasoline.

The United States Motor Truck Company featured a sprung subframe for the power plant, clutch, muffler, radiator, and special support structures for the transmission and final drive.

An amphibious truck, the "Hydromotor," was demonstrated in San Francisco.

A revolving dump body was built by the Lawrence Bruder Company. The driver could swing the load by hand to a position at right angles to the truck's center line.

The American Wagon Company developed a convertible truck body which provided fifteen different forms to adapt to different hauling situations.

Budd Wheel Corporation was formed to produce steel-disc wheels.

Municipal authorities in New York City considered mobilization of private trucks for an emergency snow-removal organization.

Vitagraph Studios used a generating plant on a 3-ton White truck for night motion-picture photography.

Packard introduced a 5-ton heavy-service model with thermostatic water control.

Knox Trucks featured fan-vanes on brake drums for cooling.

Mack had a combination cross member and bumper which swung out to expose the front end of the vehicle.

Palmer-Moore radiator was manufactured in two parts; one for each side of the engine. A cirroco-type cooling fan was used.

The new Fageol introduced several unique features: magazine spring lubrication, ventilators at top of hood, and a flexible frame with few cross members.

Truck manufacturers who built a complete vehicle, that is, all the parts used in assembly, numbered approximately 11 percent of the market. About 23 percent used partial assemblies from suppliers. The greatest majority turned to standard parts in their assembly. Yet, the assembled vehicles differed enough to provide attractive consumer variety.

Total production for 1916: 92,130 trucks.

1917

Good Drivers and Roads Scarce as U.S. Enters the War

When war was declared on Germany, the United States was adequately prepared in its numbers of trucks, but woefully lacking operators and highways for World War I. Truck manufacturers prepared to turn out 200 to 300 army trucks per day.

Inadequate roads posed the greatest problem to the future of motor truck development.

The government ordered 10,550 trucks from six commercial vehicle manufacturers and detailed plans for standardized army trucks.

New York City trained women to replace men drivers on buses.

Higher parts-and-labor costs, plus materials shortages, increased the prices of commercial vehicles.

Group assembly of the chassis was discarded in favor of a speedier progressive assembly in many truck plants.

A Packard truck equipped with nobby-tread pneumatic tires made a round trip from Detroit to Mexico (4,288 miles) to test pneumatic tires for army trucks.

The class-B standard army truck featured a radiator protector, a step rather than a running board, front and rear coil spring bumpers, and flat fenders.

Various boards for organizing the motor industry were formed by the end of the year to standardize design for war production. Large war contracts resulted in a number of mergers and extraordinary capital stock increases.

The army used specialized trucks, such as dental trucks, shoe repair trucks, truck kitchens, mail trucks, searchlight trucks, medical or ambulance trucks, blacksmith trucks.

Many companies offered commercial attachments for the Ford passenger car chassis.

Saunders Company began leasing trucks.

The YMCA provided thirty motion picture trucks to entertain U.S. forces overseas. Each truck carried a stage, props, sets, screen, curtains, electric lights, and the like.

One of the largest civilian truck contracts in history was announced between the Kelly-Springfield Company and the United States Circus Corporation for 100 trucks. The circus planned to use the 3 1/2-ton trucks instead of railcars for transporting its tent shows.

Cities adjoining Fullerton, California, provided a unique bus system to transport students to grammar schools, high schools, and junior colleges. A fleet of Moreland trucks were used as buses. They were owned by the schools, garaged on school property, driven by students, and maintained in school shops.

Chicago initiated a city bus service with fifty low double-decker vehicles with front-wheel drive.

The Wisconsin Auto Company was formed to develop a four-wheel-drive truck, based on the patents of William Besserdich. It later became Oshkosh Truck Corporation.

William C. Durant announced that General Motor Truck Company would make tractors.

A Ford artillery tractor used dual steering wheels and controls.

A truck with an 8-cylinder engine was introduced by Seagrave of Walkerville, Ontario. The engine was a Herschell-Spillman, V-8.

The Muskegon Engine Company offered truck buyers free service for twelve months.

A special hearing was held in Washington by the Bureau of Mines and the Bureau of Standards to solve fuel problems and to protect fuel purchasers from fraud.

Railroad and electric transit strikes opened new opportunities to the motor truck industry as farmers pledged to buy or rent trucks to get their goods to market.

California legislators proposed to tax buses $25 per passenger seat and to ban trucks larger than 5-ton capacity.

Truck members of the National Automobile Chamber of Commerce voted to abolish muffler cut-outs from their vehicles. The NACC asserted that the advantages of a muffler cut-out controlled by the drivers were negligible and that they were a public nuisance.

Lack of uniformity in state truck laws posed a serious problem. Many states based taxes on tonnage with no studies to justify such procedures. In many cases, the taxes were arbitrary.

New trucks introduced at the Boston Show were the: Dodge, Fulton, Maxfer, Bethlehem, Mackbilt, and Metz.

The Pull-More truck engine and cab tilted to the side for engine accessibility.

Late in the year, Dodge was in full production on a new commercial car, the famous screen-side Dodge business truck.

The Ford Motor Company entered active truck production with a 1-ton chassis. It featured a longer and stronger frame than that of the Ford passenger car chassis, a 2-foot greater wheelbase, a stiffer rear suspension, artillery-type back wheels, and worm-drive rear axle. The chassis price was $600. Production was geared for twenty-five per day.

Gersix nameplate was born as Gerlinger Manufacturing Company changed its name to make enclosed-drive trucks for the logging industry.

Oshkosh Truck Corporation was founded by B. A. Mosling and William Besserdich.

A special Mack "Wrecker Truck" helped trucks in distress.

Trailer support use increased.

Kelly-Springfield offered tires in triplet form, claiming that three

40 × 5 tires reduced wheel weight, had less wear, and cost less than two 40 × 7 tires.

The Holley Carburetor Company introduced an exhaust-heated kerosene vaporizer.

Specialized bodies were used as an advertising media.

Total production for 1917: 128,157 trucks.

1918

Yankee Ingenuity Overcomes
Shortages and Aids Victory

Critical fuel shortages of coal and petroleum existed. The fuel shortages grew from the nation's dependence on the war-burdened rail transportation. Talk of curtailing motor vehicle production, in fact, even cutting it out entirely, came from manufacturers who faced alarming shortages.

Ironically, the war's railroad congestion and labor shortages forced farmers to use trucks instead of rails to sustain the nation's food supplies.

The Council of National Defense asked retail stores to limit deliveries to one-a-day to release men for the armed forces.

The concept of a "return-loads system" was now well established in New York, Connecticut, New Jersey, Pennsylvania, Ohio, Rhode Island, and Illinois. Numerous instances of continual, cooperative deliveries were evident.

There were "heatless days" and "gasless Sundays" to conserve fuel. Everything possible was done to limit unnecessary travel.

The Motor Truck Club in Newark operated a return-load system to aid New York shippers in transferring freight from New Jersey to New York and vice versa.

More trucks were involved in overload hauls for distances as much as 750 miles.

A regular fleet of trucks ran on schedule between Philadelphia and New York. A run between Akron and Boston was inaugurated by a large tire company.

White discontinued manufacturing passenger cars to concentrate on trucks and buses. White served the Allies during World War I with 18,000 White trucks.

The U.S. government mapped army truck routes from the East to the Mississippi. The goal was to have four main highways linking the nation's great manufacturing centers with the Atlantic seaboard.

Oshkosh produced its first truck with an automatic positive-locking center differential and four-wheel drive.

Nash became the world's largest producer of trucks in 1918 with an army contract for 11,494 units of the Quad truck.

A Maxwell truck made a San Francisco-to-New York run in less than eighteen days beating freight train time by two and one-half days.

Goodyear pneumatic-tired trucks—a Packard and a White—ran 7,763 miles from Boston to San Francisco and back. The trip took twenty-one days, averaging fourteen and one half miles an hour.

The Goodyear Tire and Rubber Company announced that all its products would be shipped by truck east of the Mississippi and haul crude rubber on the return trip.

The U. S. Post Office hauled two tons of food in an experiment to reduce the cost-of-living by eliminating excessive food handling.

Cross-country operation of mail motor trucks became a huge success, according to the post master general. Thousands of army trucks were rebuilt for postal service after the war.

In vetoing a Post Office appropriation to continue the pneumatic-tube mail system, President Wilson stated that motor truck development had made tubes obsolete.

Thousands of military trucks were put into peacetime service when the war ended.

A three-wheel front-drive tractor was introduced by the Highway Tractor Company. A unique feature was that the front-wheel powerplant and cab could be turned 180 degrees to push the trailer, if desired, rather than pull it. The engine set transversely on the frame with the radiator and four-bladed fan mounted at the side of the engine.

Harsh winters loomed as a threat to the war effort. The nation's largest truck drive-away, using thirty Packard trucks, was made from Detroit to Baltimore at the height of winter—December 14 to December 28. Fighting temperatures below zero and an average snow depth on the roads of from one to four inches, the caravan proved that trucks could operate in severe winters. Future convoys were to be composed of 180 vehicles in groups of 6, leaving on the hour.

Although initially experimental when completed in January, four

class-AA standardized trucks were successfully demonstrated by
Reo, Federal, Willys-Overland, and Maxwell. The trucks were
equipped with electric starters, hot-spot manifolds, and pressure
cooling systems. In addition, an unusual feature was a crankcase,
designed so that cylinders of 3 3/4-inch bore and 5-inch stroke
were interchangeable with 4×5-inch cylinders.

Brakes controlled from the driver's seat and pneumatic tires were
being increasingly used for heavier trailers.

The war illustrated the need for good motor-truck roads and
strong bridges throughout the nation. Vehicle interests became
extremely active in seeking road improvements.

The National Automobile Chamber of Commerce called for a federal statute to control truck operation. A national road organization
was proposed to fight for reasonable laws and highway construction.

Although few new truck models were offered, two famous makes,
Chevrolet and Oshkosh, were introduced.

Pan American Motors bought Lumb Motor Truck and Tractor.

California stabilized its motorbus business with legislation that
curbed fly-by-night jitney operators and advanced the level of the
industry. Fixed-rates classification, safety, and definite routes were
some of the tangible public benefits.

The Cleveland Bureau of Child Hygiene had a special GMC truck
to serve outlying suburbs for medical examinations of children and
to transport doctors and nurses.

A 3 1/2-ton Mack truck was fitted with a special body for the
Goodyear Tire and Rubber Company. Fitted with extra-size
pneumatic tires, the truck featured a cab with a sleeping compartment: a steel box (measuring $7 \times 3 \times 4$ feet) was mounted above
and behind the driver's seat. The compartment was fitted with
mattress, bed clothing, hangers, and low rectangular sliding windows.

Standard Mack trucks featured high-door cabs which offered
protection to the drivers in cold weather. The door on the AB-
models slid sideways, while those on the AC-models opened vertically.

The Doble steam truck featured a positive temperature-control
device and a steam-pressure control that automatically stopped or
started the engine.

Frontmobile had a gearshift on its steering wheel.

The Walter 2-ton tractor had a 4-wheel drive, 4-wheel steering, and 4-wheel brakes.

Air brakes were introduced by the Parker Air Appliance Company.

Pneumatic tires were developed for 2-ton models.

Use of all-metal delivery and dumping bodies increased.

Gusseted cross members appeared on several makes.

Because of the war, accessory and automobile manufacturers offered new devices to prolong car life, and introduced carburetors to use low-grade fuel or kerosene.

Fulton truck used a triple-heating method to vaporize the mixture.

A hot-spot manifold, hot-air stoves, and other means were sought to vaporize heavy fuels.

The use of heavy fuels stimulated developments in automatic engine-temperature control and in thermostats for water-circulation systems.

High costs and frangibility began to hinder the demand for electric starters on trucks.

Engine supports were redesigned to take torque reaction and reduce noise. There was a trend to place transmissions amidships and to use center bearings to reduce propeller shaft whipping.

The Autohorse Tractor, a 1-wheel, dual-tired vehicle, was chain-driven and powered by a side-mounted 4-cylinder continental motor. It was designed to allow purchasers to use an old horsewagon.

The War Industries Board restricted truck manufacture during the last six months of 1918 to one-third of what was produced in 1917 and in the first six months of 1918.

Chevrolet became part of General Motors, rounding out the line of General Motors vehicles in every price class.

United Motors became part of General Motors. This organization consisted of companies closely related to the vehicle industry, including Dayton Engineering Laboratories, Remy Electric, Klaxon, Harrison Radiator, Jaxon Steel Products, Hyatt Roller Bearing, New Parture, and United Motors Service, Incorporated.

Officials in Washington considered motor vehicles dispensable luxuries; thus, the wartime excise levies taxed them as if they were tobacco, whiskey, furs, perfume, or jewelry.

Despite adverse legislation, the importance of the motor truck stimulated road-building. Trucks competed with railroads as war demands increased.

The war year of 1918 was unusual for the motor truck industry. Although 227,250 trucks were produced, that record total was well below 1918 forecasts which called for *over* 300,000 units. The gain of nearly 40,000 units over 1917 was a record. That gain marks 1918 the same as 1917: a year of production rather than a year of engineering design.

Total production for 1918: 227,250 units.

1919

Peacetime Move for Improved Roads

As America recovered from World War I, 1919 promised to be a year of roads. Unprecedented travel wore out many existing roads.

Transportation costs doubled because of the laborious travel on poor, rutted roads.

The demand for good roads found the nation backing road-building. More than twenty bills were introduced in the 66th Congress. The major considerations centered on a national network of highways and formation of a federal highway commission.

The Department of Agriculture estimated that $300 million of federal funds would go into road-building in 1919—half of that amount consumed by labor.

By 1919, all states had formed highway departments.

The Department of Agriculture dispersed 5,336 war trucks to various states for road construction.

Sixty-five cities now had ship-by-truck bureaus.

Cooperative Truck Line Associations were formed by farmers who were not serviced by railroads. Low rates and reliable service were the main benefits.

Chicago and New York Motor Truck Shows were revived.

There was increased use of pneumatic tires at the New York and Chicago Truck Shows.

Closed cabs were evident and visibly popular.

Few changes were made in truck designs in 1919.

The 2-ton truck model dominated production.

The chain drive continued to lose ground to enclosed types.

1917   Duplex 4-wheel-drive tractor hauling two Reo cars.

1917   First 4-wheel-drive Oshkosh truck.

1918 White army trucks carrying troops and supplies in France during World War I.

1918 The 113th motor truck train of 50 **FWD** trucks ready to depart Clintonville, Wisconsin. (*Courtesy U.S. Signal Corps*)

1918 White class-A army truck used in World War I.

1917 Trucks like this GMC blazed the trail through the tall timbers of the Northwest Pacific mountains.

1918 Chevrolet entered the truck field introducing light delivery and 1-ton models. The 1-ton model featured a 4-cylinder engine, pneumatic tires on front, solid tires on rear, wheelbase of 125 inches, and was priced at $1,545.

1918 A movable inner body reduced loading-and-unloading labor costs on this White 1 1/2-ton delivery truck.

1919 A traveling service shop was introduced by Autocar. It was one of the earliest repair trucks fully equipped to handle roadside repairs or to tow a disabled vehicle.

Truck prices continued to rise—up to 17 percent on the average.
The parts industry became a potent force in the tremendous
growth of the motor truck industry. Astute truck buyers were
frankly asking which parts—by either manufacturer's name or
tradename—were being used on vehicles. Over 200 parts makers
offered major components in 1919 truck chassis.

Pneumatic tires were optional on most 2-ton trucks.

Selective sliding-gear transmissions were on over 80 percent of the
trucks offered in 1919.

The worm-drive rear axle was used on 66 percent of the models.

The use of metal wheels grew slightly.

Electric starting systems were offered by seventy-one truck makers.

New entries into the truck field were: Oldsmobile, Paige-Detroit,
and R. E. Northway, the latter a well-known designer of engines.

Autocar introduced a service truck: a traveling repair shop equipped to handle roadside repairs or to tow a disabled vehicle.

The Diamond-T Motor Car Company opened a new concrete test
track one-third of a mile long for its trucks. Before this testing
facility, its vehicles were tested on the streets of Chicago, then on a
cinder track which did not survive the use.

The Ward special electric house-to-house delivery truck featured a
hinged dashboard that swung away for easy access and exit. A front
step also served as a bumper and was twelve inches off the ground.

The Highway Knight built by Highway Motors in Chicago had a
sleeve valve engine with a cone-shaped cap-type cylinder head and
was water jacketed.

Headlights on the Ace 2 1/2-ton truck swiveled to follow the cut
of the front wheels.

A body by the Horizontal Hydraulic Hoist Company on a Packard
chassis was all steel and could be converted for carrying any kind of
material. A two-way tailgate, hinged on the top and bottom,
functioned either for dumping or adding loading length. The tailgate latch was operated by hand from the driver's seat.

The Air-O-Flex truck frame was supported on four telescoping
cylinders working against oil and air pressure.

Fruehauf Trailers offered structural-steel channel frames with riveted and gusseted corners, proportioned to the length of the trailer
for greater stability.

A push-button, door light switch which operated when the door opened was used on an ice cream truck with a White chassis.

The Barber Motor Corporation designed a coupling unit to convert passenger cars into road tractors.

The bumper grill on the Dearborn Truck consisted of extra-heavy V-bars supported by heavy rubber cushions held by a coil spring on each side.

Emphasis was placed on weather-proofing truck cabs and on mounting cabs on springs for a more comfortable ride.

The world's first three-color traffic control was installed in Detroit. Detroit police pioneered in offering safety instruction in school classrooms.

Gasoline taxation to raise revenue for maintenance and construction of highways was first enacted in Oregon in 1919. It levied a 1 cent per gallon tax on all motor vehicle fuels.

Compounding the truckers' taxation woes was an increase in license fees.

Steel bodies were numerous.

Some closed cab models offered removable doors for ventilation during the summer months.

The Autocar Corporation formed a new legal department to combat legislation against motor trucks.

The Third Annual International Retail Delivery Association meeting endorsed one delivery a day.

Parker Air Brakes were used on Walter Trucks and Troy Trailers.

The AC-speedometer operated on a magnetic principle and featured an odometer and trip register.

Production for 1919 totaled: 275,943 trucks.

The Twenties

1920

An Era of Power Begins

Postwar enthusiasm ventured into an era of 1-ton "speed-truck" development. Although ninety different 1 1/2-ton models were popular, a trend toward lighter models was rising. Many 1/2-ton and 3/4-ton models offered superior pneumatic tires as standard equipment. The move to pneumatics was significant, forecasting a revolution to lighter truck engine design. The prior use of solid tires had required heavy, rugged engines because of severe vibrations and strain.

A trend also developed toward using detachable cylinder heads.

Parts manufacturers supplied 86 percent of the rear axles for 1920 trucks. Nearly two-thirds of the new models used the worm-driven rear axle.

Pressed-steel frames carried about 70 percent of the 1920 models, and semiflexible and flexible types were rapidly gaining in popularity.

Balloon tires were introduced for thirty-two to thirty-four pounds of air so vehicles could "float" over rough roads for a more comfortable ride.

Automatic tire pumps were introduced. A wide variety of makes and mountings were offered.

Fourteen manufacturers offered four-wheel-drive trucks.

Pneumatic tires were now featured as standard equipment on 1/2-ton and 3/4-ton trucks. They also appeared on several larger trucks.

Gasoline shortage scares swept the country once again, as an acute shortage on the Pacific Coast raised fears that prices would reach 40 cents a gallon. An Alco-gas was to be put on the market as a substitute. A Bureau of Mines report indicated that the scare was psychological, that transportation difficulties alone were responsible in the West, and that reserve stocks at the refineries totaled over 626 million gallons.

Supplies of distillate fuel on the West Coast dwindled as Standard Oil discontinued fuel distribution. The company stated that production of crude oil was insufficient to permit production of the distillate. Distillate was an early stage in the refinement of gasoline from crude oil. It cost a mere 9 cents per gallon compared to the higher 21 1/2 cents per gallon for gasoline.

The Department of Justice conducted an investigation on the Pacific Coast to determine if the gasoline shortage was artificial.

The use of trucks revolutionized the delivery of fresh fruit and vegetables. Perishability was eliminated on long hauls as trucks could go directly to railroads, eliminating in-transit storage waiting. The cushioning effect of pneumatic tires lessened bruising damage to the tender produce in transit.

John N. Willys was elected president of Republic Trucks.

A special federal tax was imposed on motor trucks which were hired and used to carry passengers. Each truck was taxed $20 when more than seven passengers were carried. The tax was $10 when fewer than seven passengers rode.

Twenty-seven New York trucking firms merged to form the United States Trucking Corporation. Three hundred motor trucks and 3,500 horses were kept in service.

Massachusetts held that lower insurance rates for fleet owners discriminated against individual truck owners and were unlawful.

Connecticut banned oil lamps as headlights on trucks because of insufficient illumination. Only acetylene or electric headlights were acceptable.

The Motor Truck Association of America was formed. The objectives of the group, which consisted of all types of truck owners, were to secure better highways, assist members in truck efficiency, and disseminate information to prevent state and federal governments from passing laws which were discriminatory to motor truck operation.

To benefit present and prospective truck owners, highway transport conferences and meetings were held each night in conjunction with the New York and Chicago Motor Truck shows.

A bill to start construction on a vehicle tunnel between New York and New Jersey was signed.

Crowley-Milner Department Store in Detroit built a 150-truck parking facility for its delivery trucks.

New York City awarded a contract for over $1 million for 212 vehicles with 5-ton capacity for snow removal and street cleaning.

The University of Michigan offered a specialized engineering and transportation course for fleet owners.

The University of Pittsburgh sent out a University on Wheels to teach repair work and truck operation. Practical demonstrations were given in garages. Movies, illustrations, and other visual aids were provided by truck manufacturers.

Apex trucks had a twin-frame construction to double reinforcement of the load-carrying space.

Autocar offered a 4-cylinder engine mounted under the driver's seat. Autocar had a special dual dump body to haul concrete. It was so well balanced that it could be operated by hand.

Diamond-T introduced a 1 1/2-ton model for farm use. A special versatile body was convertible from an express-type to grain-type or cattle-type body. The 144-inch wheelbase made it easy to handle on narrow country roads. A closed cab was also available.

Pierce-Arrow announced a new line of trucks featuring dual-valved engines for power and economy and a dual ignition with electric lights.

Schacht 5-ton trucks featured a 10-speed gearset with eight forward and two reverse speeds, plus a range of gear reductions.

Twin-City trucks featured a 4-cylinder engine with sixteen valves and removable cylinder walls.

Vacuum-feed fuel systems gained on gravity-type systems. Tanks and floats were improved to withstand vibrations, as 22 percent now used the new vacuum-fuel systems as standard.

Dry and dry-plate disc clutches replaced the cone-type clutch. A slight gain was shown in the use of wet-disc clutches.

A refrigeration body with brine circulated within its sides was exhibited by the Transit Refrigeration Company. The same system was used in meat shops. No ice contacted the goods being carried. The truck required about 200 pounds of ice per day and one icing every twenty-four hours.

The use of the Myers patented magazine oilers grew. In this system, oil was automatically filtered and fed in small quantities as required when the vehicle was in motion.

Fuel tanks on the Lorain trucks could slide into the side of the cab and be locked.

A new accessory device called "The Week's Camel" automatically kept the radiator filled. A float-control valve attached to the radiator was connected to the intake manifold. As radiator water lowered, the valve opened and a partial vacuum drew water from a reserve tank. The reserve tank featured a whistle to signal when tank water was low.

The Aluminum Casting Company introduced the Lynite wheel, a one-piece aluminum alloy casting, made in either spoke or disc-type designs.

Tail lights were mounted flush in the frame to prevent breakage.

Electric starting, lighting, and ignition systems were standard on many models in classes up to 2 1/2-ton, and in some larger trucks.

A radiator shroud was used on the Jumbo truck with manually controlled radiator shutters.

The Trailmobile semitrailer had a rear section of the frame that tilted, so that the load could be rolled off by a ratchet close to the ground. The frame was called a jackknife frame, but was really two frames in one.

A new type of truck body was developed for hauling sheets of plate glass in upright positions.

The Automatic Dump Car Company made a side-dump model.

Duplex Limited of Lansing, Michigan, set a speed hauling world's truck record at the Indianapolis Speedway in October with a 3 1/2-ton medium capacity truck. It carried a 3,300 payload and averaged 38 miles per hour on a 24-hour nonstop run of 935 miles, equal to the distance between Chicago and New York.

Mechanical loading devices emerged as labor savers for truckers.

A detachable tank body and sprayer on a 2 1/2-ton Republic truck could be interchanged with a stake and farm body.

Despite a poor business climate, the 1920 postwar truck production climbed to 321,789, an increase of 97,058 trucks over 1919.

1921

California Paves the Way

California proved that motor bus lines follow the advent of good roads. Already leading the nation with the greatest number of paved roads, California led in developing motor bus lines. Although California spearheaded the bus movement, a widespread uniform system of bus transportation was years away. Nonetheless, buses were on the move across the nation.

Many manufacturers reduced truck prices as more models became available.

A postwar recession still gripped the nation with a sharp drop in industrial activity, but new truck models continued to appear.

These favored 4-speed gearsets, dry-plate disc clutches, and pressed steel frames. Metal-type wheels showed some gain: however, wood wheels still dominated.

Speed governors on light 1-ton models were being dropped as standard equipment because the superior pneumatic tires which were being fitted permitted maximum speeds through the elimination of rough engine vibrations and improved wear.

The use of demountable bodies for trucks increased. One such example was the Roloff body, a subframe with rollers upon which the body was carried and locked in place by wedge blocks.

A rash of highway banditry between New York City and Philadelphia resulted in the use of armed guards and convoy travel.

Railways used trucks to reduce the high cost of terminal handling.

Trucks and tractors formed a line with the railroads as forests receded, and hauling logs became a problem. Trucks solved this heavy, massive problem.

The New York Central Railroad "container-car" system provided "store-door delivery." Containers or huge steel boxes were available in interchangeable sizes and could be carried by motor truck from the sender to the railroad, hoisted onto the rail car and, at destination, carried to the recipient by truck. The movement signified cooperation instead of competition between railroads and trucks.

Waltham Motors Corporation in Chicago purchased Victor Motor Truck Company.

Rumors spread that Henry Ford would bring out a 3 1/2-ton truck to sell at $1,000 or $1,200.

The National Association of Commercial Handlers held its first convention in Milwaukee, June 30, July 1 and 2.

The U.S. Bureau of Mines' tests showed that motor trucks wasted 30 percent of their gasoline due to incomplete combustion.

The Federal Highway Act of 1921 provided for the states and federal government to create a nationwide road system, with Washington paying half the cost on designated Federal-Aid roads. There were 3.2 million miles of highways, but only 14 percent were surfaced.

The Bureau of Public Roads disclosed that the use of pneumatic tires lessened road wear and gave lighter impact at given speeds. They predicted that roads in construction could bear all the loads expected.

Electric starting and lighting increased with the use of pneumatics.
Several states considered more stringent lighting laws similar to those Connecticut had previously passed for mandatory brighter acetylene or electric lights.
Yellow Cab Company entered the truck field and offered both 3/4-ton and 1 3/4-ton models.
Diamond-T introduced a contractor's special model dump truck, designed for road building. A short wheelbase enabled it to turn in an 18-foot subgrade. Two end-dump hoppers gave a total load capacity of 5,000 to 6,000 pounds.
American Truck Company of Newark, Ohio, producers of Ace Trucks, dropped all of its dealers and planned to sell directly from the factory, reducing prices as much as $500 to $700.
The Royal Rex truck was shipped dismantled to dealers. The company claimed that the truck could be assembled in four hours by two mechanics. Transportation and handling costs were materially reduced.
White Company introduced a business car model specifically for salesmen. The car was mounted on a truck chassis and the rear compartment could be fitted to accommodate various business equipment, office forms, supplies, and the like.
Mack replaced spring shackles with rubber shock insulating blocks on its new bus model. Other features were a gasoline tank at the rear of the chassis, and an exhaust pipe and muffler extended to the rear of the vehicle. An automatic light was mounted on top of the cab for night work.
Air-controlled brakes were tried on an experimental IH coach.
Larrabee-Deyo introduced its new Speed-Six: a 6-cylinder truck model with two radiators provided because of the truck's extremely slow-running capability.
International Harvester Speed Truck in the light-duty medium field was equipped with pneumatic tires.
Walter Motor trucks of New York City built electric trucks and gasoline models. The new electrics were equipped with positive-locking differential, popular on Walter gasoline models.
A special educational exhibit by Mack with a 3 1/2-ton demonstration body was mounted on a 5-ton chassis.
The Buffalo 2 1/2-ton truck had unusual features to adapt to unusual road conditions. Two 3-speed gearsets were mounted in tan-

dem to provide a gear with a countershaft in between for power takeoff (with a ratio of 130-to-1) and a low speed of one mile in seven and three tenth hours for extremely hard pulls. Two gearshift levers were mounted in front of the driver. One was used normally and the other could be brought in under heavy load. The low gear ratio allowed driving down the steepest hill without brakes.

Federal Motor Truck unveiled an elevating dump body.

Nash introduced a 2-latch dump body.

Mack used dual-reduction rear axle on 1 1/2-ton and 2-ton models.

Fageol introduced a 7-speed compound gearset with five forward speeds and two reverse speeds. The speeds were obtained by a 2-speed countershaft, so that there were no more gears than the regular 4-speed gearset.

Clydesdale trucks offered pyramidal headlamps with an octagonal front mounted at the sides of the radiator. A special instrument panel was mounted on the dash and slanted for good vision.

Rowe introduced an 8-cylinder model.

A new GMC engine featured removable cylinder sleeves for better interchangeability and replacement.

Fageol designed a bus built for rural and intercity service. The Fageol Safety Coach featured a unique low center-of-gravity construction, full height doors, a worm axle, and was powered by a Hall Scott Motor.

Improved dual-valved engines gave greater power and greater fuel economy.

Giant pneumatic truck tires supposedly gave motor trucks greater traction in snow.

The Universal Crane could be mounted on various truck chassis.

Commerce Motor Trucks introduced a truck model to serve as a grocery store on wheels.

The Amos loader enabled one man to load 1,500 feet of logs in twenty minutes. A power take-off also tightened a chain to secure the load.

United Milk Company in California installed 1,500-gallon glass-lined thermos tanks on two Pierce-Arrow trucks and on three Reliance Trailers.

"Trackless Trolleys" were tried in Schenectady, New York. The new type of trolley was operated by electricity but ran on rubber tires and did not require tracks. The pole swiveled to permit the car to pass other vehicles. The cars were built by General Electric Company.

Buses out West still used the term "stage." Eastern mass transportation was based on a rail system.

Postwar production for 1921 was down by more than 100,000 units due to depressed business conditions and to a large number of surplus army vehicles marketed by the government.

Production dropped slightly: 148,052 trucks and buses.

1922

Trucks Prove Cost Benefits

The year 1922 welcomed the start of national prosperity again—a good year for commercial vehicles.

The advantages in truck transportation continued with unrelenting upward impact—dramatically demonstrating the cost-saving benefits over hauling by horses—while truck prices steadily dropped since 1920. Quicker service, durability and lower prices widened the competitive gap between trucks and horse teams.

To facilitate travel, the National Highway Traffic Association pushed for uniform highway signs, for marking state boundaries on highways, and for uniform weights, speeds, and loads on highways.

Fourteen million passengers were carried by motorbuses in California.

New, all enclosed double-decker buses for winter service on Fifth Avenue in New York City were introduced by the Fifth Avenue Coach Company.

Rolling grocery stores increased in many communities. Although retail grocers demanded that cities restrict those vehicles to curbside locations, consumers supported the motorized stores, lauding their lower prices and convenience.

Consumers were offered a unique service by the Fay Motor Bus Service of Rockford, Illinois, whereby a woman employee would shop for country patrons reached by the bus line. Upon receiving an order, the shopper made the purchase and sent it back on the bus's return trip. A small fee was charged for the service.

Children benefited with a better education in Alabama. Forty-two trucks were used in Jefferson County to transport children in the rural school system. School attendance increased 45 percent. The annual expenditure for the trucks averaged about 6 percent of the total school budget. If it had not been for the automotive industry, Jefferson County officials stated that many of its sons and daughters would have found it almost impossible to gain an education.

The Mayo Clinic used a special bus on the Mack chassis to transport patients to its clinic. The bus had four passenger compartments, separated by glass partitions, plus a driver's compartment. Three passenger compartments had divan-deep cushion seats for three passengers. The fourth was a smoking compartment with seating for nine. Each compartment had its own door at the side of the vehicle and enclosed heating ducts. Flush lights were provided in the interior of the bus. Dual stop lights at the rear of the vehicle were brake operated. Green running lights were mounted on each side of the windshield. A lighted, nickel-plated, arm-signaling device with a red arrow was mounted to the left of the driver.

A unique refrigerator plant on a Mack truck for transporting perishables was devised by R. D. Hatch of San Francisco. Cooling of the body was achieved by the evaporation of anhydrous ammonia. Coiled pipe, insulated with ground cork and paper, lined the body of the vehicle.

The Edgewater Beach Hotel bus was equipped with luxurious seatbacks fastened on a movable anchorage to absorb driving shocks. The bus was built on a White chassis and featured doors that opened and closed electrically, controlled by the driver.

Fruehauf designed a 6-wheel, tractor-and-trailer bus with a seating capacity for sixty-six. Both the doors and brakes were operated by compressed air. Although both were operated with the same valve, to insure safety, it was impossible to open the doors without first setting the brakes.

International Harvester introduced its first speed truck, featuring a radiator mounted in front of the engine.

Various deluxe-type buses were being manufactured. Deluxe buses designed by Moele, White, and Kissel featured doors which locked automatically when closed and could not be opened until the driver released a special lever.

Many Electric railway companies were operating motor buses. Buses were exhibited at the American Electric Railway Association Convention.

A 2-car, gasoline-engine train, constructed with a steel body, was developed by the Four Wheel Drive Auto Company to demonstrate for railroads near Chicago. The 2-car train was designed for use during peak loads, featuring a capacity for forty-six passengers. Air brakes were fitted on both cars, electric starting and lighting were included, and they were heated by the vehicle's engine.

American Railway Express operated a separate body-repair building in New York City to maintain its 800 vehicles. In the largest facility of its kind, the bodies were skillfully repaired and parts replaced.

W. E. Travis, president of the California Transit Company of Oakland, sent a radio-equipped bus on a regular run to Sacramento to test the possible use of radio equipment. A 2-step shortwave radio receiving set was used with a maximum amplifier but was handicapped by an antenna too low for the vehicle. Nonetheless, the experiment was successful enough for Mr. Travis to predict that radio concerts for his passengers would soon be a reality.

For suburban passenger bus service, Fageol Motors developed a low-hung motor stage (16-inch running board height). A special, raised rear section of the frame with a worm axle provided a low center of gravity. A wheel tread of sixty-eight inches, compared to the usual fifty-six inches, added greater stability.

To curb motor vehicle thefts, a bill was introduced in the United States House of Representatives calling for federal registration of all motor vehicles.

An excise tax on gasoline was imposed by fifteen states. Other states said they would follow suit.

A demand for lighter wheels surfaced as several states threatened to limit the permissable weight of trucks. Metal wheels showed an increase over wood wheels.

To find a solution to the rapid deterioration of roads, several states required loads to be 700 pounds per inch or less of tire width, measured at the base. Truck interests claimed that other factors, such as cushioning ability—the volume of rubber in the tires—should also be considered.

Mack Trucks, Incorporated, was founded as it took over the International Motor Company.

With new management in its future, two major stockholders of the Gersix Motor Company, Kent and Worthington, took over the company under the name Kenworth.

A joint convention was held by the National Team and Motor Truck Owners Association and the National Association of Com-

mercial Haulers to consider amalgamation, among other items.
The National Motor Transport Association of bus transport companies was formed in New York City.
To keep snowbound New York roads open in winter, a fleet of four-wheel-drive snowplows was placed in service with the Fifth Avenue Coach Company by the Walter Motor Truck Company.
The Mason Road King was taken over by Durant.
Over $40 million worth of livestock was hauled by motor trucks to Cincinnati, Indianapolis, and Omaha.
Motor-driven snow removal equipment opened 27,096 miles of snow-covered highways from the East Coast through the Midwest. This was the first concerted effort by many newly established state highway departments using the motor truck in snow removal.
White Motor reported that 506 owners were operating 18,527 trucks in fleets of ten or more.
White added two new bus models and a limousine for scenic tours.
Many accessory manufacturers offered directional signal indicators.
Specifically designed for moving houses, the Acme Motor Truck Company built a trailer which moved the village of Jennings, Michigan, to Cadillac, eleven miles away.
Frank E. Smith was elected president of General Motors, replacing John N. Willys, who resigned to concentrate on his activities at Willys-Overland.
Republic Motor Truck Company was reorganized. One of its first new ventures was a Knight-Engined Bus with a unique 30-gallon capacity tank fillable through a port in the side of the body.
Only 242 truck manufacturers were listed nationally for 1922. Yet 935 organized motor transport companies operated fleets.
Total truck production for 1922 was 269,991.

1923

New Roads Bring New Taxes

Complementing the advent of increased trucking and bus popularity, 26,536 miles of new roads were opened under the Federal Road Aid Program. Twenty-five states now had a gasoline tax. Eight others were considering it.
Manufacturers expanded their model lines. Typical examples

were: Mack and Master Truck companies each offering fifteen models, U.S. Motor Trucks offering ten models, General Motor Trucks adding seven models.

Six-Wheel Truck Company and Wisconsin Truck Company combined to produce Super-Traction Trucks.

General Motors purchased the Milburn Wagon Company.

Commerce Motor Truck Company superseded Commerce Motor Car Company.

Gray Motor Corporation of Detroit entered the truck field with a light-duty model. General specifications were similar to those of the Gray passenger car which had set a world gasoline economy record of 33.8 miles per gallon on a "coast-to-coast run."

Another new entry in the truck field was Yellow Cab with its Yellow Cab Express Model.

Duplex added a 1-ton speed chassis to its line.

GMC offered an open express body with or without top and with an open or closed cab. Previously, GMC had a policy of only marketing chassis.

Brockway introduced the Model-E Highway Express Line.

Diamond-T announced a 2 1/2-ton model: The U-2.

Pacific Electric Railway Company ordered seventy-one White passenger buses to be used in conjunction with street car service.

Reo introduced a parcel delivery speed wagon. A dome spotlight was standard and the rear bumper provided a center step plate.

Reo acquired Duplex.

Autocar announced an electric truck chassis.

The MacDonald "AB" model with low-bed delivery used a hydraulic steering system.

Wood Hydraulic Hoist and Body Company built a special self-dumping steel body for Ford trucks.

General Motors Chemical Company announced the success of an "ethyl gas" in eliminating engine knocks and providing smoother operation and quicker acceleration.

The World Motor Transport Congress was held in Detroit. The aim of the four-day program was to create a better understanding of the motor vehicle in the economic development of all nations and to help solve urgent transportation problems pressing many countries of the world.

Titan Truck used a special counter-balanced crankshaft to eliminate 4-cylinder engine-vibration and gave exceptional smoothness, quietness, power, and economy.

1920 Dual concrete dump bodies were balanced and hand operated on this Autocar 2-cylinder cab-over-engine truck.

1920 Autocar trucks used by the army in marking the famous Lincoln Highway all the way across the country.

1921   Early recreational vehicles spurred a desire to visit new places. This forerunner of the do-it-yourself mobile home was an attention-getter wherever it traveled.

1921 The use of sleeper cabs such as this spacious 3-ton White was indicative of the growing interstate travel by many fleets.

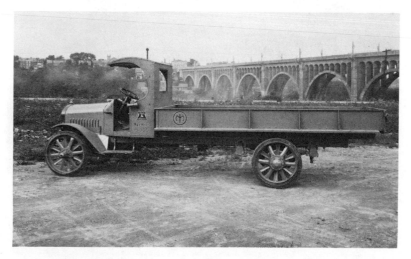

1922 Mack with Bethlehem Steel spoke wheels.

1922   Essex pickup truck by Hudson. (*Courtesy John Conde Collection, Bloomfield Hills, Michigan*)

1922   Heavy-duty GMC 10-ton tractors and trailers used hard rubber tires.

Air cleaners were used by more manufacturers and were offered as standard equipment by some.

A special van body on a Mack chassis featured a bulletproof steel cab and new Saftee glass bulletproof windshield and windows. Bulletproofing protected a driver and load from a rash of truck robberies around New York and Pennsylvania truck routes.

The John F. Ivory Moving Van proved to hold as much as a railroad box car.

Alfred Reeves, general manager of the National Automobile Chamber of Commerce, stressed the need for harmony between electric railroads and bus transportation, and urged the elimination of wasteful competition.

The army tested a 10,000-pound rubber track-laying tractor-truck which featured a suspension cable in place of conventional springs. This spread the weight of the truck over the entire chassis, allowing it to carry heavy loads over light roads without damaging them.

Champion Motor Truck used a 30-horsepower air-cooled rotary engine.

International Harvester offered a guarantee on the crankshaft of McCormick-Deering tractors for the full life of the tractor.

Chair Car Bus Service on a White chassis featured full-size upholstered wicker chairs.

The Garford 6-wheel coach-trailer had a seating capacity for thirty-six passengers although it was only 7 feet wide. The length of the combination was 36 1/2 feet.

A special luxurious motor bus was designed for Kellogg, the cereal magnate. It featured five doors, revolving seats, reclining seats which were convertible to beds, an electric range, a refrigerator, and an enclosed chemical toilet.

Ford Motor Company announced that its truck chassis and tractor production attained a new high of 193,294 units and reached record heights for its total vehicle production for the year of 1922.

A Fageol bus featured forty-eight plate glass windows, seated twenty-eight passengers with reclining seats as an added aspect, and offered air suspension at all four corners.

Direx directional turn signals worked automatically from the service brakes. The right and left signals were operated by push buttons of special design, mounted on an arm that was coupled to the steering column.

Walter offered a four-wheel-drive heavy-duty tractor for use with a 20-ton trailer. Locking differentials were used at three points.

Paige-Detroit Motor Car Company discontinued trucks because of greater demand for Paige-and-Jewett passenger cars.

Helen Schultz, age 23, owned a twenty-four bus transportation line in Des Moines, Iowa.

1923   production increased: 409,295 trucks and buses.

1924
Open Roads Lure Sightseers

Great rewards from the earlier road improvement movements and intensive highway construction became quite evident as the American public set out to explore the wonders of their huge continent. The increasing ranks of tourists with private automobiles were joined by thousands of sight-seeing bus passengers viewing the country for the first time from the windows of luxury coaches.

More than 125 different makes of buses were built by the truck industry. Many offered luxury models and parlor coaches.

White Motor Company shipped 60 buses to Yellowstone National Park for tourist transportation, bringing the park fleet count up to 279 White buses, the second largest bus fleet in the United States.

The National Automobile Chamber of Commerce urged preservation of national scenery and called for curbs on outdoor advertising to allow vision on highways and to preserve the natural scenery.

State, counties, towns, or local units removed snow in the East to keep the nation's highways open during snowbound seasons. One enterprising bus company attached its snowplows to their vehicles to assure uninterrupted travel.

Yellow Coach introduced a low center-of-gravity Y model. Its driving units were off-center to provide a central longitudinal beam to reinforce the floor—an important consideration for such a wide chassis. The engines were mounted on the left side of the chassis but, to give balance, the battery, spare wheel, and gas tank were mounted on the right.

Mack introduced a low, 1-step bus which featured a special chrome steel frame, underslug springs, and drop-type front axle to give a clearance of twenty-five inches from floor to ground.

The Reo cross-country sedan bus with red and green running lights on the back and front of the vehicle made a transcontinental trip. **Many** bus manufacturers used a 6-wheel design.

Safeway Six-Wheel Coach had a number of unusual features: the torque tube that connected the two rear axles was telescopic and filled with oil, allowing the axles to adjust for load, yet keeping them rigid in respect to each other. The spring-suspended axles allowed each wheel to be raised or lowered ten inches and still maintain contact with the road. The significance was the excellent traction it gave. Braking was on all four rear wheels. Inside, passenger grab rails extended the length of the bus; pull cords signaled the driver for an anticipated exit. An entrance safety light operated when the door opened or closed.

The Moreland Six-Wheel Double-Decker Bus featured hydraulic front-wheel brakes, pneumatic tires, drive on all four rear wheels, and 6-wheel brakes.

Scenic bus tours began on the West Coast.

The Mack-Burney safety bus had air brakes, plus air opening-and-closing doors. Air brakes were applied when the driver removed his foot from the accelerator. Its body was steel. Special, inflated rubber guards on doors further cushioned and insured passenger safety during entry or exit.

The first Kenworth truck was introduced: model KS-255.

An Armleder 2 1/2-ton model was introduced. New features included a high speed Buda engine with a 9 1/4-gallon radiator with a core where tubes could be blocked off in case of damage. Other features were an air cleaner, full pressure lubricating system, and cam-and-lever steering.

Bethlehem Motors announced four-wheel brakes as optional on its large models and on its new Airline light-truck models.

The Four Wheel Drive Tractor Truck Company truck was equipped with an air-brake system for both truck and trailer.

The Federal Motor truck made an endurance run from San Francisco to Reno (248 miles) in twelve hours, thirty-five minutes. The truck was loaded with Heinz 57-Varieties products.

A portable, radio broadcasting apparatus by Zenith Corporation was mounted on a Federal Knight truck. The purpose was to find and test the best site for a broadcasting station in Chicago.

Yellow Cab's 6-cylinder sleeve valve engine was said to give low cost on maintenance, high acceleration, fast hill-climbing ability, and smooth operation through the entire speed range.

The Atterbury Highway King model featured a 7-speed transmission on its 5- and 7-ton models.

The Baker Iron Works in Los Angeles built a 6-wheel heavy-steel frame trailer with a 50-ton capacity. The length was thirty feet and the width was eleven feet. Tires were 40 × 14. One of its first tests was hauling a 60-ton steam shovel over a mountain road, the Mulholland Skyway Drive in California.

The Moreland truck introduced a drop-frame chassis.

A Heil dump body with a hydro-assist was offered on the Warner semitrailer. The body had removable sides, an all-steel tailgate, front end, and steel subframe.

The U.S. Bureau of Standards tested vehicle brakes for a uniform national code to regulate braking for motor vehicles was necessary.

1924   production continued to increase: 416,659 trucks and buses.

1925

Highway Bus Looks to Luxury

The motor bus market continued to grow as manufacturers geared for another production record based on previous years. A statistical glimpse of 1924 reveals that over 3 billion passengers were carried by buses in the United States. Over 75 bus companies were serving the public with more than 60,000 buses. In addition, approximately 20,000 more buses were owned by rural schools.

An expansion into luxury buses spread with unprecedented force. Pierce-Arrow, Studebaker, and Ward LaFrance introduced new luxury bus models. The Pickwick Corporation even operated two parlor-buffet-type coaches, designed with individual compartments, reclining seats, a smoking section, a lavatory, and a buffet section complete with a chef.

U.S. Supreme Court decisions emphasized that no state could interfere with interstate commerce, that interstate highways must be open, and that states could not refuse to license buses operating within its borders.

Outdated war excise taxes were still on the books. Since the Federal Motor Excise Tax imposed through the 1917 War Emergency Act was still effective in postwar 1925, the NACC and AAA and numerous vehicle dealer associations urged Congress to repeal all war excise taxes on automotive vehicles.

The **National** Motor Bus Association merged with American Automobile Association's bus division.

The **American** Electric Railway Association Show opened in Atlantic City, emphasizing buses and outfitting bodies.

Hydraulic brakes and gas-electric buses were the major topics at the summer SAE meeting in White Sulfur Springs.

For **Philadelphia**, gas-electric double-deck buses were built by Yellow Coach.

The **U.S.** now had 500,000 miles of surfaced roads.

Officials of the Bureau of Public Roads were appointed to prepare a plan for uniform marking of highways.

The **New Jersey** State Highway Commission planned an exclusive truck highway to connect Newark and Elizabeth with the Jersey City entrance to the Hudson River vehicle tunnel. The distance was to be thirteen miles and would cost an estimated $12 million.

With **the** advent of balloon tires for passenger cars, truck and bus manufacturers took considerable interest in them for commercial vehicles. Despite innumerable advantages, load and inflation pressures presented a problem since balloon tires would require more owner attention, especially on heavy vehicles. Nonetheless, balloon tire use quickly increased on light delivery trucks.

Maxwell-Chalmers was reorganized as Chrysler Corporation.

Dodge purchased the majority interest in Graham Brothers. The deal merged the third largest producer of motor cars with the largest manufacturer of 1 1/2-ton trucks.

Fisher Body Corporation purchased Fleetwood Metal Body Corporation, a custom body-building company.

General Motors purchased Yellow Cab Manufacturing Company.

The **National** Automotive Parts Association was formed.

Chevrolet introduced a new 1-ton general purpose truck chassis.

Ford Motor Company added several successful truck bodies to the commercial vehicle field. Among these was the new light body "Ford Model-T Runabout with Pick-Up Body," basic price $260.

ACF acquired Fageol Motors Company of Ohio and moved operations to Detroit.

An **accessory** signal light, called the Jewel Safe-T-Lite, provided red, green, or yellow signals in addition to right and left turn signals. GO, SLOW, and STOP signals were connected to vehicle controls which operated automatically. The turn signal switch was mounted on the steering wheel's left side to be operated without removing hands from the steering wheel.

Budd-Wheel announced new all-steel dual wheels in Ford sizes of 29 × 4 inches.

GMC offered four-wheel brakes and pneumatic tires as standard equipment on 1-ton and 1 1/2-ton models.

Heil Company introduced twin hoists for dump trucks.

Master truck models were fitted with the Jackson oil engine which burned low-cost fuel and averaged 7 1/2 cents to 8 1/2 cents a gallon.

More than 150 electric railway systems now operated motor buses.

The Studebaker bus with body by the Auto Body Company featured an automatic windshield wiper, a rear bumper, and an interior rear-view mirror.

Lapeer trailer featured an automatic brake which worked with the tubular push rod, so that the trailer would not over-run the prime mover.

United States truck and bus exports for 1925 totaled 58,624 units, more than double the exports of 1924. The total value was nearly $38 million.

Truck production for 1925 was a record: 530,659 trucks.

1926

Trucks Adopt Passenger-Car Features

The passenger car influences offered logical transitions to motor truck construction, specifically in the use of the 6-cylinder engines with their quicker acceleration, smoother power, and high average speeds. Also highlighted into trucks, were more driver comforts, closed cabs, better lighting, low-pressure tires, windshield wipers, air cleaners, and ease of handling.

The emphasis in bus design shifted from appearance to maintenance, accessibility, and reduced operating costs.

The Interstate Commerce Commission announced an investigation of motor truck and bus operations to determine the connection or competition with railways.

There was a move to amend state highway statutes to allow increased use of trailers and semitrailers by recognizing load distribution over additional wheels and longer wheelbases. Most states had maximum axle allowances for trucks only, not trailers.

Pontiac offered a light 1 1/2-ton 6-cylinder delivery truck.

Ford introduced a custom-built Fordson truck rather than a production unit. It was a 2-ton cab-over-engine type, fitted with a high rack stake body.

The Pac-Age-Kar was introduced at the Chicago Delivery Truck Show, featuring an engine and transmission at rear of chassis.

Henrickson introduced its famous equalizer beam suspension. It coupled two rear axles by means of an underslung beam centrally pivoted and combined with conventional leaf springs mounted on the pivot saddle.

National Motors purchased the Day-Elder Company.

C. T. Truck Company absorbed the Electruck Company.

A Yellow Cab truck with a Buick 6-cylinder engine was announced by General Motors.

Rear "under-frame" tire carriers were numerous.

White introduced a heavy-duty dump truck featuring an auxiliary transmission for increased pulling power. Rounded corners in the body bed and a double-acting tailgate controlled by the driver were other features.

Some manufacturers at the New York Show displayed 4-cylinder models and offered 6-cylinder engines as optional.

Service trucks were equipped with oil filters and booster brakes. The brake system used an intake manifold vacuum to amplify the driver's foot pressure on the brake pedal. The oil filter and rectifier removed dust and other foreign matter from oil in the crankcase and vaporized unburned fuel in the oil.

Commerce Truck Company introduced Relay-Drive trucks, wherein a gearing arrangement in the rear wheels was connected with the engine, and a flexible connection between the axle and frame moved the chassis up and forward to an overbalance position.

Walter Motor Truck offered a mechanism for dumping semitrailers by means of an elevated fifth wheel.

New models introduced in 1926 included: GMC's "Big Brute"; Yellow Knight's "Money Maker"; International Harvester's "Special Delivery"; Durant's "Compound Fleetruck"; Federal's "Scout"; Selden's "Pacemaker"; Gramm's "Fast Freighter"; National's "Speedway Six."

The GMC "Big Brute" line had a Fisher Body all-steel cab as standard equipment. An automatic windshield cleaner, sliding Pyralin curtains, folding doors, a cab mounted with shock absorbing rubber discs held in metal containers, channel bumpers, radiator guard, and tow hooks were also featured.

The flat-rate truck service and repair method gained popularity.

Continental Motors introduced a single-sleeve valve engine built under the Argyll patents acquired by Continental. The Argyll-type engine had only one sleeve per cylinder and, in addition to an up-and-down motion, each sleeve rotated in the cylinder. Quieter operation, longer life, better fuel economy, lower production cost, less vibration, and decreased weight were advantages claimed for the engine.

Metropolitan Coach and Cab Company exhibited an eight-wheel, thirty-two-passenger bus. All four front wheels steered.

The door on the Graham Brothers' bus controlled the air brakes in an "on" position for six seconds after passengers left the bus.

Six-Wheel Company offered air brakes as standard equipment on its motor coaches.

A Baker steam bus was introduced.

E. G. "Cannon Ball" Baker drove a fully loaded 2-ton GM truck from New York to San Francisco in record-breaking time—five days, thirty minutes.

General Motors bought Fisher Body Corporation.

American Car and Foundry Motor Company bought Fageol Company.

Ford inaugurated a 5-day 40-hour work week.

Dr. Graham Edgar devised the octane scale for gasoline.

SAE issued a new standard on oil viscosity and introduced SAE designations SAE 10 through 70.

Union Trailer designed a semitrailer for use with the Ford 1-ton truck.

Ball and socket tie rod ends were used by some makers.

Pneumatic tires had surpassed solid rubber tires by 1926, saving taxpayers millions of dollars in repairing road surfaces which would have been pounded to pieces by solid rubber-tired wheels. They also eliminated difficult miles of bone-shaking rides caused by hard rubber tires on poor roads and provided driver comfort with an air-cushioned ride.

Electric Truck Manufacturers Association disbanded. All activities and committees were transferred to a new electric truck committee of the National Automobile Chamber of Commerce.

Trucks accounted for nearly 12 percent of the automotive-industry output.

Total truck production for 1926: 608,617 units.

1927

Power Brake Use Accelerates

Power brake use on trucks grew, stimulated by increased traffic and strong safety need. Good acceleration was as important.

Bus activity continued to expand and followed many of the motor truck trends: 82 percent of the buses used 6-cylinder engines, 73 percent used four-speed transmissions, and 88 percent used pneumatic tires.

It was estimated that of the 80,000 buses in use, some 30,000 were owned by public or private schools.

Twin Coach, ACF, and Versae exhibited buses in which the entire length of the vehicle was available for passengers. The driver sat at the very front of the vehicle, which was similar to a street car. Engines were placed either at the rear or side of the body in compartments.

Under an agreement between the International Harvester Company and the American Car and Foundry Motors Company, salesmen of ACF would sell IH buses and trucks. IH branches would stock parts for ACF buses and Hall-Scott engines.

Commerce Motor Truck and Service Motors merged to form the Relay Motor Corporation.

Republic Motor Truck acquired the Linn Tractor Company.

Roy D. Chapin succeeded Colonel Charles Clifton as the new head of the National Automobile Chamber of Commerce.

The Motor Truck Association of Chicago was formed by representatives of practically all leading makers of trucks sold in that city. The primary aim was to improve truck merchandising. Other states were said to be considering the idea.

Mack introduced a model powered by a 110-horsepower diesel engine with a Lanova precombustion-chamber cylinder head.

Twin Coach started production in Kent, Ohio.

Willys entered the light commercial vehicle field with its introduction of a Whippet chassis in seven body styles.

Hug Company introduced a dump truck for hauling wet concrete; the batch was remixed at dumping.

Ford introduced a 1 1/2-ton truck model with a 40-horsepower, 4-cylinder engine, multiple disc clutch, 3-speed transmission, and 4-wheel brakes. The price was $460. It was based on the Model-A.

The Dodge Brothers coupe and roadster models offered telescoping drawers in the rear of the vehicles for $100 extra.

Chrysler introduced a duplex channel frame.

More than 1 million Ford 20-horsepower trucks were operating all over the world.

International Harvester announced a business coupe, mounted on a 3/4-ton truck chassis. The low side body was designed to appeal to specialty salesmen.

The new Reo Speed Wagon Junior featured a rubber-suspended engine, a 7-bearing crankshaft, Lockheed four-wheel hydraulic brakes, and Hotchkiss drive.

Divco-Detroit Company introduced a door-to-door delivery truck. The truck could be driven from the driver's seat or side platforms midway between the front and rear wheels.

AC Spark Plug Company introduced a mechanically operated fuel pump consisting of a diaphragm pump, operated by a lever driven from the push rods, tappets, or eccentrics on either side of the camshaft.

Fageol Brothers organized the Twin-Coach Company and produced the first "integral" bus with underfloor engine amidships.

All windows on the Murray Duralumin coach were fitted with Protex safety glass. The windshield was Triplex glass.

Jones Gear of Benton Harbor, Michigan, manufactured a Hi-Life dump body which could be raised eight feet vertically for dumping.

Warner Manufacturing Company, a trailer manufacturer, offered an electric brake for trucks and trailers. It was connected to the truck's regular electric system.

Total truck production for 1927: 464,793.

1928

Color and Design Brighten Light Trucks

Trucks with contoured, streamlined fenders and sparkling hues of coordinated color brightened the New York Show in 1928. Nickeled headlamps, belt moldings, sun visors, and other luxury passenger car improvements began to appear on light trucks.

The popularity of 6-cylinder engines continued, while the 4-wheel brakes assumed greater importance as speed and power increased.

Demand for high-speed vehicles with pneumatic tires in 1927 was so strong that increased conservatism in truck selling methods occurred, that is, reforms on used truck trade-ins and caution in credit selling surfaced.

Steering gears became more powerful to reduce driver effort.

The steering wheel was placed at a more comfortable angle and more manufacturers were fitting booster mechanisms for braking.

Pressure lubrication became standard on many makes.

Many manufacturers increased the cooling capacity of their models. Thermostats in cylinder heads were finding wider use.

A trend in bus bodies included the observation-type coaches with full head room in the aisle, leather air-cushioned individual seats with adjustable seat backs, mirrors, ashtrays, and individual lights.

The first highway interchange was built in New Jersey.

Highway expenditures for 1928 totaled well over $500 million.

An Interstate Commerce Commission attorney examiner, Lee J. Felymo, recommended federal control of buses and trucks involved in interstate commerce. The recommendation was based on an ICC investigation conducted throughout the country since 1926. At a hearing on February 10 in Washington, a spokesman for the automotive industry voiced strong objections to any federal regulations of the motor truck.

A special truck for road patrol and maintenance was built by the Greenville Manufacturers Works. It was called the Omort truck, an acronym for a "One-Man Operated Road Truck."

Chrysler Corporation purchased the Dodge Brothers, Incorporated, outright on an exchange-of-stock basis.

Brockway Motor Truck merged with Indiana Truck Company.

Nash discontinued the Quad truck.

The 1928 Ford truck chassis was upgraded to an increased payload of 1 1/2 tons. The higher capacity necessitated a more massive frame, a heavier transverse front spring, and comparably stronger components. Its driveline was also stronger with a 2-piece driveshaft, larger radius rods, and a heftier worm axle.

The Federal Motor Truck used a driveaway system with one driver in charge of three trucks. By this, the company hoped to lower F.O.B. prices of their vehicles.

World Motors Company introduced an 8-cylinder model truck.

GMC expanded and improved its 1 1/2-ton to 4-ton models with Buick engines. The 1-ton Buick-engine model was discontinued.

The sporty Luxford taxicab was unveiled. Smart in appearance and speedy, the unconventionally low body was built on a standard Model-A chassis. It was designed by Edsel B. Ford.

The Hendrickson two rear-driving axles of its six-wheel model featured a 3-point mounting, wherein the weight of the truck would take care of most of the torque reaction of the axles. Additionally, two worm housings were connected by ball joints through a torque arm connected to the frame.

The Four Wheel Drive HT-Model had a manually operated differential lock so the driver could cut differential action in the center and rear axle differentials on extreme road conditions where loss of traction might result. Four power take-offs were provided for winch, air compressor, boring units, or other mechanisms.

Studebaker offered a new parking brake on its truck models. The brake consisted of a 14-inch cast steel disc, mounted on the driveshaft with a pair of shoes clamped on each side of the disc to effect the braking.

Autocar featured a rotary dump hoist with a maximum dumping angle of 60 degrees.

Mack introduced a 6-cylinder engine in its 3- to 4-ton BJ Model. Gasoline feed was by Triplex electric pump.

The Yellow Truck Division of GMC introduced a small bus powered by a Cadillac V-8 engine. Additional features included four-wheel hydraulic brakes, self-adjusting ball-and-socket tie rods, front and rear bumpers, automatic windshield wipers, and a blower-type heater.

Fargo Motor Corporation, a division of Chrysler, introduced a 1/2-ton 4-cylinder model, called "Packet" and a 3/4-ton model designated the "Clipper."

Mack introduced a hypoid bevel gear, with a single-reduction rear axle on its Model BB. The advertised advantage of new drive was that it could be mounted above the axle and give straight-line drive under full load. It was also quieter, simpler, lighter, and more efficient than double reduction drive.

Pierce-Arrow introduced a 10-ton model "RG" with dual ignition systems that were entirely separate and individual.

Lockheed hydraulic four-wheel internal brakes were standard on Federal trucks.

New models offered were: American LaFrance "Chief"; Reo Speed-Wagon "Tonner"; Selden "Pacemaker"; Pierce-Arrow "Fleet Arrow"; Autocar "Trail Blazer"; Durant "Rugby Fast Mail"; Maccar "Sure-Trac"; Indiana "Ranger"; IHC "Six-Speed Special"; and the Hug "Express Flyer."

Bender Body Company developed a bus body with a roof to carry luggage inside the bus on shelves over the seats.

By 1928, all forty-eight states had imposed gasoline taxes, ranging from 2 to 5 cents per gallon.

Graham Brothers of Chrysler introduced three new motor coaches, embodying a number of improvements in performance, safety, and comfort. All models used the Dodge Senior-Six engine with four-wheel hydraulic brakes, radiator shutters and thermostat, gasoline and oil filters, adjustable driver's seat, and recessed seating for increased knee room.

Delling Motors developed a 3-cylinder double-acting horizontal steam powerplant mounted amidships of its twenty-seven passenger bus. A horizontal fire tube boiler was mounted under the hood. The makers claimed that fuel costs would average 5 to 6 cents per gallon, give better acceleration, better hill climbing, and longer life for the engine.

Graham Brothers' twelve-passenger coach had individual bucket seats.

Eleven percent, or 315,000 trucks, of all commercial-vehicle registrations were operated in fleets of ten or more trucks.

Texaco was first to market gas in all forty-eight states.

Pickwick added an all-metal coach called "Nitecoach," featuring sleeping compartments. The unit body coach accommodated twenty-six passengers and was 34 feet long, 10 feet high, 8 feet wide, and constructed of Duralumin. Compartments were in an upper-lower level arrangement, with chairs that converted into berths.

The year 1928 was the greatest production and export year to date.

1928 truck production totaled 583,342 trucks.

1929

Door-to-Door Delivery Develops

A trend to door-to-door delivery trucks developed in 1929, and the last defense for horse-drawn vehicles began to collapse. The often-cited advantage of using the horse for delivery because he "knows the route" lost ground to the speed, efficiency, durability, and range of the motor truck.

Smart businessmen noted the easier door-to-door truck trend, and a mobile grocery store movement surfaced again.

Numerous advantages claimed for balloon tires—lower cost, better mileage, better traction, softer cushioning, and speed—hastened their use on light trucks.

Optional axles were interchangeable. Radiator shells, springs, drag links, clutch pedals, spring hangers, and shackles were becoming interchangeable between various truck models.

Intrigued with the potential of diesel engines, many truck manufacturers experimented with it for practical use. But the advantage of its fuel savings equated against high initial production costs, delayed its use. The diesel's weight and complicated structure delayed its progress.

Aluminum use increased in trucks and trailers because of its lightness. This gave trucks greater load capacity.

Because many states limited gross vehicle weight for highway vehicles, the gain in payload from lighter bodies helped offset the higher cost of aluminum.

Republic Truck and American-LaFrance agreed to consolidate, subject to ratification by their stockholders. The new company came to be known as the LaFrance-Republic Corporation.

Four Wheel Drive Auto Company acquired Menominee.

The U.S. Supreme Court ruled that interstate carriers were subject to state insurance laws.

Hudson Motor Company entered the light truck field with the Dover model.

Hug Company offered a 5-ton Roadbuilder with the engine overhanging the front axle. The front bumper was of channel steel.

Larrabee-Deyo stressed interchangeability of many parts in its model lines. All models used four-wheel hydraulic brakes. Those over three tons supplemented the hydraulic brakes with a vacuum booster. Six-cylinder Continental engines were standard.

1923 Ward's drop-frame electric anticipated the low cab-forward movement that came back in styling in later years.

1924 Steel-hauling Mack Bulldogs were part of the Ryerson steel
fleet.

1926   This White 3 1/2-ton heavy-duty model with stake body still used hard rubber tires despite the growing use of pneumatic tires for heavier models.

1926 Typical of the many highway buses serving the tourist boom, this White 6-cylinder model featured a 100-hp overhead valve engine, double drop frame, and 4-wheel air brakes.

1928 The grocery store on wheels complemented door-to-door delivery trucks. This special body was built on a 1928 Dodge chassis. (*Courtesy National Automotive History Collection, Detroit Public Library*)

1928   White 2 1/2-ton model 51-A supplying the power to clean streets in Augusta, Kansas.

1929   Dodge truck with high-stake body was popular in farm delivery work.

Allison Engineering Company joined General Motors.

Reo Motors introduced its 6-cylinder Gold Crown engine, featuring a vibration dampener on the front of the crankshaft, a combined fan-and-water pump unit driven by an adjustable V-belt, cylinder blocks of chrome nickel alloy iron, oil pressure regulator, and removable water-jacket plates for cleaning the jackets.

Sanford Motor Truck introduced the Cub series.

Studebaker introduced a straight eight 115-horsepower engine on its truck and bus chassis. An automatic choke and a dual-ignition distributor with two sets of breaker points were included.

Studebaker offered three body heights and four loading lengths on its three 6-cylinder models, a total of thirteen body choices.

A 100-horsepower White Model-59 tractor truck was built from standard units and sold only on specifications to meet users' needs.

A trend in ice truck bodies developed to eliminate a truck roof, to allow quicker deliveries. The express-type open body could be used in other hauling jobs during slack seasons.

The increased use of trailers spurred truck operators and manufacturers to perceive the need for a fifth-wheel standardization for interchangeable use on tractors and trailers.

Mack manufactured four-wheel trailers of 5- and 10-ton capacity. The trailers housed a main frame and two subframes. A new line of dump bodies was also offered.

Stewart Motor Corporation became the first chassis manufacturer to use aluminum for covering all outside body parts.

Brockway Indiana introduced a six-wheel model SW-40, incorporating a Timken tandem worm-drive rear axle assembly. Westinghouse air brakes were standard equipment and its air tank was mounted above the step brackets.

International Harvester introduced an A-Line of light and medium 6-cylinder trucks up to a 5-ton payload. A bus chassis was included in the line.

The front drive on the Freeman four-wheel-drive trucks used a double-bevel gear assembly universal joints.

Coleman "Roadster" Truck Company introduced six four-wheel-drive models. A low-sided body and a spare tire mounted at the rear of the cab allowed snowplow mounting.

The Maxi Six-Wheeler featured four chain-driven rear wheels.

Dual Duty Company of Alma, Michigan, introduced a four-wheel chain-drive unit for Ford trucks.

Autocar introduced two 6-cylinder engine models: the Six-Cylinder Dispatch SA and SD. Hydraulic brakes were used on the front wheels, mechanical brakes on the rear.

Chevrolet added a sedan delivery model to its truck line. W. S. Knudsen, president and general manager of Chevrolet, outlined plans for production of 1,250,000 cars and trucks in 1929.

Diamond-T models featured brightly colored, lacquered bodies, four-wheel hydraulic brakes with vacuum booster, and nickel-chromium plated head-and-cowl lights.

Ford raised its wage scale to $7-a-day minimum.

Ford used a 6-brake system on truck models similar to that used on Ford passenger cars.

Gramm offered a choice of four to five wheelbases in its line of light trucks.

Fruehauf introduced the 3-ton "Flyer" trailer with cast steel wheels, pressed steel frame, wheeled supports, and a broad-faced fifth wheel tipped toward the rear of the trailer for each engagement. An automatic locking device was an additional feature. Connecting or disconnecting could be completed in thirty seconds, according to the manufacturer.

Motor Car Carrier Company exhibited a double-deck semitrailer. The unit was used for delivering automobiles to dealers in Michigan within a few hundred miles of Detroit.

Leland James organized Consolidated Freightway Truck Lines for versatile, all-purpose freight hauling. It was individually designed to shipper's specifications. The truck line later became Freightliner.

All-steel welded road service bodies were designed for the Ford chassis.

Special bodies for hauling ready-mix concrete long distances were introduced. Agitation of the batch was provided by either power take-offs from the engine or from a separate engine on the chassis.

Timken-Detroit Axle Company developed a self-contained tandem axle four-wheel-drive unit equipped with air brakes. Although intended primarily for original equipment, the unit could be used to replace single driving axles.

Cotta Gear offered a constant-mesh transmission with five forward and two reverse speeds, all controlled by one shift lever.

The use of dry ice in refrigerated truck bodies was replacing the old water-ice method.

Leece-Neville introduced the voltage regulator.
Bethlehem Steel developed an adaptation of a torque amplifier for power steering.
Manufacturers adapted the ventilated disc-type driveshaft brake.
Adjustable steering columns, sun visors, and 4-wheel brakes were offered on many truck models. Sixty-one percent of the 4-wheel brakes were hydraulically operated.
Total production for 1929: 881,909 trucks.

The Thirties

1930

Business Collapse Slams the Brakes on Truck Industry

The stock market crash in late 1929 and the dim business climate in 1930 witnessed a movement to "super trucks" designed for heavier loads and competitive export. Economizing on operating costs was the number one problem facing most fleet owners.

Typical of the heavy-duty model was a 6-wheel truck equipped with 4-wheel drive, a large 6-cylinder engine, a 12-speed transmission combination, air brakes on all six wheels, and a Timken-tandem rear axle.

Aluminum alloys gained wider use in truck and trailer manufacturing. Its weight-saving feature was a plus at a time of cost consciousness.

Most manufacturers offered engine options to prospective buyers.

Heil Company built aluminum truck bodies and tanks, and claimed a weight savings to 50 percent over steel and an increase of 20 to 25 percent in load.

A diesel passenger test car was driven from Columbus, Indiana, to the New York Auto Show by C. L. Cummins, president of the Cummins Engine Company. The engine was a marine-type diesel, installed to test the fuel system under normal road and driving conditions. On the 792-mile trip, the car's average speed was 31 2/3 miles per hour. Fuel cost $1.38, with diesel fuel priced less than 5 cents a gallon.

In nine state legislatures, 1,400 of 15,000 bills introduced affected the vehicle industry. The majority of the bills were directed at the motor truck and motor bus and were restrictive.

Dodge Brothers used "standard" and "heavy duty" to distinguish between its two truck lines.

The smallest commercial delivery vehicle was introduced by American Austin, featuring a 4-cylinder, 45.6-cubic inch engine, the first of the compact trucks.

Studebaker and Pierce-Arrow announced a new joint manufacturing and marketing arrangement through a new organization: the

S.P.S. Truck Corporation. A. R. Erskine was president of the new corporation.

Diamond-T Motor Car Company celebrated its silver jubilee and introduced new models in the low-price market.

International Harvester dropped the name Harvester and called the new models International Trucks.

International Trucks used 'removable' cylinder sleeves as a standard feature.

Manufacturers continued naming engines: Autocar's "Blue Streak"; Reo's "Flying Cloud"; Sterling's "Petrel."

Chevrolet's 1 1/2-ton model offered pressed steel wheels, heavier rear axle, articulated shoe brakes, and an option of dual rear wheels at $25.

Day Elder introduced the "Super Service Six" models.

A new line of trucks called the "Fisher-Standard" was introduced by Standard Motor Truck Company, Detroit.

A six-wheel unit for Ford trucks was offered by Martin-Parry.

General Motors Truck offered a light-duty model.

Stewart Motor Truck Company and the Graham-Paige Company entered the delivery field.

Timken offered double-reduction drive as a substitute for standard rear axle units.

Twin Coach manufactured a house-to-house delivery truck with unit body and frame construction. Sliding doors were mounted behind the front wheels. Design was similar to a small bus.

An 8-cylinder engine was introduced by Ward-LaFrance on its "Bustruk" chassis.

Far ahead of its time, the Buda high-velocity engine called "Hivelo" stressed interchangeability of parts and a crankcase ventilator system through the air cleaner.

The Sterling Petrel engine was the largest 6-cylinder engine in the truck field with a 5 1/4-inch bore, a 6-inch stroke, 779.3-cubic inch displacement, developing 185-horsepower at 2,200 rpm. Dual carburetors with hot spots were used. Heat control could be manual, semi, or fully automatic. Two spark plugs per cylinder were used.

A growing impetus toward power steering began on special purpose trucks, although initial experiments began several years earlier.

Total production dipped in 1930 to: 575,364 trucks.

1931

Refrigerated Trucks Open New Vistas

Although business was still depressed, a new science of quick-freezing opened fresh markets for the fast-growing ranks of refrigerated vehicles. Rapid distribution of produce by the cooled motor trucks provided citrus and other fruit growers with a healthy year-round market. Fresh fruits and vegetables all year were welcomed by truckers, grocers, and consumers alike.

More than seventy-five firms were building refrigerated bodies.

Southern Freight Lines of California tested the feasibility of long-distance hauling in a coast-to-coast run. A GMC refrigerated truck and trailer carried a 21-ton payload of fruit perishables from Los Angeles to New York in 117 hours (a few hours under five days) at an average speed just over 27.3 miles per hour.

The Chicago, North Shore, and Milwaukee Railroad carried piggyback trailers or "ferry trucks" to terminals where road tractors hauled them to their consignees. Railroad flat cars were equipped with locking devices to hold the trailers fast.

New truck restrictions were adopted by eighteen states to lessen the effects of heavy loads on road surfaces. Some states permitted pneumatic tires only on highways. Many states refused to be guided by federal agencies, a major cause for the lack of uniformity in motor vehicle laws.

Five more states added a ton-mile tax, which brought the total to seventeen states imposing such taxes as a fixed rate. The tax varied from two-thirds of a mill to two-thirds of a cent per ton-mile based on gross weight.

The SAE formed a committee to study truck ratings and to devise an acceptable standard of rating trucks.

Railroad freight rates were reduced on completed trucks. The estimated savings would save the truck dealers and operators between $1.5 million and $3 million.

Ford entered the house-to-house delivery field with a "Standrive" model.

A Dodge house-to-house delivery truck was introduced.

Exhibits at the New York Auto Show proved that the trend toward stylized appearance and sharp color hues was still strong.

The 4-cylinder engine previously used in the 1 1/2-ton class suddenly made a comeback after losing ground to 6-cylinder engines. **Bevel** gear drive and full-floating rear axles became popular. **Most manufacturers** offered either 4-cylinder engines or 6-cylinder engines or two sizes of sixes. **Optional** wheelbases were commonplace. **General** Motors Truck Company manufactured semitrailers in addition to its truck lines and featured interchangeable parts between the trailers and trucks. A standard-type fifth wheel could couple with other trailers and adapt to other makes of tractors. **Pierce-Arrow** reentered the truck field with six models, ranging from 2 to 8 tons. A **Cummins** diesel-powered truck was driven coast-to-coast from New York to Los Angeles. **Cummins** founded the Cummins Engine Company to manufacture diesel engines. **White's** house-to-house delivery model featured a single pedal for both clutch and throttle. **The first** V-12 engine in the truck field was unveiled by American-LaFrance and Foamite Corporation. The engine had two banks of six cylinders at an angle of 30 degrees with four ignition distributors, and twenty-four spark plugs with a single overhead camshaft. **The ACF** Highway Express Model had front fenders fastened to the front bumpers and a frame which narrowed toward the rear end of the chassis. Aluminum pistons in the engine had six rings. **Checker** Cab Manufacturing Corporation introduced a utility model which could be used as a light truck or passenger car. It converted from one to the other by folding seats. **Federal** Motor Truck introduced a six-wheel model with two-wheel drive. Only the forward axle of the two rear axles was a driving axle, although both axles were mounted as a unit with parallel, inverted semielliptical springs. **Ford** truck and light delivery car lines offered fifty body types for mounting on Model-A or Model-AA chassis. Price reductions ranged from $5 to $15. A new town car delivery was available in a number of colorful combinations. **Marmon** Herrington offered four- and six-wheel-drive trucks with air-operated brakes on all wheels. The emergency hand brakes were of the disc type with multiple shoe and located between the main and auxiliary transmission to operate brakes on the driveshaft.

Steward introduced an 8-cylinder model.

Reo introduced a line of low-priced semitrailers to complement its 1 1/2-ton speed wagon.

Fruehauf introduced a line of pressed steel frame semitrailers with fully automatic couplers.

Relay Motors Corporation offered a 2-engine, dual-drive truck. Two 8-cylinder engines, either of which could be cut out when desired, drove two rear axles and had individual transmissions with air shifts. Power steering was achieved through hydraulic pressure. Brakes were of the 6-wheel air-controlled type with a vacuum booster. Three gasoline tanks were supplied.

Lee Tobin Company announced manufacture of a small truck called "Toby" for $450. Selden-Hahn assembled the truck.

Gunite Corporation introduced a brake drum with radial fins in back covered with a thin plate. This construction acted as a centrifugal fan to draw air to cool the brake linings and shoes.

The Schacht 10-ton model was equipped with an auxilliary gasoline tank of 35 gallons on the side of the frame in addition to the regular 28-gallon tank under the seat.

Hug Company introduced a new front-spring mounting called the Front Spring Rocker to allow the front axle to rock under the frame without twisting. The strain on engine supports and twisting of radiator, cab, or hood was relieved. The construction of the unit consisted of a U-shaped rocker-bar equalizer with the rocker bar attached to the rear ends of the front springs by double shackles for universal movement.

Four new model Timken four-wheel drive tandem axle units included dual balloon tires and were offered with worm or double-gear reduction drive.

Alabama limited drivers' hours of service.

Federal used bevel gears in its four-wheel rear-tandem unit.

Hydraulic brake control outnumbered mechanical control in most new models offered. Power assist also increased, especially in larger classifications.

Lycoming designed two 8-cylinder engines for trucks and buses.

The Vickers hydraulic-steering system was used on a Mack bus.

A Powermatic ramp was developed by Griswold Powermatic.

Consolidated Freightway Truck Lines merged with Fedral Auto Freight. The new name was shortened to Consolidated Freightlines.

Trucks accounted for 27 percent of the total automobile tax revenue although they comprised only 13 percent of total vehicle registrations.

1931   production continued low for the seventh year with a total of only 432,262 trucks produced.

1932

Federal Regulations
Dim the Dawn of Diesels

Truck interests vigorously opposed the Federal Motor Carrier Act of 1932, which gave the Interstate Commerce Commission regulatory powers over buses and trucks operating in interstate commerce. Truck interests argued that of the 3.5 million trucks and buses in the United States, 86 percent were privately operated and not subject to public control.

The Indiana Motor Truck was the first to offer a model with a diesel engine. The engine was a Cummins diesel.

Cummins diesels were also offered by Sterling and Kenworth trucks.

A Mack-BK bus fitted with a Cummins Motor H diesel engine successfully completed a transcontinental run.

Duplex announced a 32-passenger bus built on its 2 1/2-ton Duplex chassis.

Purity Stores Limited of California put into regular delivery service a White truck with a Cummins diesel.

White announced plans to market the Indiana-assembled truck through its own dealers.

Ford introduced its first V-8 for commercial application.

Eleven manufacturers offered multistop house-to-house delivery trucks. They were: DeKalb, Divco-Detroit, Dodge, Ford, Kenworth, Step-N-Drive, Thorne, Twin Coach, Walker, Ward, and White.

The Relay truck used a hot water heater for its cab. The truck featured twelve forward and three reverse gear ratios in its unit-mounted transmission combination. The latter comprised a 4-speed transmission with a 3-speed auxiliary transmission attached to the rear of the 4-speed transmission.

Four Wheel Drive Auto Company introduced a front-wheel-drive model. The front drive featured a ball-and-socket joint at the end of the axle allowed steering, and a universal joint also transmitted the drive.

The American Association of State Highway Officials adopted the first recommendations on vehicle size and weight limits.

Trailer use and development continued upward. At least thirty firms were now manufacturing semi and full trailer units with wheels and axles in various combinations. The units were stronger, lighter, cheaper, and adaptable to more varied work situations than previous models.

Sterling purchased Republic-LaFrance.

A general trend emerged in the use of a third axle. Its advantage of running twice as much payload appealed to more and more owners, and the increased capacity far exceeded the increased cost of the axle. An added plus, often overlooked, was the addition of two more brakes on such trucks.

Twenty manufacturers offered ready-mix concrete truck equipment.

The National Highway Users Conference was organized.

The federal government enacted a 1 cent excise tax on all gasoline used in the United States.

Bendix introduced the Startix system to actuate the starter motor when the ignition switch was turned on. The company also unveiled an automatic choke.

Sterling featured a chain-driven four-wheel bogie for tandem trucks.

In 1932, the movement of freight by trucks across the United States amounted to 34 billion-ton miles.

Production in 1932 dropped to 228,303 trucks and buses.

1933
Engineering Design Meets
Challenge of Restrictive Legislation

This year dawned with both manufacturers and users apprehensive about pending legislation in federal and state legislatures; however, a new voice was added in defense of the truck industry. The farmer and his spokesmen, the National Grange and the American Farm Bureau Federation, spoke against high gasoline taxes and unnecessary restrictions on truck development.

A survey by the National Highway Users Conference showed that thirty-nine states limited the number of hours that a truck driver could drive on a continuous basis.

Legislatures in New York, Massachusetts and Connecticut sponsored legislation to prohibit truck trailers on the roads. But advances in engineering saved the day. As the effects of federal restrictions continued to mount, innovations like lighter materials, short-coupled combinations, streamlining, drop frames, and unusual shapes were but a few of the successful design features engineers ingeniously employed to overcome the legislative hurdles.

Autocar designed a special front end to meet legislative restrictions on length. Placing the engine under the seat and chopping the front end solved that problem.

General Motors Truck Company built all of its own engines.

The National Transportation Committee, appointed by nationwide groups of insurance companies and railroad-interest groups, comprised such notables as Calvin Coolidge, Clark Howell, Alexander Legge, Alfred Smith, and Bernard Baruch. In its report regarding transportation, the committee stated: "One thing is certain, automotive transportation is in advance in the march of progress. It is here to stay. We cannot invent restrictions for the benefit of railroads. We can only apply such regulations and assess such taxes as would be necessary if there were no railroads and let the effect be what it may."

The American Highway Freight Association and the Federal Truck Association merged into the American Trucking Associations.

Congress legalized the sale of 3.2 percent beer and, with that move, reestablished a lucrative market and historic business ally of the trucking industry. With the brewing industry as one of the nation's biggest truck users, it was reported that the dollar value to the trucking industry would approximate from $32 to $42 million.

The Federated Truck Association of America was formed in Washington at the truck operators' convention. A tentative code for carriers of property by motor or horse-drawn vehicles was submitted to the National Recovery Administration.

The annual SAE meeting in Detroit considered the future of the automotive industry. Topics discussed were fifty miles per gallon, streamlined vehicles, nonshattering flexible windshields and windows, automatic clutches and transmissions, and 2-cycle engines.

The Automotive Parts and Equipment Manufacturers, Incorporated, was organized to represent parts and accessory makers.

Bell Motors introduced its new model, 15-FR, featuring a tubular frame, front-wheel drive, spring sliding in rocker arms, and a low center of gravity.

Diamond-T designed a unique 1,500-gallon, streamlined tank truck. The engine was longitudinally mounted in the rear with the radiator crosswise behind the storage tanks. Double-plated curved windows provided an unobstructed view.

Dodge offered a sedan which was convertible to a commercial sedan by removing steel panels behind rear side windows. An upholstered rear seat was removable through a wide rear door.

Dodge also featured a novel spare tire carrier on its 2-ton model. It was located under the rear of the frame with a supporting carrier plate on rails.

Ford uprated the V-8 to 75-horsepower for its commercial cars and trucks at $60 for trucks and $50 for commercial cars.

Fruehauf unveiled a deluxe semitrailer, featuring modern styling on a drop-frame chassis with a new enclosed support mechanism that prevented shifting of the support under strain or shock.

International Harvester introduced a 1/2-ton delivery model "D-1" to sell for $360.

Hudson reentered the commercial car field with the Essex-Terraplane models in the 1,000-pound category.

Marmon-Herrington offered a line of twenty-one models, ranging from 1 1/2 to 20 tons. All-wheel drive was featured with one of the series offering a Hercules diesel engine at extra cost.

Oshkosh offered a new line of 7-ton to 10-ton four-wheel-drive trucks.

Reo offered a door-to-door delivery model.

The Sterling tilt-cab model's engine was mounted in a compartment between the two seats in the cab. Brakes and clutch were operated by air.

White announced a new city bus with a horizontally opposed 12-cylinder "pancake" engine mounted underfloor.

The Stutz rear-engined Pak-Age-Car was controlled by a single lever for throttle, clutch and brake, eliminating pedals. The front and rear wheels were independently suspended. The engine was removable with the radiator, and a unit-body construction was featured. Front tires extended beyond the front to act as bumpers.

Esco Motor of Pittsburgh was a newcomer in the truck field.

Automatic devices were the star attractions at the New York Auto

Show, where automatic spark advance, automatic choke, automatic starting by use of accelerator pedal, and automatic operation of the clutch were highlights, initiating a trend to make driving easier. Although the new devices required little maintenance, they required regular inspection.

An "electric eye," which turned vehicle lights on or off automatically, was introduced as an accessory item.

A unique maintenance scheme was used by John A. Wanamaker's fleet of 150 trucks in Philadelphia. A different color grease was used each month to ensure proper lubrication.

A semitrailer by Booster Trailer Corporation of Iowa carried its own engine, transmission, and drive line to assist the tractor engine up-hill or in tough going.

The new Ford V-8 engine featured a dual intake manifold and dual carburetor by Stromberg.

American Diesel Engine Company developed a monovalve diesel engine using a single valve per cylinder to give advantages in mixture turbulence. The engine required fewer parts and kept the valves cooler.

Doman and Marks offered a line of air-cooled engines.

Butane gas was used experimentally on the West Coast as an automotive fuel. Several fleet operators using specially designed carburetors reported a 25 percent increase in miles per gallon over gasoline.

The Stromberg automatic choke was offered as a replacement unit on 1933 and 1934 Chevrolets.

Hendrickson signed an exclusive contract with International Harvester Company to provide tandem suspensions.

Thornton Tandem developed a dual-ratio positive four-wheel drive. The 2-speed transfer case with two helical gear trains was carried on cross tubes to provide ratios of 1,176 and 2,023.

Bendix-Westinghouse Automotive Air Brake Company developed an air-steering control unit.

Aluminum alloy used in Gulf Oil Company tank trucks saved approximately 40 percent in weight over steel.

Anodized, the use of color in aluminum, was developed by Consolidated Stamping Company of Detroit.

A special alloy steel with copper-chrome-silicon was used in the carbon-cast crankshaft.

Many sedan delivery models changed to hood-and-radiator designs similar to passenger models.

Plans to merge White Motor and United Truck were abandoned.

More than 300 automotive vehicles were used regularly on the construction site of the Boulder Dam.

Excise tax on gasoline increased from 1 cent to 1 1/2 cents on all gasoline used in the United States.

Three million registered trucks paid $303,467,000 in registration fees, gasoline, and excise taxes in 1933. Trucks represented only 13.5 percent of the motor vehicles registered, but paid 27 percent of the special motor vehicle tax bill.

1933   total production moved up slightly to: 329,218 trucks.

1934

Cab-over-Engine Stages a Comeback

To alleviate the problems of overall length and axle load restrictions, several manufacturers offered engine-under-the-seat models or "camel backs" as they were popularly called. One prophetic sales organization aptly used the term "cab-over-engine" to describe the arrangement.

Camel-back models were offered by Autocar, Mack, Sterling, and Hendrickson.

West Coast fleets used butane fuel under the trade name B-Gas. Increased power at a lower operating cost was claimed and estimates for conversion per truck totaled $240 or $260, depending on the size of tanks. Difficulties in refueling, with a pressing lack of facilities, continued to be major problems.

The Wisconsin Public Service Commission barred trucks weighing more than 6,000 pounds from the state's main roads on Saturdays, Sundays, and legal holidays.

Virginia and Connecticut required mechanical turn-signaling devices on trucks.

To unify tax laws, a Western Truck and Bus Conference was held in Salt Lake City, while the Eastern Truck and Bus Conference met in Harrisburg, Pennsylvania. The conference hoped to develop a nationally uniform plan of truck and bus taxation and uniform motor transport laws.

Since repeal, highjackers switched from stealing bootleg booze to valuable cargo handled by legitimate haulers. The problem on the

Atlantic Coast alone amounted to millions of dollars.

The American Trucking Associations, Incorporated, requested an opportunity for the truck industry to regulate itself under a Code of Fair Competition. In a letter to the federal coordinator of transportation and to members of the Senate and House on the interstate commerce committees, it was pointed out that because of the wide diversity and far-flung nature of the industry, more effective control could be achieved with the Code rather than through a federal agency.

Autocar offered a sleeper seat next to the driver that could extend to a full-length couch or recline to any position desired. A foot and leg rest folded under the cowl when not in use.

The Chevrolet truck now differed from the passenger lines in appearance, as the forward movement of the engine and greater ground clearance gave it a distinct appearance.

Fram introduced a replaceable cartridge oil filter.

Diamond-T had a complete new line of twelve models from 1 1/2 to 5 ton. The gas tank filler was concealed behind a door in the corner of the cab.

Hug Company offered a commercial series to its road building line.

Fruehauf introduced a semitrailer dump body operating on a direct drive through the fifth wheel.

Dodge added a 1 1/2-ton model.

The Euclid Trac-Truck was designed for road building and other heavy-duty work.

The world's largest trailer was used at Boulder Dam and weighed forty-one tons. A total of thirty-two Goodyear solid tires supported the load with two axles at each of four corners.

Federal entered the low-price truck field with a new 1 1/2-ton model, the 15-X. Fuel lines were carried outside the frame and the fuel pumps were shielded from engine heat to prevent vapor lock. Indirect lighting illuminated the instrument panel.

Ford announced 1935 model lines with a new gasoline tank filler location, plus insulated roof and cowl. Safety glass was now standard on windows, doors, and windshield. A coupe-type, all-steel cab was equipped with an adjustable, tilting driver's seat.

Driver comfort became an important issue to Mack trucks when two new cab-over-engine models called "traffic type" models were introduced. The cab's driver-comfort design included leather-covered, deep-comfort spring seats and back cushions. Drop-type ventilator windows, special door ventilators to draw off warm air inside the cab, dome light, coat hooks, and an electric ventilator fan were added for driver comfort. The engine was located between seats and floor boards, and was covered by a hinged, heavy-insulated, sheet-steel housing that was heat tight, gas-proof, sound proof.

The GMC cab-over-engine model provided a wind tunnel engine shroud which took hot air and gases from under the hood to under the body. Interior cooling was facilitated by a ventilation system. Fresh air was drawn through three ducts above the windshield into the cab through adjustable doors in the roof. Air was exhausted through roof ventilators back through ducts in the cab roof in front of the vehicle. The engine was mounted on a subframe with rollers to allow removal by sliding it from the front of the vehicle after the stud-attached bumper was removed and hinged-grill swung out.

International Harvester built its own 1/2-ton model, designated the C-1.

Ward La-France introduced a line of diesel-powered tractors and a cab-over-engine Model-K.

White offered two 12-cylinder "pancake engine" truck models. The engines had horizontally opposed cylinders and were located under the floorboards of the cab.

White also offered a new multistop delivery truck with a drop frame.

Consolidated Freightlines built their first COE model.

The first diesel-fuel service pump appeared at the Associated Company in Los Angeles.

Automatic and semi-automatic transmissions for trucks received increased attention by researchers. The Mono-Drive Semi-Automatic Transmission was used on a General Motors bus. Shifts were controlled by the accelerator pedal.

The Newell-Swift streamlined coach was equipped with an electro pneumatic gear shift.

A frameless aluminum alloy semitrailer with a chassis was designed for the Baltimore Transfer Company by Fruehauf. The trailer weighed 3,705 pounds, was 219 inches long, 94 19/32 inches wide, and 7 feet by 4 7/8 inches high.

Buda offered two full-size heavy-duty diesel engines built under a license from M.A.N. Company of Germany.

Federal excise tax on gasoline was reduced to 1 cent.

1934 production jumped sharply to 576,205 trucks and buses.

1930 Indispensible to firefighting and rescue work was this Kleiber searchlight truck of San Francisco's Fire Department.

1931 Federal 6-wheeler hauling a Heil 600-gallon petroleum tank.

1932 Cummins tested his diesel engine coast to coast in a Mack bus. The New York to Los Angeles trip of 3,220 miles took 78 hours. (*Courtesy Cummins Engine Company*)

1932 Cummins demonstrated the economy and durability of his 6-cylinder diesel engine in this Indiana truck's cross-country tour. He proved speed and economy, traveling 3,214 miles in 97 1/2 hours with a fuel cost of only $11.22.

1932 Purity Stores of California bought five trucks with Cummins Diesel "H" engines. (*Courtesy Cummins Engine Company*)

1932 Dodge with a special custom-built body for unusually large hauling loads.

1933 Essex-Terraplane-6 enclosed panel delivery truck for multipurpose services.

1934 Chevrolet Six with new stake body mounted on a 131-inch wheelbase.

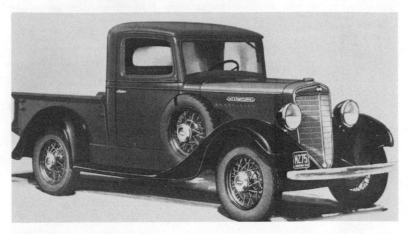

1935   The International 1/2-ton C-1 pickup model featured an all-steel body with attachments to accommodate a special slip-on top and side curtains for cargo compartment.

1935   Rugged Linn tractor powered by a Cummins diesel engine.

1935   Sporting new streamlined styling, tank body on a Dodge chassis fitted to petroleum delivery.

1936 Henry Ford and his son Edsel stand next to their 3 millionth truck—an important Ford milestone. (*Courtesy Ford Archives, Henry Ford Museum, Dearborn, Michigan*)

1936 Dodge 1 1/2-ton panel truck, popular with retail stores, laundries, groceries, bakeries.

1936   Breweries continued to be major truck users.

1936   The Stutz Pak-Age-Car was a familiar sight in most neighborhoods as door-to-door delivery service became commonplace.

1935

Diesels, Streamlining, Lead Prosperity

The year saw a new upswing toward prosperity, with truck production exceeding the pre-Depression boom of 1929.

On-going improvements in diesel development resulted in successful performance of the diesel truck engine. This success culminated years of expensive and difficult experimental research for solving overwhelmingly complex problems for reliable operation of powerful diesel assets into motor trucks. Lower "fuel cost" was a prime asset of the diesel engine. It used fewer pounds of fuel for a given horsepower output than comparable gasoline engines. But controlling undesirable diesel exhaust fumes, high initial costs, unavailability of specialized or experienced repairmen were major problems that had retarded diesel progress.

Persistence and success in engineering nonetheless led to widespread diesel demand among truckers, especially for long-distance up-hill hauling where greater power with fuel economy spelled the difference between profit and loss.

Diesel fuel—once tax free—was now taxed in thirty-three states.

Cummins introduced a 331-cubic inch 6-cylinder diesel, developing 85 horsepower at 200 revolutions per minute, weighing 1,200 pounds. The engine was cast en bloc.

Other smaller diesel engines were: Buda-Lanova, 275-cubic inch, six cylinders, and the Hercules models, 260 and 280-cubic inch models.

Sterling offered a forwardtilt-cab diesel made mostly of heat-treated aluminum alloy, especially designed for hauling an aluminum tank trailer.

Autocar offered Waukesha diesel-powered trucks.

The excitement of streamlined automobiles and trucks paralleled the intrigue in diesel engines.

Autocar offered a streamlined tanker.

The Diamond-T 1936 streamlined models featured new rubber engine mountings, redesigned grill, cab, fenders, and a V-type windshield which sloped to 30 degrees.

Reo introduced a streamlined 1 1/2-ton model and built a streamlined tanker for Sunoco.

White introduced a new line of streamlined trucks designed by the famed industrial designer, Count Alexis de Saknoffsky.

Indiana entered the low-price market with a streamlined model.

Amidst the excitement of new designs, President Roosevelt signed the Motor Carrier Bill for federal regulation of motor carriers.

The Interstate Commerce Commission created a Motor Carrier Division to regulate motor trucks. The division would have fifteen to twenty district offices throughout the country with the central staff headquartered in Washington.

Seven state legislatures proposed legislation to require licensing of automobile mechanics.

The U.S. Supreme Court declared code regulations, such as the National Recovery Act trucking code, as unconstitutional. An emergency meeting of American Traveling Association was called to reshape policies. It was decided to continue supporting the Eastman Bill with amendments to increase the size of the ICC, establish a Highway Division for Regulation, permit membership of individual operators, and to support all divisions within ATA for over-the-road haulers and other groups.

Autocar introduced three 4-wheel-drive models.

Reo offered a 1/2-ton pickup model.

The Dearborn cab-over-engine model was offered by Transportation Engineers through Ford dealers.

Ford had produced 3 million trucks.

Hendrickson Motor Truck Company developed a combination highway and rail truck.

International announced a 4- to 5-ton streamlined tractor-semi-trailer.

The Mack Traffic Models CH and CJ had roll-out engines for easy maintenance, short wheel base, and an all-metal roof built integral with the cab. Doors were hinged at the rear and access was by a step in front of the fender with an assist bar.

Reo introduced a short wheelbase cab-over-engine model, the Speedwagon.

Studebaker introduced the Metro-Cab forward model in the 1 1/2- to 2-ton field and gave distinctive names to all four chassis models in its new lines: the 1 1/2-ton Ace, 2-ton Boss, 2 1/2-ton Mogul, and the 3-to-4-ton Big Chief.

Truck Equipment Company introduced torsion-bar suspension to replace conventional leaf springs.

The Waukesha-Hesselman diesel engine was available for trucks. The engine weighed only thirty to fifty pounds more than an equivalent gasoline engine. Ignition was by electric spark. The engine was started with gasoline, carried in a separate tank, and, after several revolutions, normal operation on diesel fuel began.
Marvel Carburetor Company experimented with direct fuel injection for trucks and buses.
An increased number of directional signals were offered in the accessory field.
Deep-skirted fenders had popular impact on most makes.
Mack had a combination gasoline and crankcase oil gauge. By pressing a button, the driver could instantly tell the quantity of oil in the crankcase.
Marmon-Herrington introduced a complete line of four- and six-wheel-drive trucks, ranging from 8,400 pounds to 52,000 pounds. Also new was ALL-WHEEL-DRIVE construction on a Ford V-8 truck. The cost: below $1,500.
Among many adaptations for Ford trucks was one where a manufacturer mounted an additional engine with a driveshaft at the driver's side to drive a third axle. It featured cab-over-engine.
Four Wheel Drive Intercity Special Model X6 had a 50-gallon tank mounted on the running board.
Steward introduced a 3 1/2-ton model.
Many companies were experimenting with independent front-wheel suspension for trucks up to 2 to 3 tons.
Many fleets used "decal transfers" for lettering their trucks.
Rumor had it that supercharging truck engines to improve performance was in the near future.
A sprayed-on porcelain enamel finish was used on a Langendorf bakery truck on the West Coast. The porcelain enamel was sprayed on, then baked at 1,700 degrees for five minutes. The process was said to be cheaper than normal paint refinishing and would last a minimum of ten years.
Delaware and California required directional signals for loaded vehicles if the loads obscured hand signals.
Long-distance truck travel became commonplace and the successor to the American "cowboy" emerged. Hollywood produced a full-length feature movie about a long-haul trucking company, starring James Cagney, entitled "The St. Louis Kid."
Growing competition among fleet owners influenced them to out-

fit their drivers with a "uniformed look." A prominent early sartorial look featured the black celluloid bow tie.

1935   production increased to: 697,367 trucks.

1936

Long-Distance Hauling Concept Begins

A feasibility test run for long-distance hauling was made from Chicago to Los Angeles by Keeshin Transcontinental Freight Lines, Incorporated. Terminals were spaced as near as 200 miles apart. The round trip run took 223 hours (nine days, six hours) to complete 4,894 miles.

General Motors inaugurated the Parade of Progress Tour of 200 miles. The tour had twenty-eight GMC trucks with bodies where the upper half of the sides lifted up and the lower sides were let down to join two trucks for exhibition purposes.

Recognition of the importance of weight distribution provided by trailers was evidenced by laws in forty-two states that favored the tractor-trailer combination over the four-wheel truck. Twenty-five states favored the tractor-trailer over the six-wheel truck in the amount of gross weight.

Emphasizing the difficulties of trucking fleets, it was reported that the forty-eight states and the District of Columbia had forty-nine varieties of regulation for safety and equipment.

A poll of 150 fleet owners indicated that 72 percent credited longer engine life and fuel and oil economy to the use of engine governors. On the negative side, half of those polled cited the interference with power in the middle gears.

Inconsistent legislation within states continued to affect truck and trailer development and design. Restrictive legislation on lengths, widths, axle and gross weights, brakes, lights, etc., varied so much that many operators welcomed the Interstate Commerce Commission and its regulatory powers, hoping for reasonable and uniform requirements.

As fuel prices continued to rise, there were more advocates of alcohol-blended gasolines.

Mack entered the low price truck and bus fields with the Mack Jr. models. The new line was a radical departure from the previous policy of manufacturing only heavy-duty vehicles.

Marmon-Herrington converted a Ford 1/2-ton V-8 model for army utility which inspired later Jeep-type vehicles.

Some states adopted compulsory vehicle inspection laws.

A 1 1/2-ton model B Chevrolet truck was modified to a six wheeler with Thornton four-rear-wheel-drive unit. The truck hauled a 22-foot Trailmobile with a payload of 30,620 pounds over 2,639.9 miles in a certified economy run. Running time was 134.01 hours (approximately five days, eight hours), with an average speed of 19.7 miles per hour, at just over five miles per gallon. Three and seven tenths quarts of oil were consumed.

Chevrolet truck introduced an all-steel cab.

Dodge truck offered "fore-point" load distribution, which placed more of the payload on the front axle.

LeBlond-Schacht and Ahrens-Fox Fire Engine companies merged and retained the Ahrens-Fox name.

Reo Motor Car Company dropped passenger cars to start exclusive production of trucks and buses.

Ford assembled its three millionth truck on May 12 at the Rouge Plant in Dearborn, Michigan.

Bantam announced that its commercial models would run forty-five to fifty miles per gallon of gas at speeds up to sixty miles per hour.

Sears, Roebuck and Company initiated a program where all its drivers and helpers were trained and qualified in first-aid. Each truck carried a first-aid kit.

An automobile fitness law in Chicago rejected 60 percent of the passenger cars tested as faulty and unsafe. Only 10 percent of the trucks tested were rejected and the majority of those were owned by private haulers. Fleet equipment passed all tests.

The Interstate Commerce Commission published proposed safety regulations for motor vehicles involved in interstate or foreign commerce. The publication was designed to encourage criticism and initiate a public hearing for revisions of the regulations.

The National Automobile Dealers Association moved its headquarters to Detroit's Hotel Statler.

Some states initiated port-of-entry legislation whereby fees could be collected, permits checked, weights and loads checked, and clearances issued.

The Dodge 1/2-ton commercial car adopted a truck-type double drop frame which had deeper side rails and five cross member with rear support for the engine.

International Harvester added eight 6-wheel models to its model line. Three models had 2-speed rear axle combinations. Two of the models had driving third axles, while six had trailing third axles. The combination provided a 6-wheel truck with eight forward speeds and two reverse speeds.

Federal developed a 1 3/4-ton, 4-cylinder truck for light delivery.

Fruehauf offered a new refrigerated semitrailer.

Oshkosh built a special four-wheel-drive tractor for earth moving.

Terraplane introduced a 3/4-ton panel delivery.

Chevrolet trucks were equipped with hydraulic brakes.

The Hug Lugger model 95, a front-and-rear-drive dump truck model, had front and center steering.

International introduced a 1/2-ton milk-delivery model.

Gramm announced a new line of ten truck series.

Mack developed an automatic fifth-wheel safety-device parking brake which remained set when the landing gear was down. It was impossible to raise the landing gear until the coupling was correct.

Reo's new streamline model 2-D4M offered an optional 2-speed axle and double reduction differential.

GMC offered a rear bumper to avoid rear collisions where cars telescope under trucks and trailers.

Studebaker offered the automatic hill holder on truck and bus models. The device was located in the hydraulic brake line and maintained brake pedal pressure as long as the clutch pedal was kept depressed.

Four Wheel Drive introduced a T-40 model for high-speed heavy-duty hauling.

Walter six-wheel truck had driven front and rear axles.

Diamond-T displayed a light diesel truck at the Chicago show.

Poloroid glass was introduced and tested for headlight lens.

New metals in trailer construction made it possible to construct trailers without a chassis. The construction was termed "monocoque" and transferred the weight-carrying capacity from the chassis to the girder-built body.

A hot spark ignition for oil-burning engines was offered by the Mallory Electric Corporation.

Chevrolet added a coupe pickup to its line of vehicles. The pickup combined the passenger-car look with the utility of a truck.

1936   truck and bus production showed a steady climb to 782,220.

I937

Traffic Safety Becomes a National Concern

The Automotive Safety Foundation was organized this year by top-ranking executives of automobile, truck, accessory and finance companies. A half-million dollars were spent by the foundation in 1937 to promote safety.

Reflecting the nationwide concern for safety, the Interstate Commerce Commission established new regulations covering driver qualifications, driving rules, accident reporting, and new standards for safety equipment. The requirements for safety equipment were:

Brakes—Two separate means on all four wheels (except trailers under 300 pounds). On all trailers over 300 pounds with breakaway brake, brakes must stop within thirty feet at twenty miles per hour (brakes on all four wheels). Where brakes are not on all wheels— forty-five feet at twenty-five miles per hour.

Chains—Vehicles outside of corporate limits must carry tire chains. Trailers must have a stay chain or cable to prevent breakaways.

Fire extinguishers—Every truck and tractor must carry at least one fire extinguisher.

Flags—A red cloth flag twelve inches square must be used when projecting loads are carried. Outside corporate limits: two red flags.

Flares—Three flares or three red lanterns must be carried on every truck and tractor, unless operated solely on lighted streets.

Fuel tanks—Main and auxiliary tanks must be permanently attached with no projection beyond side of truck.

Glass—Safety glass must be used in replacement for windshield, rear window, and driver's side window.

Lights—Two headlights, one taillight, and one stoplight. Clearance lights were required on front and rear near top of the vehicle. One spare bulb for each type of light must be carried on vehicles operating outside of corporate limits.

Mirror—Every vehicle must be equipped with a rear view mirror.

Reflectors—Red reflector on each side of rear of vehicle.

Windshield wipers—One device controllable by driver for cleaning snow and rain from the windshield.

The West Coast surpassed the East in diesel use. In the West, better size and weight limits, longer distance hauling, and lower fuel prices were more evident.

Trends noted in truck design were: all-metal bodies with emphasis on strength and lower weight; cab-over-engines; more powerful and better-balanced engines; hydraulic valve lifters; and synchromesh transmissions.

Not only was the truck expected to handle its load with ease, it had to look better and do the job better. Trucks tended to be larger, heavier, with a wide choice of transmission options. As the trucks grew in size, engineers were faced with the demand for better fuel economy and performance.

Aluminum was increasingly used, and tubular body frames with all-welded construction were on the horizon.

Use of synchromesh transmissions and high-heat conductive cylinder heads increased.

International Harvester offered twenty-six new models in its D-line, featuring heavier, more powerful brakes, adjustable seats and back cushions, roomier cabs, styled harmoniously with the sweeping fender lines and overall streamlined look. International Harvester also introduced its first diesel-powered cab-over-truck model "C-300."

Federal Motor supplemented its 1937 models with a line of oversized "H" models for heavy-duty applications. Heavier rear-end, larger axles, springs, brakes, universals, and tires added 300 to 400 extra pounds to the trucks.

General Motors formed a Diesel Engine Division to manufacture Winton diesels in a new plant constructed in Detroit.

Air-Cooled Motor Corporation, a manufacturer of heavy-duty air-cooled engines, announced the acquisition of Franklin Automobile Company's name, trademark, and patents. The new company had acquired the plant and assets of Doman-Marks Engine Company a short time earlier.

General Electric offered refrigerated bodies, including automatic power take-off, hold-over, and dry-ice types.

Interpretation of the Federal Motor Carrier Act in determining common carriers, contract carriers, and agents continued to be confusing. The American Trucking Associations formed a Private Carriers Division to represent that view. Small operators claimed that ICC decisions favored big operators.

GMC offered a complete series of cab-over-engine models, the F-series. Dual-tone paint combinations were offered as standard.

Studebaker announced a new 1/2-ton "Coupe-Express" model which featured its automatic hill-holder that kept the truck from rolling down hill after coming to a complete stop.

Plymouth introduced pick-up and sedan lines.

Luce Manufacturing Company (body builders) streamlined the "*Mechandor*," a special-delivery model.

Hudson announced its "Big Boy" 3/4-ton commercial vehicles.

New models for the year included: Studebaker's cab forward 1 1/2-ton; Mack's EN truck and EQ tractor; Plymouth's commercial pickup and commercial sedan; White's two streamlined Indiana models; Diamond-T's two diesel models with 2-speed rear axles.

International dump models featured an "armor-plate shield" extending over the top of the cab protecting cab and driver.

Studebaker added a diesel-engine model to its truck lines. Offered in three wheel bases—138, 162, and 180 inches—the model used the Hercules DJXB engine.

White Merchander model mounted the engine back of the front axle under the floor. Access was by means of large trap doors flush with the floor. Capacity of the light delivery truck was 350-cubic feet, 318 of which were in back of the driver's seat.

Gramm Motor Truck announced a new line of trailers and semi-trailers with trailer ratings from 18,000 to 42,000 pounds. New radius rods and springs were featured along with a double-line vacuum brake hook-up with built-in slack adjusters.

United Parcel developed its own cab-over-engine package delivery truck, which featured tubular frame and unique steam-cooling system with roof-mounted condensors.

Ozone generators were used to sterilize and deodorize food truck bodies. The floors were dampened and the ozone generator turned on. Upon opening the body doors, the ozone was dissipated by fresh air. The system saved time and left no chemical traces.

"Cle-Air," a combined air-cushion and shock-absorber for commercial vehicles, was developed by Cleveland Pneumatic Tool Company. The device was designed for use with the rear springs and provided a varying rate of deflection for a soft, controlled ride on severe road shocks.

The Society of Automotive Engineers annual meeting provided a forum for truck operators to voice complaints and solutions to ease the problem of maintenance. Although GVW ratings increased, engine size had not kept pace, and a better balance for uniform performance was required.

Vacuum kits for brakes on Chevrolet and Ford trucks were introduced by several accessory manufacturers.

Ful-Ton Truck Company introduced a door-to-door delivery.

International Harvester offered vacuum-suspended boosters as standard equipment on some large models and air brakes on the DR70 and larger six-wheel models.

Best Company of Los Angeles built a motorized semitrailer with power applied to the front axle by a standard Ford or Chevrolet engine with clutch, transmission, and drive units. Control between the trailer and tractors using identical drive unit was hydraulically synchronized.

Temperatures in the body—built by the General Temperature Control Corporation of Milwaukee—could be maintained automatically at any given temperature. Temperatures could be dropped from 70 to 35 degrees F in 35 minutes or kept high enough to incubate eggs.

A power-elevator tailgate was developed by Lang Industries of New York. The unit, called "La Tro," could be built into new or old bodies, and was powered by the truck engine with a control lever on the side of the body.

Walter Snow Fighter had "four-point positive drive" on its four-wheel-drive truck. The system provided correct automatic differential action between all wheels, front and rear, left and right.

An estimated 2,500 diesel trucks were on the road.

The fleet used by the Civilian Conservation Corps totaled over 10,000, the majority of which were trucks.

1937   trucks and bus production: 891,016.

1938

Use of Cab-over-Engine Accelerates

A close-coupled or cab-over-engine design became a pronounced trend in 1938. Other names for it were the cab forward, engine under seat, and camel back. The design was to reduce truck length, shorten wheelbase, and make handling easier.

Improved insulation and refrigeration of bodies promoted shipping of perishables.

Sparkling colors and new finishes expanded as an advertising plus.

Ford introduced its new cab-over-engine models in 101-inch and 134-inch wheelbases. A stronger front end was provided by a cross member for support and an additional cross member to take driving and braking stresses. Fuel, oil, and water were refillable without opening the engine cover.

Chevrolet's "Montpelier" cab-over-engine model was introduced on a 1 1/2-ton chassis. A new feature was a forward-tilting hood for engine accessibility.

Diamond-T announced its *Fast Dispatch* series with exterior metal parts in gleaming stainless on deluxe models and polychrome silvergray finish on standard models. Five cab-over-engine models were introduced.

GMC announced a new "Special Delivery" model for "stop-and-go" delivery. The model was a cab-over-engine design with engine access through an insulated hatch mounted flush with the floor next to the driver's seat.

Reo introduced a new line of cab-over-engine models.

Federal featured a streamlined look on twelve new models. Liberal use of chromium complimented its swept-back hood and cab lines.

Mack offered six new cab-over-engine models.

American Bantam purchased the former Austin Car Company plant and produced a line of 1/4-ton panel and pickup trucks, called "Bantam 60."

The Oregon State Highway Department had 678 pieces of mobile equipment for road work. Two hundred forty nine trucks were regularly used in snow removal.

Autocar developed a new 6-man cab on its U.B. chassis.

Despite the desire of many fleet operators to install two-way radios, the problem of securing suitable airwave channels from the Federal Communications Commission could not be overcome. Primary criteria for granting a license was proof of service to the public interest and substantial contribution to the development of radio art. Radio use was limited primarily to emergency vehicles.

A number of congressional proposals for super highways made good politics; however, suggestions for toll charges were viewed in light of failures of such systems in Europe.

State bills for super highways were introduced in New York and Pennsylvania. The New York bill failed, but Pennsylvania approved the Pittsburgh–Harrisburg super highway.

A survey by the Automobile Manufacturers Association listed 149 of the largest truck fleets, owned mostly by private shippers. More than thirty-four were headquartered in New York. Other than Bell Telephone Company, which listed 13,725 trucks, the Railway Express Agency, with 9,306 trucks was the largest private fleet in the world. Other large fleets included: Borden's Milk Company, 6,706 trucks; Hertz Drivurself, 1,810; Jewel Tea Company, 1,546; and Dugan Brothers, Incorporated, 1,225.

Through a sampling of 22,532 carriers, employing 128,038 drivers, the Bureau of Motor Carriers of the ICC determined that the average driver was five feet eight inches tall, thirty-three years old, with 13.6 years of driving experience.

The first blanket labor contract in the truck industry for 180 truck operators and their 7,000 drivers and helpers was signed by the Pennsylvania Motor Truck Association, Philadelphia chapter and Teamsters local 1107.

A telemobile unit was used by NBC on two Mack trucks. One truck housed the cameras and microphone, while the other transmitted the program to the NBC television station on the Empire State Building tower.

Thirty-one states required direction signals when trucks were so loaded that hand signals could not be seen.

Driving time was limited to ten hours of driving in any twenty-four-hour period by the Interstate Commerce Commission. The regulation required an eight-hour off duty rest period. Weekly hours of service were limited to sixty hours.

Bohn Aluminum and Brass Corporation and American Liquid Gas Corporation took a Ford V-8 with a 2-ton load on a 3,000 mile run to test Algas, a blended butane-propane fuel.

The highway user was subjected to more forms of taxation than any other group, according to the *Commercial Car Journal*. In addition to regular taxes, the motorist paid over $1.3 billion in 1937. Increased gasoline taxes were sought by eleven states. There were attempts to reduce tax rates in some western states, but movements to increase taxes on diesel fuel developed.

In Congress, demands for proper use of vehicle taxes were voiced in Section 12 of the Hayden-Cartenright Act, which stated that it was "unfair and unjust to tax motor vehicle transportation if the proceeds of such taxation were not applied to construction, improvement and maintenance of highways."

Many states began to modify carrier regulations to harmonize with the Federal Motor Carrier Act.

A diesel firetruck was built by Stutz. The model was designated FD and was powered by a 6-cylinder Cummins engine with 150-horsepower.

A Mack armored vehicle had a special turret-top design to repel projectiles.

Fruehauf introduced the Merchandiser trailer and designed it to be pulled behind an automobile so that loads not heavy enough for large semitrailers could be accommodated. The model filled the gap between commercial and passenger car trailers.

Diamond-T's super deluxe model featured extensive use of chromium in the new front end design.

General Motors announced a 3-, 4-, and 6-cylinder, 2-cycle diesel engine with a Roots-type supercharger in the 71 series. Additional engine features were reversible block and interchangeable parts.

Walter developed a 10- to 15-ton dump truck, designated the ADV model. Powered by a Cummins 150-horsepower diesel, the model also featured a transmission with six forward and two reverse speeds. Hydraulic steering was also available.

Federal added new six-wheel models which featured full-floating, rear-spring suspension.

International Harvester introduced a multistop truck, model D-2-M with a Metro body. Metro later became an IH-owned subsidiary.

Dodge emphasized low-cost operation with its "Econ-o-miser" models. High-compression cylinder head, vacuum-spark advance, and fuel-feed efficiency were cited as prime economy features.

Studebaker "Fast-Transport" featured two-stage rear springs.

Hug model-99S used a double-reduction dual-drive rear axle with equalizing beams and torque rods.

White introduced a low-priced 1 1/2-ton model, the 700.

Marmon-Herrington Company adapted its all-wheel drive Ford V-8 to traverse all types of terrain. Flotation and traction were obtained by mounting 13.50 × 24 tires on the 135-inch wheelbase. The model was designed for oil-industry exploration and was called the "Marsh Buggy."

Willys introduced an Economy Cab Pickup model and a door-to-door 1/4-ton model.

Walker Vehicle Company introduced the "500 Dynamotive" gas-electric model. The driving motor was incorporated in the rear-axle assembly with final drive through a pinion, two idler gears, and an internal gear on the wheel.

Four Wheel Drive Company introduced a highway maintenance model.

Oshkosh line consisted of twelve models. The lightest model offered was a 2-ton GCB model.

Walker introduced a line of light duty electric trucks.

Diamond-T engine, radiator, clutch and transmission were withdrawn as a unit for overhaul.

GMC offered three fast-duty models, whose improvements included dual-tone appearance, increased driver comfort, and the lowest price in the field for cab-over-engine models.

Ford introduced a new 1-ton V-8 model.

Divco introduced a new streamlined Divco-Twin, door-to-door delivery model.

Sterling offered air brakes as standard.

GMC introduced a new light-duty truck line in 3/4- and 1-ton capacities. Double-wall, coppered-steel tubing for hydraulic brakes was standard.

Surge tanks to recover antifreeze or vapor from the radiator were offered as accessories by several manufacturers.

Tire experts recommended the use of balloon tires rather than high-pressure pneumatics.

The Teleoptic Company introduced turn signals which were controlled by a switch mounted on the gear shift ball handle.

White dissolved The White Company and centered both manufacturing and selling in the White Motor Company.

Truck and bus production dropped drastically to 488,841 units.

1937 Dodge road service truck shows the influence of new streamline designs.

1937 Dodge police patrol body was fitted on a 1/2-ton truck chassis and was capable of seating 12 passengers.

1938 White super-twin articulated bus gave easy maneuverability around corners of city streets.

1937 Mack tractor with Fruehauf trailer.

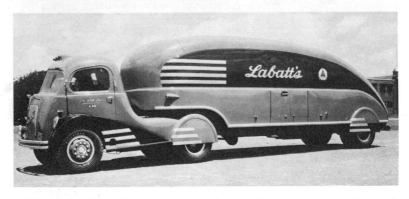

1937 This White Streamliner served the Labatt's brewery with ample cargo space. It was custom designed with a Smith body that hauled a special Fruehauf trailer with a drop-center frame.

1938   Dodge introduced a cab-over-engine model for 1 1/2- and 2-ton chassis.

1938   The Bantam "68" elegant boulevard delivery truck.

1937   Beauty and dependability were emphasized on this International DR-70 model. The distinctively styled model was powered by a 6-cylinder valve-in-head engine of 401-cubic inch displacement.

1939   The Grico two-engined highway tractor was developed by Gear Grinding Machine Company of Detroit. The second engine, mounted behind the cab, powered a separate drive shaft and axle to assist in heavy load hauling. (*Courtesy National Automotive History Collection, Detroit Public Library*)

1939
World War II Armies Move on Wheels

The sound of cannons echoed as once more Europe was enmeshed in war. The Second World War immediately demonstrated the automotive achievements developed during twenty years of peace. The "Blitzkrieg" unleashed by Adolf Hitler in Europe served notice that the modern army moved on wheeled and tracked vehicles. Mobility was the key word.

The Society of Automotive Engineers investigated the position of the United States auto industry in the event of mobilization. With the war still an ocean away, the year 1939 in America started on a high note as New York hosted the World's Fair.

The Fair promoted motor trucks. They were always in view. A fleet of 107 vehicles was in use daily to produce the Fair, recording over 60,000 miles a month, and requiring 147 men for driving and maintenance.

On another happy note, Dodge made a Pan-American Goodwill tour of 14,000 miles from Mexico to Peru. A load of Peruvian artifacts and antiques was carried to the World's Fair for exhibition.

Dodge entered the diesel field with a 6-cylinder diesel engine offered on the 3-ton model. The new engine featured two fuel filters, one between the tank and transfer pump, the other between the transfer pump and the fuel injection pump.

International Harvester transported two traveling display trailers around the country and demonstrated the development, theory, and operation of the diesel engine.

A 3-ton Dodge diesel truck set a transcontinental record from New York to Los Angeles to San Francisco and back to New York in seven days, eighteen hours, and thirty-three minutes, a distance of 6,378 miles.

Waukesha Motor Company introduced a multifuel polycycle engine which would operate on oil, gasoline, butane, or natural gas.

Federal Motor Truck entered the low-priced light truck field with 3/4-ton models available with 4- or 6-cylinder engines.

Ford also introduced a 3/4-ton series. Four body styles were available with V-8 engines.

Peterbilt introduced its first truck lines after T. A. Peterman bought the Fageol Truck and Coach Factory.

Four Wheel Drive Auto Company introduced an HG model designed primarily for road maintenance. The driving mechanism, including the front axle steering, driving knuckles, and full floating axles, were fully enclosed. Another model, a cab-over-engine with a 32,000 GVW rating was also announced.

The Gear Grinding Machine Company of Detroit developed a twin motor highway tractor called the "Grico." A standard Ford cab-over-engine, short wheelbase truck was used, and behind the cab, a second engine was mounted to power an independent drive shaft and rear axle. The unit could use both engines for heavy loads and a single engine for light hauling. The combined power of both engines was 190 horsepower.

International Harvester offered two all-steel streamlined multi-stop delivery trucks with sliding front doors.

Chevrolet increased the number of cab-over-engine models and added 2-speed axles and optional power brakes.

Mack introduced the "Thermodyne" engine which gave high power and torque through combustion control. The new overhead valves with larger and freer porting gave more direct flow and greater cooling. The shape of the chamber was a half-dome with a new kidney-shaped offset combustion chamber in combination with a dome piston.

Mack introduced another engineering feature on its CM bus—an automatic clutch and synchromesh transmission.

Studebaker offered a 1-ton "Fast Transport" model.

Gramm Trailer Division offered vacuum-operated brakes on trailers with an automatic brake lock in case of trailer breakaway.

Weber Trailer of Los Angeles developed a telescoping frame on its dual-axle semitrailer. The trailer measured twenty-six feet in a closed position and could be extended to varying lengths up to thirty-three feet. The automatic brake lines were made of brass and also telescoped with the frame.

Kingham Trailers introduced a novel suspension with two individual full swivel axles attached to the frame side-by-side at the rear of the trailer with four wheels that moved independently.

Pullman Standard Car developed the Antarctic *"Snow-Cruiser."* The special vehicle was fifty-five feet long, and nineteen feet eight inches wide. Wheels were ten feet in diameter. A complete scientific laboratory was carried on the vehicle with accommodations and one year's provisions for a crew of four. An airplane was carried on a special top deck.

Diamond-T took over the sale and service of Pak-Age-Cars.

Consolidated Freightliner changed its name to Consolidated Freightway, Inc., and built its first light-weight aluminum high gross and became one of America's leading haulers.

The first mechanical transport refrigeration unit was offered by Thermo King Corporation. The unit was mounted under the truck.

The American Association of State Highway Officials adopted the AASHO code for uniform size and weight standards.

Interstate Commerce Commission's Motor Carrier Safety Regulations prescribed a system of marker and clearance lights.

Production gained in 1939: 700,377 trucks and buses produced.

The Forties

1940

Defense Production Begins

As the war in Europe accelerated, the Atlantic Ocean did not seem quite as wide as it once had to most Americans. National defense and the lend-lease programs profoundly affected United States industry. U.S. subsidiary plants in Europe were converted to military production. Military contracts at home also increased.

First prototypes of 4 × 4 "Jeep" were: American Bantam, Willys, Ford, respectively, in late 1940.

Autocar received over $16 million in contracts for half-track scout and personnel cars.

White also received an order for half-track and four-wheel-drive scout cars.

Dodge built 20,000 special trucks for the army.

Reo received an order for 300 army trucks.

Ford was building Pratt and Whitney aircraft engines.

Packard was building Rolls Royce aircraft engines.

Gramm received an order for sixty-one van-type trailers.

An automotive committee for Air Defense was formed to facilitate aircraft production.

The nation again took a hard look at its roads and discovered immediate improvements were in order.

Of the 75,000 miles of strategic highways, more than 14,000 miles had insufficient surface strength, 4,000 miles and 500 bridges were less than eighteen feet wide, 24,000 bridges were below strength standard, and more serious, 2,900 miles of military access roads needed immediate improvement, estimated $194 million.

President Roosevelt signed the Federal Aid Bill for highway improvement.

Other transportation problems became evident as varying state regulations obstructed full use of interstate motor transportation.

Caterpillar Tractor Company introduced a 90-horsepower diesel engine for automotive vehicles.

Diamond-T announced two new 1 1/2-ton models: the Cab Forward line, model 306 SC, rated at 11,000 pounds; and the model 404 SC, rated at 13,000 pounds.

Federal introduced a Model 16 with a heavy-duty Hercules 6-cylinder diesel engine.
GMC offered thirty-four 6-wheel trucks ranging from 22,000 pounds to 90,000 pounds. A new trailing axle setup used tandem level-drive axles with independent propeller shafts to a torque divider behind the transmission to give separate drive to each axle.
Chevrolet adopted hypoid rear axles throughout the complete line.
Dodge introduced a new 1 1/2-ton series which included a cab-over-engine model and offered 105-inch and 129-inch wheelbases. A 3-ton diesel-engine model was also available.
Ford offered the broadest line in its history: forty-two body and chassis types, six wheelbases and three V-8 engines. Hydraulic brakes were used on all models. The 1940 Ford trucks included new Shiftoguide speedometers which were marked so that the driver could know at which speed he should shift gears for greatest power and economy. A battery-condition indicator was also a new instrument.
GMC introduced two special delivery models.
International Harvester had four new cab-over-engine models in the medium and heavy duty fields. The engine was removable through the front of the cab.
Mack introduced the "Retailer" on a special chassis of 120 1/2-inch wheelbase.
Mack introduced a heavy duty LM model. Safety glass was standard throughout and the V-type windshield sections opened individually. The driver's seat was separate and adjustable.
Merry-Neville Manufacturing Company in Birmingham, Michigan, designed a twin engine, 7-axle tractor trailer combination for forestry and long distance hauling. A Ford V-8 cab-over-engine model was modified for the conversion.
Third axle use grew as increased payload, better weight distribution lowered costs. More and more six-wheelers were purchased.
White announced an unusual model in a rear-engined air-cooled general delivery truck. The model, the "200," was available from 1 1/2- to 3-tons with a GVW rating of 10,000 pounds.
Chevrolet established a new world's record for the longest truck run ever, conducted by the American Automobile Association. A 1 1/2-ton Chevrolet truck was selected at random from assembly lines in Flint, Michigan, by AAA officials on January 10, 1938. It

traveled over 100,000 miles on a tour of three countries, which ended on January 20, 1940.

Edwards Iron Works introduced light-weight semitrailers in eight models with capacities from 16,000 to 30,000 pounds. Frames and body were constructed from high-tensile steel.

Gramm offered a model line from 6,500 to 25,000 pounds GVW. Unusual service brake arrangement had the brake pedal-control shaft routed through the frame to the outside where the master-cylinder synchronizer and vacuum booster were mounted. Gas tanks were mounted outside the frame on the larger models.

Trailmobile developed an outside frame semitrailer. Carried underneath the trailer was the narrow frame to the outside of the body and used as a load-bearing beam for supporting the entire width of the trailer.

An all-wheel-drive truck for highway construction was offered by Marmon-Herrington. The model was a standard Ford cab-over-engine model converted to all-wheel drive by Marmon. A wheelbase of 101 inches gave a very short turning radius. Marmon-Herrington conversions were available for all Ford models.

A 6-cylinder diesel engine for Ford trucks was announced by the Buda Company. In a demonstration run, the new diesel was mounted in a standard Ford chassis. It pulled a full load, averaging eleven miles per hour.

Cummins Engine Company offered a 100,000 mile or one-year warranty on all of its diesel engines.

Fluid flywheels were used on eleven heavy-duty Dart trucks at the Mesabi Iron Range to dampen vibrations and to reduce shifting operations of the Fuller 8-speed transmission. The fluid fly-wheel was mounted between the conventional clutch and the engine.

Push-button door latches were on White trucks.

A shift lever on the Linn Convertible Road Tractor would change wheels to tracks and vice versa.

Standard Bread Company of Los Angeles replaced the entire company fleet of 214 delivery trucks with new *White Horse* 99 models. Each truck had special glass display racks for curbside selling, and musical horns that played an identifying tune.

Hercules announced a new series of horizontal, or pancake, diesels designed for underfloor mounting.

Clark Equipment Company developed an automatic power booster for 1 1/2-ton Chevrolet trucks. The unit consisted of an auxiliary

4-cylinder Hercules engine which gave added power and acceleration for hills. Automatic controls brought the booster in and out of
operation without driver assistance.

Brown Trailers introduced a full-size demountable container
body for Ocean Van Lines.

Ford advertised for its customers to try an "on-the-job" test or a
free demonstration of the new Ford trucks or commercial cars.

The National Council of Private Truck Owners, Incorporated,
established in 1939, held its first national convention and opposed
ICC recommendations that private carriers be subjected to the
same regulations as the common and contract carriers. On August
1, private carriers involved in interstate or foreign commerce were
subject to ICC regulations. Then this was delayed to October 1.

The Pennsylvania Turnpike, with 160.8 miles of super highway,
opened on October 1. Tolls ranged from $1.50 to $10 one way.

Freightways, Incorporated, built a cab-over-engine model.

Fruehauf offered stainless-steel trailers.

SAE recommended that maximum engine horsepower should be a
measure of the load that could be pulled.

Federal excise tax on gasoline increased from 1 cent to 1 1/2 cents
again in the United States.

Total truck production in 1940: 754,901 trucks and buses.

1941

Nation's Defense in Full Gear—
War with Japan at Year's End

A state of limited national emergency was proclaimed by President
Roosevelt on May 27.

Over $1 billion cumulative war orders were placed with the au-
tomotive industry early in the year. Later, an additional $4 billion
more were placed.

The Office of Price Administration was created by executive order.

Ford developed the "Pigmy" truck for the army. Officially, the
truck was a "command reconnaissance" 4 × 4. The engine was a
4-cylinder 42-horsepower model with a top speed close to sixty
miles per hour. The truck also had six speeds forward with the
four-wheel drive. The front axle could be used as an idler.

Willys-Overland received an order from the War Department for light reconnaissance cars with four-wheel drive.

Fruehauf Trailer received an order from the air force for 237 drop-frame Aerovan trailers. The trailers were equipped with dollies for conversion from semi to full trailers.

A nationwide census of trucks and buses was held to provide vehicle information to the War Department.

The Office of Production Management (OPM) initially requested, and the automotive industry agreed, to reduce production 20 percent so that manpower, materials, and plants were available for defense. The cut was later reduced to 10 percent.

The OPM also set priority ratings for vehicle production on a three-month period.

Despite an emphasis on defense, state legislatures continued to introduce bills that would increase taxes for truckers. However, a growing number of states revised their weight limits upward.

Crosley announced five commercial models: The Parkway Delivery, Covered Wagon, Panel Delivery, Pick-Up Delivery, and Station Wagon. All were 1/4-ton models capable of attaining fifty miles per gallon of gasoline. Prices started at $299.

Chevrolet models were restyled with new front appearance. An oversized engine was available for the heavy-duty models.

Dodge continued to increase its model lines and, as the 1941 models were announced, a total of 112 standard models were available. Oil bath air cleaner, carburetor, mounted fuel filter, and floating-type oil pump screen were improvements designed to increase engine life and add to performance.

Ford introduced a 4-cylinder, 30-horsepower, economy engine as optional in the light commercial and multistop models, and late in the year made the 6-cylinder engine available in commercial vehicles.

GMC introduced an economy engine with a special velocity-inducing intake manifold, a Turbo-Top piston for turbulence, special economy jets in the carburetor, and a metal shield to deflect cooling air so that the warm-up period was shortened.

International offered a new K series with five models ranging from 1/2- to 1 1/2-ton. Also new was the Green Diamond engine, which featured fuel economy and quieter operation. A redesigned combustion chamber, manifolding, and spark plug location were several features which gave better gas mileage.

Mack introduced heavy-duty trucks—LF and LJ series, and LFT and LJT tractors—and six-wheel units (LF and LH) with emphasis on sturdiness and streamline appearance. The Mack Thermodyne gasoline engine, or Mack Lanowa diesel engine were available on all models.

Plymouth presented a 1/2-ton truck chassis for its new commercial models, a pickup, and a chassis with cab for any type of special body. A Panel Delivery and Utility Sedan were also announced.

Reo announced two special heavy-duty models, one powered by a 310-cubic inch engine for off-highway work, called the "Loggers Special." The other was for a long-haul tractor with a 404-cubic inch engine. Five more heavy-duty models were added included hydraulic brakes, plus provisions to be fitted with air brakes.

Studebaker announced three new series: the Coupe Express, the Standard, and the Heavy-Duty. All models featured a three man all-steel cab, hood lock inside cab, adjustable seat cushions and seat backs, and provisions for radio.

The new White Horse model featured an air-cooled engine, called the "Seal-Vac," which was a sealed crankcase, except at the suction side of the sirocco-type fan. This setup created a vacuum in the crankcase to remove condensation and blowby gases.

Willys introduced a semicab-over-engine 1/2-ton panel delivery.

A 3-axle truck featuring dual front wheels was developed by E. Garnett of Garnett Truck and Coach Company.

A post office on wheels was put into service between Washington, D.C., and Harrisburg, Virginia, a distance of approximately seventy miles. The post office was mounted on a White chassis and was similar to railway post offices.

Several new engines evident during the year were: Continental B-600 series for heavy-duty trucks (using deflectors in the intake manifold to aid fuel distribution); Ford 6-cylinder engine, interchangeable with the V-8; and GMC's 236-cubic-inch valve-in-head engine as standard on 2-ton models.

Wagner Electric Corporation introduced the "Hi-Tork" brake where both brake shoes divided the load equally, requiring less brake line area. This permitted a bigger drum size and good heat dissipation and ventilation. Both International and Studebaker used the brakes on larger models.

American Chain and Cable Company introduced Tru-Stop emergency brakes. The brakes were disc type and ventilated.

The results of ICC braking tests performed in late 1940 on 1,700 interstate vehicles in thirty states revealed that only a few trucks and buses tested met the ICC requirement of stopping in thirty feet from twenty miles per hour.

ICC asked Congress to regulate sizes and weights of trucks where state limitations restricted interstate traffic.

Two Mack trucks conducted engine speed tests on the Pennsylvania Turnpike, running at speeds up to seventy miles per hour for four months. They ran three 8-hour shifts a day, five days a week. Each truck was equipped with an array of instruments to record the effects of strenuous operation on the engines.

Liberty Aircraft Products purchased 66 percent of the outstanding stock of Autocar Company.

In September, the first order was issued limiting production of replacement parts for medium and heavy duty trucks and buses, plus limitation on production of buses and medium-heavy trucks. **The limitation** on production of light trucks occurred in October.

The Automotive Council for War Production was organized December 31, less than a month after the U.S. declared war on Japan.

Freightways, Incorporated, changed its name to Freightliner.

Chrysler achieved mass production of tanks, delivered its first anti-aircraft guns, and proceeded with scores of defense contracts.

Dodge built 20,000 special trucks for the United States Army.

Studebaker took a contract to produce aircraft engines.

Willys started delivery of a reconnaissance car, soon to be popularly known as the "Jeep."

White produced half-tracks, tank destroyers, prime movers, and cargo trucks.

General Motors Divisions began production of machine guns.

Pontiac began work on Oerlikon anti-aircraft guns.

Ford began production of combat cars.

The industry applied its full facilities to production for the armed forces. For the first time, the army moved entire regiments by trucks.

Total production jumped to 1,060,820 trucks and buses.

1942

The Industry at War

America was deeply involved in war against the Axis powers of Germany, Italy, and Japan. The automotive industry had proven its capability in providing defense and Lend-Lease materials. But now, the totality of war production demands amid growing shortages of materials and labor posed a herculean task. Yet, within a few months, the complete conversion of automotive plants and equipment to war production was achieved.

There were 1,038 automotive plants producing war goods in thirty-one states, with 316 of the plants in Michigan. On January 1, the sale of passenger cars and trucks was frozen, and five days later, export of cars and trucks was frozen.

Tire rationing began early in January. Truck rationing went into effect in March. Civilian truck production was halted in March.

Gas rationing went into effect in seventeen eastern states in May.

A national speed limit of forty miles per hour was put into effect. Later in the year it was reduced to thirty-five miles per hour.

All states agreed on reciprocal truck licensing laws for the duration of the war.

The army ordered 880,000 heavy-duty trucks. Over 40 percent of the trucks urgently needed were models 2 1/2-ton and over.

The War Production Board approved plans to convert light trucks for heavy duty use by adding third axles and auxiliary engines.

The War Production Board also named five classes of users who could purchase trucks. The move dropped sales of rationed trucks drastically as only 640 users qualified out of 33,000 applications.

Nonmilitary highway trailer production ceased in June.

A steel shortage slowed war production.

The government requested vehicle owners having excess tires (more than four) to turn them over to the government.

The automotive industry produced $4.665 billion in arms.

Secretary Ickes paid tribute to the truck industry for its cooperation in the war effort.

Chevrolet 1942 trucks had few changes from the 1941 models.

Dodge Deluxe Cabs for 1942 featured adjustable sun visors, electric windshield wipers, dome light, and leather upholstery.

Ford trucks emphasized increased durability and redesigned front end styling. A total of 126 chassis and body combinations were available.

Ford production of the Willys model MB 1/4-ton 4 × 4 truck and an amphibious model were started at the Rouge plant.

Marmon-Herrington announced a six-wheel-drive cab-over-engine Ford conversion model.

Reo added three heavy-duty models powered by Waukesha engines of 381, 404, and 517 cubic inches. All engines featured an electric fuel pump.

White introduced "Power Pilot" control for shifting its 2-speed axle automatically. A push-button control preselected either high or low gear by easing up on the accelerator. The shift occurred by means of a vacuum control.

Willys new pickup truck emphasized economical operation.

The Office of Defense Transportation adopted a new system of truck rating which used gross vehicle weight (GVW) instead of tonnage.

Civilian production dropped: 818,662 trucks and buses.

1943

The Industry at War

The first twelve months of total war production ended with automotive war goods being produced at an annual rate of $7 billion. New war orders on the automotive books totaled more than $20 billion.

After a year of turning out primarily defensive materials, the demand switched to offensive weapons and new engineering changes to keep pace with rapid turnover from one war product to another. In several companies, as the demand for military vehicles lessened, the slack was taken up by the manufacture of a 4,500-pound amphibious truck called "the duck." Within five weeks after receipt of the letter of intent from the War Department, the manufacturers completed and were testing the vehicle. By early June, aircraft production supplanted military vehicles as the number one war production job in the automotive industry.

The industry was geared for swift action. Converting from tank hulls to aircraft wing sections could be accomplished in an amazingly short time by many companies.

The president decreed a forty-eight-hour week for all war industries. With labor shortages a continual problem, the employment of disabled war veterans was a welcome addition to the work force. The industry worked with rehabilitation centers in supporting the movement and establishing standards for employment. The value of disabled veterans for productive work was supplemented by the morale that their presence brought to the other workers.

1940 Plymouth panel delivery on the Roadking chassis with streamlined styling, unusual load-carrying space, steering post gearshift, and individual coil-spring front suspension.

1940 Freightliner trucks were introduced with enclosed van bodies for freight.

1941 Chevrolet cab-over-engine model served as a mobile display room.

1941 All-wheel drive with dual differentially connected wheels was demonstrated on this Ford tractor by Differential Wheel Corporation. The arrangement claimed to prolong tire life by 50 to 100 percent and increase gasoline mileage. (*Courtesy National Automotive History Collection, Detroit Public Library*)

1945 Greyhound Bus on Pennsylvania Turnpike. (*Courtesy Standard Oil Company*)

1946 This White bus was powered by a 12-cylinder underfloor engine. Also featured was an automatic transmission.

1942   Industry converted to production for World War II. These Chevrolet 4×2 and 4×4 military truck chassis await shipment.

1943   A convoy of World War II army 2 1/2-ton trucks—workhorses of the army.

1943   Foamite fire truck by American LaFrance.

The War Production Board authorized production of 7,500 heavy-duty civilian trucks for the second half of the year.

War production continued to rise in the automotive industry and, by the year's end, had filled more than $13.5 billion worth of war orders. More amazing was the fact that price reductions in products actually pushed the physical output higher than the dollar volume indicated.

Manufacturing efficiency resulted in lower price reductions and voluntary refunds.

Aircraft production was eleven times greater than it was at the beginning of 1942. Military vehicle production had tripled and more than eight times as many tanks were being produced.

Despite the satisfaction of success in the war effort, the automotive industry experienced a great loss when, on May 26, 1943, Edsel Ford died at the age of forty-nine. Mr. Ford had been president of the Ford Motor Company for twenty-four years.

Henry Ford II assumed duties in the direction and management of the Ford Motor Company after being placed on the inactive list by the navy.

GMC added buses to its line which reflected a new name: GMC Truck and Coach Division.

Civilian production almost at a standstill: 699,689.

1944
The Industry at War

The automotive industry began the year with a backlog of war orders in excess of $14 billion.

The axis powers had begun to feel the effects of U.S. mechanization. Allied forces landed on the beaches of Normandy and the drive for Germany was underway.

The type of war goods in demand changed as the tides of battle shifted. The war in Europe now required heavy-duty trucks, new bomber engines, and fighter planes. Those items received high priority. However, cost reductions continued as production technology improved. Tanks, certain types of bombers, and various weapons were delivered at half the price paid a year earlier.

Reports from the war fronts more than ever dramatized the importance of American trucks as the great allied war machine swept onwards toward its goal of victory.

War needs continued to fluctuate and contracts were sometimes cancelled even though production had just begun. Months of preparation, plant building, and tremendous investment were often scrapped as emphasis shifted toward more urgent demands.

Morale was high and some thoughts and plans for reconversion surfaced.

On the homefront, the production of heavy-duty civilian trucks for stateside transport was increased to about six times the number turned out in 1943.

A new production record was set this year as the industry turned out war materials to the tune of 9.32 billion.

America's war production figures to date were announced in early December. Those of significance to the automotive industry were: 1.8 million trucks, 68,000 tanks, and 187,000 planes.

The War Production Board announced the formation of an Automotive Industry Advisory Committee to study reconversion problems.

The Office of Defense Transportation assumed the responsibility of rationing trucks and commercial vehicles.

President Roosevelt announced a 40 percent cut in war production and a return to the forty-hour work week.

Synthetic tires became available for nonessential driving.

Butyle rubber appeared in truck tire tubes, a synthetic with a future.

In November, the War Production Board authorized manufacture of the first light civilian trucks since early in 1942.

Studebaker was the second largest producer of 2 1/2-ton 6 × 6-wheel-drive military trucks.

Dodge produced more than 300,000 trucks for the war effort.

Kenworth became a division of Pacific Car and Foundry Company.

Production of civilian trucks during war year: 737,524.

1945
Reconversion as War Ends

Confident of final victory and an end to world conflict, the automotive industry looked toward reconversion and the resumption of peacetime production.

Approval was granted by the War Production Board for production of $50 million worth of machine tools and related equipment for auto production.

Gasoline rationing ended August 15, 1945. All restrictions on truck production were lifted August 20, 1945.

The automotive and truck industry had been a potent force in the final determination of the outcome of World War II.

More than 20 percent of the national output of war products was delivered by the automotive and truck industry. Never before had an industry produced more goods in such a short time. The automotive industry alone had accounted for: 2,600,887 military trucks, 54,173 tanks, 22,160 airplanes, 529,647 trailers, 4,131,000 engines (aircraft, truck, boat and tank), and 5,947,000 weapons.

The Automotive Council for War Production was dissolved in October. The 613 members had delivered war products to the allied cause, valued at nearly $29 billion.

As the industry prepared to change over to peacetime production, truck manufacturers reported that emphasis would be on the production of current models. Major design changes would not occur until 1947.

Truck and trailer rationing ended December 1, 1945.

The GMC "duck" amphibious vehicle featured a novel, central tire inflation system whereby any or all of the tires could be inflated or deflated with the vehicle moving on land or water.

Ford Motor Company offered a driving kit for amputee WWII veterans to be installed in any Ford, Mercury, or Lincoln—old or new model. The order was placed with any Ford dealer who would advise Ford headquarters of the veteran's condition, whereupon the proper kit was supplied. Ford Motor Company paid original cost of equipment and installation.

International Harvester military vehicles M-1-4 and M-5-6 were replaced by the KB-line as peacetime production resumed.

American Trucking Associations reported that almost 200,000 trucks on U.S. highways were 1928 models or older.

Henry Ford II was named president of Ford Motor Company, succeeding his grandfather, Henry Ford I.

Marmon-Herrington announced production of the DeliVr-All, a house-to-house delivery truck featuring front-wheel drive, independent rear suspension and a completely detachable unit.

Heil offered a Hydro-Steer unit for road trucks and equipment. Movement of the steering wheel controlled hydraulic pressure on individual wheel cylinders, which caused front wheel movement left or right.

Cessie Cummins and a relief driver set a nonstop truck-driving record of 14,600 miles at Indianapolis Speedway to prove the endurance of the diesel engine. Cummins and the relief driver circled the track day and night for fourteen days.

Civilian truck production still low: 655,683.

1946

Peacetime Production Resumes

Truck registration reached a new high to almost 4 million by 1946. But an insatiable demand for more indicated this was only the beginning. Trucks brought a new age of transportation, fanning out onto new roads into remote communities across the nation, bringing prosperity with them. Trucks gave employment to 5.5 million men. But peacetime reconversion after the war presented new challenges.

A coal strike caused steel shortages which hampered truck production. An erratic flow of materials to the plants caused intermittent production. Strikes, slowdowns and shutdowns, in combination with critical shortages of copper, lead, and lumber, provided a gloomy outlook for this year.

The Office of Price Administration (OPA) was officially discontinued on July 1, but was restored again within a month.

The consensus at a special truck meeting by SAE was that truck improvement must be directed toward driver comfort and safe operation. Priority needs were: better seats, ventilation, visibility, soundproofing, and accessibility of controls.

The American Association of State Highway Officials (AASHO) developed a Size and Weight Code for trucks and truck trailer combinations. The code was adopted by a majority vote of State Highway Departments.

Gimbels, the famous New York City department store, offered surplus army trucks for sale, among which were the 2 1/2-ton

Studebaker, 1 1/2-ton Chevrolet, 5-ton International Harvester.
Autocar featured a new step-type gasoline tank, mounted under cab, easily removable, constructed of twelve gauge metal, and with the filler cap located at the front of the tank.
Chevrolet offered an unusually wide range of ninety-nine truck models on nine wheelbases, ranging from 4,000 pounds to 16,000 pounds. Vacuum power brakes were standard on the heavy-duty models and optional on medium models.
Dodge introduced the Power-Wagon model, featuring four-wheel drive, dual power take-off with a front power winch, and a tail shaft drive for pulley, machinery, and the like.
Dodge featured a manually controlled valve to regulate air in the seat cushion for accommodating the driver's weight or preferred driving position.
Eisenhauer Twin Engine Truck by Eisenhauer Manufacturing Company, Van Wert, Ohio, offered a heavy-duty 20-ton long-distance model, featuring a twin Chevrolet engine, four front steering wheels, and three rear axles with a special compensating spring suspension.
Federal trucks had an automatic under-the-hood light. A mercury switch in the base of the lamp activated when the hood was opened. Illumination was supplemented by a cadmium-plated reflector.
Federal introduced four new heavy-duty models equipped with air brakes in front and rear with maximum-size brake shoes.
Ford built over 100 chassis and body combinations in four major groups.
Bostrom introduced a hydraulic seat for driver comfort.
Ford Motor Company of Canada introduced a new line of Mercury trucks with thirty-nine models, ranging from 1/2 to 3 ton.
GMC offered forty-eight basic models from 4,600 to 55,000 pounds GVW.
Hudson's entry in the commercial market was a 3/4-ton pickup with independent front-wheel suspension, center point steering, and a hydraulic brake system with a reverse mechanical system on the same pedal.
White offered "Super Power" models and engines with pressure cooling systems and expansion tanks, duplex carburation, sodium-cooled stellite-faced valves, and zero lash hydraulic valve lifters.
Leece-Neville introduced its first alternator for all types of motor

vehicles. The alternating current was changed to direct current through a Selenium-plate rectifier.

International Harvester offered two "Western Freighter" highway models with a choice of gas or diesel engines.

Nash announced plans to reenter the truck field with three models: 1/2, 3/4, and 1 1/2 ton, for the first time since 1929.

Mack introduced the mono-shift, vacuum-controlled 10-speed transmission with preselection of compound ratios for heavy-duty trucks. The transmission allowed the preselection of lower gears and completion of shifts without engine racing.

Studebaker announced truck models in the light and medium range, a 1/2-ton and the 1 1/2-ton coupe express.

Walter Trucks featured 4-point positive drive, involving three differentials, suspended double-reduction drive wherein differentials were mounted outside the axles and driven through internal gears on wheel hubs.

White featured an "economy range finder" that enabled the driver to read the engine speed from the speedometer dial and select the best transmission gear.

The major industry-wide problem in the production of new trailers was the scarcity of tires.

A trend toward prefabricating and standardizing body parts was developing among trailer and body manufacturers.

The use of magnesium in truck and trailer bodies increased.

American Bantam announced a line of supercargo trailers.

For lighter weight, easier maintenance, Consolidated Freightways designed new flooring for truck and trailer bodies of channeled aluminum. Weight-saving was 700 to 800 pounds per body.

Bantam trailers offered Quadri-point suspension. Aluminum truck axle housing, hubs and brake shoes by Timken Axle cut weight by 220 pounds.

Fruehauf trailers showed an elevating endgate which lifted and lowered heavy loads by hydraulic power and operated through the truck's engine. Capacity was up to 1 ton.

Fruehauf "multi-rate" suspension with an arrangement of leaf springs and rollers and radius rods provided flexibility.

Fruehauf also adopted a new tandem-axle trailer-suspension system, designated the "Gravity Torsion Bar Suspension," under an exclusive license from Truck Equipment Company, the basic patent holder. The system consisted of longitudinal torsion bars—two for each axle. They merged into two torque divider gear boxes forward of the front axle and were fixed in shackles at the rear. The axis of the shackles and torsion bar were inclined toward the center of the chassis, imparting self-steering to the rear wheels. Also, a new "feather-ride" coil-spring suspension for trailers was introduced.

Gar Wood Industries developed an all-enclosed refuse collector with hydraulic hoist for dumping.

Knockdown all-steel van bodies were available from Kruger Steel Sections, Incorporated, and Reynolds Metal Company. The bodies were offered in 10-foot, 12-foot, and 14-foot lengths, 7-foot widths, and 6-foot headroom. They could be assembled by two unskilled men and mounted on a chassis.

A variable-pitch, thermostatically controlled engine fan for heavy-duty trucks was introduced by Evans Products. When the engine was cold the pitch of the fan blades was zero. As the engine warmed, the pitch was automatically controlled by a thermostatic-control activated by engine coolant.

Two-way radio telephones were installed on five units of the Willett Company.

Air intake heaters were introduced for Hercules diesels.

Allegheny Ballistics Lab in Cumberland, Maryland, tested rockets on a Jeep for a one-time emergency stop. Stopping distance was cut in half.

Vickers developed hydraulic power steering for trucks.

Wagner hydraulic brakes were self-adjusting and self-positioning.

Monroe E-Z Ride truck seat used double-action hydraulic shock absorber and a variable-rate coil spring.

A new Warner dual electric braking system was introduced with electric retarders on tractor and trailer and with an electric shoe-type brake.

Spicer Manufacturing changed its name to the Dana Corporation.

Vanette, Incorporated, a Detroit-based company, announced three delivery models available on Ford 1 1/2- and 1-ton chassis.

Continental engines featured Thompson "Roto Valve" rotating exhaust valves to prevent valve burning, corrosion, and to keep valve seats clear.

Truck registrations reached 5,982,389.

Truck production for 1946 was 951,185 units.

1947

Wartime Technology Sets New Pace

Over 18 million trucks had rolled off assembly lines and onto streets and highways by 1947. This heralded a better way of living, more employment, productivity, and prosperity.

Not all wartime trucks were successful for peacetime use, but the successful performance of six-wheel trucks during the war convinced manufacturers that they could be produced as dump trucks and highway tractors. The low-cost wartime supply of aluminum used in fighter bomber construction found its way into truck construction after the war. The benefit of wartime technology contributed to a trend toward heavier trucks.

Increased postwar labor costs in 1947 led a trend toward using heavier trucks by reducing the number of drivers required by smaller and lighter fleets. The liberalization of road weight and length restrictions in many states stimulated the move to heavier models.

GMC introduced eight heavy-duty diesel models and ten gasoline models. Oil cooling and pressurized cooling were several outstanding features.

International Harvester produced nine heavy-duty KB models with all-steel safety cabs and five sizes of 6-cylinder valve in head engines, ranging from a 250-cubic inch engine developing 99.8 horsepower at 3,200 rpm to a 586-cubic inch engine developing 200 horsepower at 2,600 rpm.

Mack announced a super-duty 6-wheel model, LTSW-L, to handle off-highway type requirements. Two independent air brake systems were used. A power divider between the two drive axles gave better traction and reduced backlash.

Federal Motor Truck added four heavy-duty models to its line. The four models ranged from 30,000 pounds to 55,000 pounds GVW and were designated 65 MA, 663MA, 664MA, and 664 MAB. The latter three models were six-wheelers.

Dodge introduced its "Job-Rated" heavy-duty truck models up to 20-ton GVW, available with either a 282 or 331-cubic inch displacement engine.

White continued its 3-ton heavy-duty line with the WB-28 and WB-28T models.

Walter Motor Truck offered its Four-Point Positive Drive Models of 5-ton, 8-ton, and 12-ton capacity.

A folding crane, stowed into the floor of a pickup truck bed, converted a regular pickup truck into a wrecker. The conversion was called the Canfield and was distributed by Walter Williams.

Fruehauf Trailer Company entered the truck-body manufacturing field with a new line of all steel bodies in 12, 14, and 16 foot lengths.

International Harvester reduced prices on trucks and farm equipment. The reductions resulted in an estimated $20 million savings annually for IH customers. Chairman of the Board, Fowler McCormick, stated, "We believe there is nothing more important to this country than to lower the prices of the goods that people buy."

Chevrolet "Advanced Design" models featured driver comfort and eye appeal in design of cabs and bodies.

General Motor's experimental engine with 12.5 to 1 compression ratio improved fuel economy by 35 percent.

Spangler truck manufactured by Hahn Motors was powered by two Ford 100-horsepower V-8 engines and also featured dual wheels on all four axles and walking beam front and rear bogies to equalize load distribution.

Willys introduced new two- and four-wheel-drive utility models, rated 4,700 pounds GVW.

Several manufacturers showed electrically and mechanically operated sanders for trucks and buses.

Two-way radio use was growing.

Los Angeles purchased a fleet of twenty-one Willys-Overland Jeeps to maintain traffic signals, paint driving lanes, and perform other safety functions at the city's 1,100 intersections. Two-way radios on the vehicles were to aid in traffic emergencies.

Pittsburgh Coal Company and the Standard Oil Company of New Jersey announced plans for a combined venture to build a $120 million plant near Pittsburgh to convert soft coal into gasoline, diesel oil, fuel oil, and alcohol.

A 1/2-ton delivery truck, "The Delcar," was introduced by American Motors of New York. An unusual suspension system carried the load on rubber cords operating on vertical guides. The conventional chassis was replaced by an underbody box frame.

Federal offered a positive crankcase ventilating system which utilized the force of the engine to extract water, fuel, and acid vapors from the crankcase.

Crosley introduced a 1/4-ton light pickup model.

Ted V. Rodgers retired as president of the American Trucking Associations. He had served as president since its formation fourteen years ago. He was replaced by Edward J. Buhner.

Diamond-T located the air cleaner outside the hood on tractor models.

Federal's engines, the R-6602 Continental, could be converted to burn butane gas.

Leece-Neville offered a new AC-generating system for vehicles with extra electrical equipment, using an alternator with a copper sulfite rectifier to convert AC current to DC, and a load relay to regulate voltage and current.

White offered two-way adjustable driver's seat and a new heating and ventilating system on its WB cabs.

Freightliner, a subsidiary of Consolidated Freightways, was incorporated. A new plant was built in Portland, Oregon, to manufacture Freightliner trucks.

Peacetime production increased to 1,284,843 trucks and buses.

1948

Shortages and Strikes
Mar Production Mark

Strikes, short supplies, higher prices, even work stoppages could not halt the high tides of record production reported by manufacturers: 1948 was the greatest year in truck history to date. Total production reached 1,349,582 units.

Dodge introduced new door-to-door delivery vehicles, called Route Vans, with fluid drive offered as optional. One beam axle supported the load, and a swinging-type driving axle and offset engine with angled drive complemented the new vans.

Fleet owners reported that truck replacement parts, especially sheet metal parts, were in short supply.

Chevrolet's light truck model featured a foot-operated parking brake with its release control on the dashboard. In the medium and heavy-duty models, a 4-speed transmission was offered with a synchro-mesh and helical gears in second, third, and fourth speeds.

Foot-operated parking brakes, a steering-column gearshift, push-button starting, and ride stablizers were standard equipment on Chevrolet's new "Advance-Design Forward-Control Models."

Dodge introduced a six-wheel model B1-VX featuring a tandem axle drive, mounted in a special bogie with torque rods.

Ford introduced two heavy-duty models rated up to 21,500 pounds GVW. The new models emphasized driver comfort and redesigned V-8 and 6-cylinder engines.

The Ford F8 tractor featured a new 145-horsepower V-8 engine, dual-throat carburetor, power-operated 16 × 5 inch hydraulic brakes with double cylinders. Heavy-duty, 5-speed transmission with overdrive was optional.

Diamond-T designed a "quickly detachable fender" for its 3-ton and greater capacity models. The fender assembly was carried by two braces and six mounting bolts.

White series WC super power trucks featured dual carburetion and a closed pressure cooling system.

The American Association of State Highway Officials revised recommendations for width, length, height, speed and load. (The association initially recommended standards on November 17, 1932, and modified them for the war emergency on May 27, 1942.)

Requirements established in 1937 for equipment to reduce wheel spray or splash with splash guards were now being enforced in the State of Washington.

The Federal Communications Commission assigned eight frequencies in the 30 to 40-megacycles bands for intercity truck radio service.

Los Angeles County operated a "diesel patrol" to help combat smog. Two cars with trained inspectors patroled the highways in Los Angeles County to inform drivers of the state laws regarding excessive diesel smoke and to levy fines for repeated violations.

General Motors Truck and Coach established a training school for motor coach mechanics on maintenance and overhaul of General Motors series 7000 diesel engines.

Three series of cab-over-engine trucks were offered by GMC, providing eleven models in the medium-duty range.

International Harvester purchased Metropolitan Body Company of Bridgeport, Connecticut.

Brooks Stevens designed a special truck for the Miller Brewing Company known as WK-65. Built on a Dodge chassis, the new heavy-duty had a 136-inch wheel base, was 96 inches wide, and 113 inches high.

A **convertible** haulaway trailer to eliminate "dead heading" (eliminating haulaway trucks returning empty) was designed by W. O. Bridge, a Detroit motor freight carrier. The drop-frame trailer carried freight on the lower level, cars on the upper level.

Fruehauf introduced combined automatic coupler and automatic support legs for trailers. When the trailer was uncoupled, the supports were automatically lowered and automatically raised when coupled.

A new flooring for trucks and trailers was announced by Brown Industries, called "Caralite." The flooring was .09-inch corrugated aluminum and allowed for fabrication without seams.

Dorsey Trailer Manufacturing introduced a new frameless trailer. Its top and bottom rub rails, combined with light-weight steel cross members, provided a rugged light-weight van body.

Pacific Car and Foundry introduced "Cargovan," an aluminum-alloy panel delivery truck body for 3/4-, 1-, and 1 1/2-ton chassis. The body featured an increased payload.

A new type fire truck, designed by Ansul Chemical Company's Fire Extinguisher Division, used dry chemical as the primary extinguishing agent. On a FWD chassis vehicle, 2,800 pounds of the dry chemical and 250 gallons of water were carried.

Reynolds Metal developed an aluminum "Trailerail" container for use on special trailer frames transferred to railway flat cars. Built-in hydraulic lifts, winch, and cable systems provided the means for shifting the container from trailer to flat car and vice versa.

Reflective materials for trucks and buses were available for fleet operations.

The Connecticut State Police announced that radar traffic-beam instruments would be used to measure the speed of motor vehicles on state highways.

GMC introduced its hydraulic V-Drive automatic transmission, produced by Allison. An angle drive to the rear axle was featured.

GMC Truck and Coach offered its 40-foot transit models, which seated fifty to fifty-five passengers.

National Truck Body Manufacturing Association (later TBEA) was organized.

Total production increased to 1,349,582 trucks and buses.

1944 Marmon-Herrington H-542 heavy-duty army tractor fitted with a fifth wheel to pull a trailer.

1945 White Motor's sturdy 4-wheel armoured army scout car.

1943 The M-10 military tank testing its tractive paces.

1947 Peterbilt models featured driver comfort and convenience which eased the burden in heavy-hauling situations.

1948 "Advance design" Chevrolet cab and chassis with 137-inch wheelbase to accommodate bodies up to 9 feet long.

1949 Seventeen passengers could travel in this special Northern Pacific Railway Transport which also carried freight in its rear 18 × 18 cargo area. The Bruck, as it was called, was built by Kenworth to supplement short-line rail service.

1949 Studebaker truck with stake body featured a two-piece slanted windshield and distinctive grill and curved bumper.

1949 Crosley panel delivery truck, emphasized low cost ($879), speed, maneuverability (15-foot turning radius), and full economy with 35 miles per gallon.

1949 White model 3016 built for Coca-Cola Bottling Company.

1949

Steel Strike Stalls Production

Material shortages, labor problems, and strikes continued to hold the reins on the automotive industry. The seemingly perpetual steel shortages and threats of strikes had manufacturers stockpiling metal whenever possible. Despite those efforts, the effects of the steel workers' walkout for a month prevented a third consecutive record year for truck production. However, demand for the new models was evident and the industry continued to expand.

Coast-to-coast trucking increased as the leading truck firms reported large tonnage through Chicago terminals. The three major long-distance firms were Denver-Chicago Trucking Company, Incorporated, Pacific Intermountain Express Company, and Consolidated Freightways, Incorporated.

Diamond-T introduced a heavy-duty diesel tractor 910N. The model was offered as a four- or six-wheeler capable of maintaining highway speeds with total train weights to 36,000 pounds.

The Diamond-T model 650T was offered in the medium-duty highway tractor field. Powered by a 6-cylinder, 140-horsepower engine with a displacement of 427 cubic inches, the air intake featured an oil-bath air cleaner mounted outside the hood.

Ford introduced the F-3 Parcel Delivery chassis. Air brakes were optional.

Ford increased the wheel base on several models.

Federal Motor Truck Company added a new model, 15 M light-duty series, for general hauling and utility work. The model featured an all-steel cab, adjustable seats, dual wipers, sun visors, and arm rests. Two new high-speed diesel series were also introduced.

International Harvester announced two new diesel models for heavy-duty operation. Mounted outside at the right rear of the cab was a new muffler—5-feet long, 6-inches in diameter, with a 4-inch exhaust stock.

International Harvester introduced a heavy-duty L series with a "Comfo-Vision" cab, featuring a one-piece curved windshield and new Silver Diamond and Super Blue Diamond engines.

Mack introduced three new diesel engines, the 457, 510, and 672. These featured a new system of timed injection, Syncrovance, synchronized to the speed of the engine.

Eaton introduced electric control for 2-speed axles.

Peterbilt acquired MacDonald Truck and Manufacturing Company, builders of low-body and lift trucks.

Reo announced its Speed Wagon pickup truck, model D-19X. A new series R-23 was also announced and featured hydraulic brakes with a reserve tank as standard and air brakes optional.

Reo introduced a new truck and tractor model, the E-22, powered by the new "Gold Comet" heavy-duty engine which developed 140-horsepower at 3,200 rpm. The engine was "square," 4 1/8-inch bore and stroke, and featured "wet sleeve" cylinders which were both replaceable and interchangeable.

Reo also introduced a new tandem E-226 line in five wheelbases from 150 to 203 inches.

GMC coaches used hydramatic automatic transmission.

A Studebaker 1/2-ton pickup model made a cross-country tour in a safety promotion. The pickup featured an overdrive transmission, automatic windshield washers, hill-holder, radio, heater, and back-up lights.

The Studebaker 16A and 17A models offered Adjusto Air seat cushions, adjustable to the driver's weight. A plate on the underside of the seat sealed in the air and contained a valve to control the amount of air inside the cushion.

White Motor Company celebrated its Golden Anniversary with a new model 3000 series with a hydraulically power-operated forward tilting cab, allowing accessibility to the engine in 30 seconds. This was fundamentally a new concept in truck design. The model featured a shorter wheelbase, lower driver position, widetread front axle for better weight distribution, and a greater payload capacity. White took a bow, literally.

White series WC super power trucks featured dual carburetion and a closed pressure cooling system.

Freuhauf used a combination of steel, aluminum, and magnesium parts in the manufacture of their new trailers. The weight savings totaled 1,250 pounds.

Trailmobile introduced an all-aluminum Model AA van-type trailer. Built of special alloys and special extruded-aluminum forms, the trailer also featured wheels cast of aluminum alloys.

Freightliner introduced its first sleeper cab, model 900.

A new forward-control truck body was developed by Lindsay Corporation. The unit was offered in lengths of 9 1/2, 10 1/2, and 11 1/2 feet. Overall width was 80 3/4 inches and the inside height was 68 inches.

Pittsburgh Steel Products Company designed a "Speed-Rack" tarpaulin carrier to provide a hand-crank operation for opening and closing the tarpaulin over the trailer.

Strick produced a roll-off roof for van trailers.

Andrews Industries, Incorporated, produced an all-aluminum fabricated trailer.

Holland Hitch Company developed a safety fifth wheel mounted on a swiveling baseplate with a 4-inch offset in the pivot to keep it parallel with the trailer axle.

Dodge expanded its truck line with the introduction of a B-2 series of cab-over-engine models. Interior features included a hand-pull parking brake control mounted under the center of the cowl, and a steering column gearshift to provide more floor space.

Production this year totaled 1,160,568.

The Fifties

1950
Business Improves Despite
Strikes, Shortages, and Korean War

Despite a coal strike, steel shortages, a 100-day strike at Chrysler, and the Korean War outbreak, this year's production of new trucks was 1,377,261—an all-time record and 200,000 units higher than 1949.

Hostilities in Korea started June 25, followed by rumors of rationing, shortages, and governmental controls. Yet, it was business as usual for most of the industry.

United States Army tests on the Reo Eager Beaver 2 1/2-ton trucks were so successful that $25 million were added to the original order of $31 million.

The National Highway Users reported that 57 percent of all trucks in service were used for hauling food and dairy products. Lumber industry use ranked second and accounted for 11 percent.

International Harvester introduced two refrigerated trucks for multistop delivery.

The Boeing Engine Company built a 160-horsepower gas turbine engine for land vehicles. The model "502" weighed 185 pounds.

Kenworth Motor Truck Corporation roadtested a gas turbine-powered experimental truck. The turbine engine was a 175-horsepower light-weight model, also built by Boeing Airplane Company, and was mounted in a 10-ton chassis for trial runs.

A new Autocar cab stressed driver comfort with a wider five-way adjustable seat and new systems for fresh air, heating, defrosting, and ventilating. Driver vision was improved with a curved windshield for 56 percent more visibility.

Chevrolet added the Suburban Carryall to its truck lines.

Dodge announced its Y and YA models with payload allowances of 19,800 pounds. Wheelbases were from 130 inches to 190 inches, the longest trucks ever offered by Dodge.

Ford introduced a forward-control F-5 parcel delivery chassis which could accommodate a 12 1/2-foot body. The truck was powered by the Ford Rouge 226 6-cylinder engine.

Freightliner introduced a "short tractor" with a 112- to 118-inch wheelbase to meet overall 60-foot length limitations, hauling two 24-foot trailers.

Federal introduced the "Style Liner" series, featuring a fender that swung up for accessibility to the engine. It used a hinged instrument panel for access to the wiring.

GMC introduced two light-weight diesel tractors known as Series 640 and 650 in the medium-priced field. The diesel engine used was the 2-cycle, 4-cylinder unit weighing 1,583 pounds.

New Mack engines featured sodium-filled valve stems with rotators and direct water cooling for the exhaust valves to increase their life.

Peterbilt featured a hinged fender for access to the engine for minor repairs, and a tilting cab for complete access.

Reo introduced a E-20 series powered by a 255-cubic inch Gold Comet engine. A series of tandem-axle trucks were also offered and designated the E-226.

A new Sterling "TG" cab-over-engine model featured an all-steel cab with four-position, adjustable steering wheel and power ventilation. The length of the cab was reduced, permitting the use of longer bodies and improving maneuverability by its reduced turning radius.

Ford sold manufacturing and sales rights of motor buses to Marmon-Herrington Company, Incorporated. Distribution continued through the same Ford distributors.

Twin Coach Company introduced a new concept for a freight hauling truck with the Fageol Super Freighter. The vehicle was basically a trailer fitted with a single-driving axle, underfloor engine, and transmission. An unusual steering arrangement had the front axle pivoting on a platform around a fifth-wheel kingpin. The arrangement allowed use of dual wheels on the front axle.

White introduced a 3014 model truck tractor for city delivery service. A shorter wheelbase and wide tread permitted a savings of two feet in overall length. A lowered frame reduced lifting in loading and unloading. A sleeper cab was available on the White 3000 series tilt cab tractor.

Greyhound introduced its first high-level Scenicruiser. It featured a new system of air suspension.

The National Highway Users Conference continued to speak out against a growing tendency of some states to divert part of their highway funds from gas tax yields to nonhighway purposes.

The American Trucking Associations continued its push for reciprocity so that any motor vehicle properly licensed in one state would have the right to operate in another state without additional license plates or registration fees.

Oregon classified its highways according to their load carrying capacity. Heavier trucks used only the highways built to take the heavy gross loads.

The U.S. Bureau of Public Roads reported that the frequency of axle loads of 20,000 pounds or more per 1,000 vehicles had doubled since the end of World War II and more than tripled since before the war.

Fuller produced 10-speed, single-level "RoadRanger" transmission.

Total production increases to 1,377,261 trucks and buses.

1951

Military Contracts Increase

The National Production Authority indicated that strict limitations on some materials would occur because of the Korean conflict.

Wage and price controls and job priorities were secondary problems to the growing manpower shortage. Yet, truck production continued at a record rate.

Military contracts to the automotive industry continued to increase as production gained momentum.

Defense Transport Administrator, James Knudson, warned the governors of the forty-eight states that artificial barriers to highway transportation could impede mobilization in a time of national emergency.

The Interstate Commerce Commission proposed changes to update Motor Carrier Safety Regulations. The updating called for physical exams for drivers, accident record and violation requirements, and driver inspection of equipment. The observance of speed limits in the driver's scheduling and adequate equipment requirements were also proposed.

New York State enacted a ton-mile tax which increased truck taxes on a graduated scale. Estimated cost to New York taxpayers was

$30 million a year. Motor Carrier Association of New York announced that they would test the constitutionality of the tax.

Brown Equipment and Manufacturing Company introduced a cab-over-engine model LS Tandem Tractor and a drop frame tandem trailer.

Dodge introduced a B-3 series.

Federal Motor Truck Company introduced its 3400 series Style-Liner models with a range of wheelbases from 136 to 250 inches.

Freightliner introduced a cab-over-engine diesel tank truck for bulk petroleum transport.

GMC introduced a light duty line replacing its former FC 100 and FF 350 models.

GMC built a 6 × 6 tactical vehicle designated the M-135. The major innovations included: hydramatic with automatic front wheel drive, torque-rod front wheel suspension, and "snorkel" devices for traveling submerged in deep water fording situations.

International Harvester introduced six cab-forward models, called the C series, featuring increased vision with curved windshields and wide dual rear windows.

International also offered free inspection for all IHC trucks on the road. The service was available at the 5,000 IH sales and service outlets for ninety days.

Kenworth introduced a combination passenger and freight model called the "Bruck." The bus-truck provided seating for twenty-one passengers in the front and a freight compartment of twenty-four feet at the rear.

A fleet of Mack buses in New York City was equipped with fluorescent lamps in the interior and ventilators above the seats.

Reo developed a Liquid Propane Gas (LPG) conversion system for its Gold Comet engine. The engine was also available as a replacement package.

Twin Coach added a new bus called the Fageol-Liner. The model offered improved structural components, greater engine accessibility and choice of gasoline, propane or diesel engines.

White Motor Company designed its "Mustang" engine which developed 150 horsepower with a compression ratio of 6 3/4 to 1. The engine featured individual intake manifold ducting, a redesigned combustion chamber, and a new duplex carburetor with two venturi, one for each three cylinders.

White and Freightliner signed an agreement whereby trucks manufactured by Freightliner would be sold and serviced exclusively through The White Sales organization. A new nameplate was born: White Freightliner.

White acquired Sterling Motor Truck Company, Incorporated, of Milwaukee and established the "Sterling White" nameplate.

Trailmobile offered a light-weight model A trailer which reduced unladen weight by 240 pounds, yet increased strength and rigidity. The price of the trailer was reduced by $480.

Distribution and servicing rights for Freightliner were handled through White Motor in the western states.

San Antonio Transit Company converted sixty-two of its Twin Coach bus fleet to propane gas.

Twin Coach introduced a 35-foot long coach, convertible into a truck. Quick removal of seats and partitions, and folding baggage racks, provided 321-cubic feet of cargo space.

Detroit Diesel announced an option on its series 71 diesel engine so either diesel or natural gas could be used as fuel. GM 4-71 and 6-71 diesel engines advertised a "fuel moderator" in the governor assembly to control the amount of fuel injected at speeds below 1,500 rpm.

Despite high truck production since the end of World War II, one of every three trucks was of 1940 vintage or older.

Record production: 1,450,596 trucks and buses.

1952

Good Roads Movement

A national good roads movement again surfaced with the formation of "Project: Adequate Roads" (PAR).

The Interstate Commerce Commission's annual report concluded that long distance highway transportation of freight continued to increase and that standardization and interchange of trailers was increasing rapidly.

Short-haul transportation of mail was transferred from railroads to trucks. The switch was said to reduce delivery costs.

Chicago opened a planned "truck town" to house forty terminals, recreational facilities, eating and sleeping facilities, and repair shops. The terminal area covered twenty square blocks.

More than half the states were considering toll roads. Some had legislated their construction.

The Korean War continued to affect the industry.

Critical material shortages developed and defense officials feared shut-downs of steel furnaces.

The automotive industry cut back vehicle production, and saved millions of pounds of critical materials for the defense program.

The Army Ordnance Corps produced a 2 1/2-ton truck with hydraulic drive.

The United States government purchased 9,000 GMC trucks for the armed services. The total cost was $30 million.

Business volume was rising as were costs and taxes. Wages kept pace. Tire and battery prices were reduced by the rubber industry.

The ruling of the constitutionality of the states ton-mile tax was to be appealed to the United States Supreme Court.

Chevrolet van delivery models featured a special body with a hydraulic liftgate which was an integral part of the rear enclosure.

Diamond-T designed two models with diesels up to 300 horsepower. The 950 and 951 series were the largest and most powerful ever built by Diamond-T. The trucks were built for maximum loads in the Pacific Northwest mountain states and Pacific Coast, specifically in lumber logging, but also for oil fields.

Federal's new 4400 series tractors were equipped with Swing Lift fenders for access to the engine and a hinged instrument panel for access to dash and instruments.

Ford offered three overhead valve engines, a 6-cylinder model, and two V-8s.

Fruehauf introduced a van-type aluminum trailer called the Road Star. Panel sides, wheels, landing gear, flooring and wheel plate were all aluminum. The manufacturer claimed strength and durability, as well as weight savings.

GMC package delivery model P-150-22 was equipped with an automatic transmission as standard equipment.

GMC introduced a 3-cylinder, 2-cycle diesel in its 2 1/2-ton model D-450-37. Also noteworthy was a combination air-hydraulic brake system. Hydraulic brakes were operated by a unit which changed air pressure into hydraulic pressure at dual cylinders in the front and rear.

GMC offered trucks in the 20,000 to 35,000 pound GVW range. Hydramatic transmission was made available on 3/4-ton models. **GM** offered its first air-suspension bus.

International introduced six cab-over-engine models and offered LP-gas engines as options.

Ocean Van Lines began container service from Seattle to Alaska.

A Kenworth gas turbine truck completed a 1,445-mile test run from Canada to Mexico in less than sixty hours.

The Mack A 55T diesel tractor was equipped with an ether-injection starting system.

Reo introduced an L-P gas engine as factory equipment in its larger trucks, and entered the diesel field with its F-23 DT model. The gross combination weight was 50,000 pounds for the new tractor.

White introduced a new steering pusher axle on its 3000 model and diesel tractors. The unit was a separate steerable axle coordinated with the front axle. The extra axle allowed 6,500 pounds more load.

Trailmobile introduced an exterior post semitrailer.

ACF-Brill Motors Company merged with Foremost Dairies, Incorporated.

Production dropped to 1,238,193 trucks and buses.

1953
Highway Development Gains Momentum

The national movement to improve the nation's highways continued. Diversion of highway funds surfaced as the newest problem. One bright note was that three states outlawed the practice.

In the campaign for better roads, PAR was active in twenty-nine states. The national movement was sponsored by the National Highway Users Conference.

Many states viewed toll roads as a solution to highway problems.

An increased interest in "piggy-back" (hauling highway truck-trailers on railroad flat cars) surfaced as shippers and motor carriers looked for ways to combat highway problems.

California increased trailer lengths from thirty-five feet to forty feet.

New York State Supreme Court upheld the ton-mile tax.

1950 This multipurpose Willys Overland 1/2-ton Jeep truck, featuring new body styling and a high compression "Hurricane" engine, drove on terrain over which many vehicles could not travel.

1951 Reo "Eager Beaver" 2 1/2-ton army truck cruising through the waters in Chesapeake Bay, Maryland.

1951   Rugged Ford F-5 model stake truck with "5 Star Extra" cab designed with added driver comfort.

1952   Ford F-6 series truck cab and chassis, available with 106-horsepower big six engine and designed for heavy-duty hauling.

1953 International introduced this R-line multistop delivery truck with Metro all-steel body.

1954 The Kenworth cab-beside-engine design gave the driver an unsurpassed view of the road. The cab was half the size of conventional cabs, had a single door, and tandem seating with the passenger behind the driver.

1953   Heavy equipment work to construct the interstate highway system. Pictured is the interchange between the Edsel Ford and John Lodge expressways in Detroit.

Ohio passed a weight-distance tax which, in effect, imposed a fee or toll to operate a truck in Ohio.

Construction began on the Ohio Turnpike. The 241.4-mile super highway from the end of the Pennsylvania Turnpike to the Ohio-Indiana border was scheduled for completion in June, 1955.

A highlight of the year was a commemorative postage stamp honoring the truck industry's fiftieth year. It was issued by the Post Office in conjunction with the American Trucking Associations' annual convention in Los Angeles, October 26–30. This came fifty years after competitive truck test trials were a hit on Broadway in New York City in 1903.

A two-month steel strike curtailed truck production; yet, the industry demonstrated that civilian needs could be met despite the Korean War. The lack of skilled labor posed a serious problem.

Weight reduction was stressed; magnesium truck bodies were manufactured.

Companies introduced new models: Diamond-T's model 723 offered a lightweight diesel; Reo F-50 series featured a heavy-duty tractor with a 160-horsepower engine; Mack B series, a complete new line, featured engine accessibility for service and maintenance, and a "Flag Ship Cab" for driver comfort and safety; International Harvester introduced a complete new line known as the R, RA, and RD series; Ford models ranged from F 100 to F 900 and featured a new frame, which had been strengthened and ran parallel from front to rear rather than tapering as in previous models.

Reo began coast-to-coast truck leasing through its subsidiary, Reo Truck Leasing, Incorporated.

Chrysler Corporation used plastic dies to stamp steel panels for Dodge trucks. Time saved in die manufacture and low cost were the chief advantages.

Beetle Plastics Corporation manufactured a 3,400-gallon fiberglass reinforced plastic tank to mount on a semitrailer for hauling formaldehyde. The combined weight of trailer and tank was 7,025 pounds, half as heavy as the former steel tank and trailer.

Fruehauf introduced a new haulway trailer for automobile shipping. The length of the trailer was thirty-five feet.

Automatic transmissions were introduced by Ford on F100 and pickup models, and by Dodge on 1/2 and 3/4 models.

GM replaced conventional chassis springs on buses with a bellows and compressed air system.

Freightliner added a COE highway linehauler with a pancake engine and 4 × 4 drive.

The new Greyhound order for 400 series GM coaches specified hydraulic power steering.

Waukesha Motor Company added turbochargers to three of its diesel engines for truck and transportation.

Turn-signal laws were passed in many states.

White Motor Company acquired Autocar Company of Ardmore, Pennsylvania, in exchange for White Motor preferred stock.

White discontinued making buses.

White sold the Sterling plant, integrated the operations into its business, and discontinued the Sterling-White nameplate.

Navajo Freight Line, Incorporated, merged with Fleetways Incorporated. The merger was approved by the Interstate Commerce Commission. The new company retained the name Navajo Freight Lines, Incorporated.

Omnibus Corporation purchased the Hertz Driv-Ur-Self system from General Motors.

General Motors acquired Euclid Road Machinery Company.

Roger M. Kyes, general manager of GM Coach and Truck Division, became deputy secretary of defense, joining Wilson, Summerfield, and McKay in the Eisenhower administration.

Production still declined to 1,216,879 trucks and buses.

1954

Production and Sales Falter
But It's Still a Record Year

Despite a drop in production and sales, 1954 was a record year in the truck industry. As sales declined, the manufacturers geared production proportionally.

Government truck orders were also reduced. However, the manufacturers welcomed another government move, which saw a record $966 million authorized for an interstate highway system linking major cities in the United States. With the prospect of a national super highway system, the burden of increased state highway taxes did not seem quite so grim. To everyone's benefit, the taxes collected on trucks and other motor vehicles helped highway growth.

Sixteen states cancelled reciprocity with Ohio because of that state's weight-distance tax.

Trucks from states which did not accord reciprocity to trucks from Georgia were required to pay a permit and round trip fee to operate in that state. The action was in response to the Ohio mile tax.

Eighteen states required mud guards or mud flaps on trucks and trailers.

Diamond-T's tilt-cab model 723C tilted forward by counter balanced springs.

Ford trucks offered two new overhead valve V-8 engines with 239 and 256-cubic inch displacement. They were of the over-square, short-stroke design.

GMC offered a new automatic transmission with seven speeds coupled to a 3-speed reduction gear box. The combination provided twenty-one possible gear reductions.

Folding seats and floorboards, and a removable "humpcover," provided above-frame engine accessibility in the GMC cab-over-engine models, called the "stripaway system." Counterbalanced hinges allowed exposure of the engine in thirty seconds.

GMC offered the Hydramatic automatic transmission as an option up through the 4-ton series with eight speeds forward. Power steering was also optional on all models from 2 ton up.

Counterbalancing was also used on the International tilt cabs, so that one man could raise it. A special hatch was in the top of the cab for entrance and exit if the side doors were blocked.

Kenworth introduced a cab-by-engine design to provide a smaller cab (less than half the width of regular cabs) with one windshield, one windshield wiper, one door, and one front seat. The second seat was behind the driver.

Air brakes were standard equipment on the new Mack four- and six-wheel tractors. Maintenance features included detachable panels between the fenders and hood for engine work, detachable inside door panels which housed the door, window mechanism, and glass. A panel behind the glove box carried the fuses.

Mack designed a cab with a special rear contour for trailer corner clearance and long-pin location, a foot-and-a-half forward of the rear axle. Mack also offered a short tractor 90-inch BBC.

Chevrolet introduced completely new models for 1954. Engine, chassis, and body were modified and reengineered for the first time since 1947. Three new engines, Thriftmaster, Loadmaster, and

Jobmaster were introduced.

Reo celebrated its golden anniversary and announced a new V-8 engine, the Golden Comet.

The White WC-24 TD tractor measured only ninety-six inches from bumper to back of the cab. The engines were tilted twenty degrees to the right to accommodate the short wheelbase.

Willys developed a Jeep-type vehicle with right-side steering for mail delivery.

Dorsey light-weight trailer freight vans featured plastic roof caps with a translucent section to admit outside light.

Fruehauf announced forty-four new trailers featuring greater space, strength, and increased payload.

Strick Company introduced a new refrigerated truck trailer which used reinforced plastic panels and beams. It weighed 11,800 pounds, with tandem wheel assembly.

Boyertown Body Works designed two trailers which converted into a traveling auditorium that seated 100 people comfortably.

Freightliner introduced a new model with a 75-inch BBC.

Truckstell Company developed a swivel frame that allowed the front and rear portions of the truck to rotate independently. This eliminated distortion of truck running gear and body parts.

A number of firms offered swing-up rear doors for trucks and trailers.

Tandem axle manufacturers emphasized lighter construction.

Plastic fenders were used by Chevrolet on its fleet of tractor-trailers for the All Star Show.

Automatic transmissions were available on all lines of GM trucks.

Demand for power steering increased.

Michigan Trucking Association elected Gladys M. Wright president of the association. Wright owned the Intercity Trucking Service in Detroit.

Mailing of Trucking Stamp first day covers topped an 875,021 mark, and set a new record for philatelic envelopes.

The Virginia Museum of Fine Arts used a specially designed Fruehauf trailer to show painting exhibits throughout the state. Called the "Artmobile," the 45-foot aluminum trailer had special walls, built-in ceiling lighting, sound system, air conditioning, and carbon dioxide fire preventive system.

Air-suspended trailers were offered by Fruehauf, Brown, and Strick.

Nash and Hudson merged to form American Motors Corporation. *Production faltered to 1,029,312 trucks and buses.*

1955

Heavy-Duty Trucks Spur V-8 and Diesel Sales

Activity in V-8 and diesel engines complemented a demand for heavy-duty trucks. Models over 26,000 pounds GVW recorded a 58 percent increase in production over 1954 totals. Close to 65,000 units were manufactured. The use of shorter compact engines, such as the V-8s, allowed short-nose cabs, and shorter, over-all cab lengths meant increased payloads. Proposals involving new super highways also looked inviting to heavy-duty long-haul truckers.

Pacific Intermountain Express Company built an experimental tractor with a Cummins pancake diesel engine, air suspension and two sets of steerable front wheels on tandem axles.

Cummins introduced its 6-cylinder, 175-horsepower JT turbo-diesel engine, which weighed 1,615 pounds with accessories.

Dodge added five V-8s and two automatic transmissions, the Powerflite and the Super Truck-O-Matic.

Four Wheel Drive Auto Company announced two highway tractor models, a 4 × 4 model T47 and a 6 × 4 model T 647.

International Harvester announced nineteen new models and two new engines, the Black Diamond and the Royal Red Diamond.

GMC added new valve-in-head V-8 engines featuring aluminum parts to save weight.

Reo offered a 100,000 mile warranty on its Gold Comet engines.

Ford introduced the Cargo King V-8 engine line with sodium-cooled exhaust valve stem and cobalt-chrome seat insert combined with valve rotation.

Ford offered vacuum power brakes on all its 1955 models and standard on the 600 and larger models. A new spark plug "Turbo-Action" (Champion 18mm) featured a tapered seat which eliminated the need for gaskets.

Chevrolet extended its V-8 option to all truck models except forward-control models. Chevrolet also introduced the new V-8 "Trademaster" for light and medium trucks.

Chevrolet introduced a Cameo Carrier model featuring a reinforced glass fiber plastic body.

Oshkosh had a new four-wheel-drive ready-mix concrete truck with a cantilevered engine forward of the front wheel.

Chrysler Corporation tested an all-aluminum 2 1/2-ton army truck which weighed 9,000 pounds as compared to the over 14,000 pounds of a conventional 2 1/2 ton. The special model featured air-assist hydraulic disc brakes, independent torsion bar suspension, automatic transmission, and a fuel-injected air-cooled engine.

The number of railroads offering piggyback service increased to twenty-two. A year ago only nine offered the service.

The concept of "fishy-back" grew as the Maritime Commission and Interstate Commerce Commission studied new proposals for permission to construct "roll-on, roll-off" ships to carry up to 300 trailers.

A portable steel shipping container called "Mobilvan" was announced by Clark Equipment Company. The container was half the size of a semitrailer, had automatic locking devices for securing to semitrailer or railcar and had a capacity of 20,000 pounds.

The use of fiberglass-reinforced plastics for truck bodies and trailers received increasing attention in the industry.

Montpelier Manufacturing Company built a fiberglass-reinforced plastic milk truck body.

Strick Trailers developed an all-plastic refrigerated trailer and an open top trailer with an aluminum roof that moved forward or backward to allow crane loading.

Bassons Industries Corporation introduced a three-wheel delivery truck of fiberglass-reinforced plastic.

GMC displayed an experimental panel truck, *"Le Universelle,"* at the GM Motorama in New York. Its front-wheel-drive setup used an inverted hydramatic transmission; a 288-cubic inch V-8 engine was mounted behind and beneath the driver.

Flxible Company developed a two-level, 37-passenger bus called the "Vista-Liner." Air conditioning, reclining seats, and individual radio speakers were featured.

FWD Company, in cooperation with the army, built the "Teracruzer," an experimental personnel and cargo vehicle. Engineered for rough terrain, it had pneumatic tire bags of low pressure furnished by Goodyear. The measurements of the vehicle were: length, twenty-five feet; width, twelve feet; and height, ten feet.

Union Switch and Signal Division of Westinghouse Air Brake Company designed a platform mounted on a trailer for launching jet planes.

Dorsey offered its "Giant" (deep frame platform) trailer of all-welded construction. Two additional bodies, grain and livestock, were also available.

Fruehauf Trailer Company introduced an all-aluminum truck body, the Cargo Star.

The Columbian 6,600-gallon steel tank trailer had sections of graduated diameters with the middle section tapered to match the larger rear section.

An adjustable fifth wheel was developed by Transportation Engineering Sales Company. The fifth wheel was hydraulically adjustable so that the trailer could be pushed backward or moved forward to meet different load and length limits.

The Automobile Manufacturers Association and the Truck Trailer Manufacturers Association proposed jointly that an auxiliary emergency braking system for truck and trailer combination be required.

The Federal Communications Commission approved radio frequencies for local and intercity bus and truck fleets.

The nation's major eastern railroads and trucking companies formed a policy board to maintain peace in the transportation industry. It was known as the Council of Eastern Rail and Trucks Common Carriers.

The Central States Motor Freight Bureau filed a petition with the Interstate Communications Commission for a compulsory rate increase on traffic for all for-hire truckers operating in its area.

The American Trucking Associations reported that United States trucking doubled its fleets of trucks and tripled its tax payment from 1954 to 1955.

Tubeless tires were available for large trucks.

Negative grounding of storage batteries was adopted as an SAE standard (SAE J-538).

Dana Corporation purchased the Auto Frame Division of Murray Corporation of America.

White acquired Superior Diesel.

Warner and Swasey Company acquired Duplex Division of Reo.

Federal announced its "Golden Eagle" line featuring a driver's seat mounted on individual hydraulic cylinders.

Spencer-Safford introduced the "Loadcraft" air suspension system, featuring two air pillows per axle that could be installed on existing equipment.

Production rallied upward to 1,253,672 trucks and buses.

1956

"Heavies" Lead the Way

Heavy-duty trucks were again the talk of the industry as they recorded an increase over 1955 by 26.6 percent. The number of units produced was 220,265 compared to 173,966 in 1955.

Diesels increased 53 percent over 1955 production.

New favorites coming were tilt-cab and four-wheel-drive models.

Chevrolet introduced a line of heavy-duty trucks for the first time and extended its GVW range up to 32,000 pounds. The company added forty new models in the 2 1/2-ton class which brought the total to over 100 models.

Dodge added a line of six-wheel tandem-axle trucks with power as high as 220 horsepower and GVW up to 46,000 pounds.

Ford's complete truck line offered over 280 models with eight new engines and increased horsepower. Tubeless tires, 12-volt electrical systems and safety steering wheels were standard.

International introduced three new V-8 engines specifically for heavy-duty models. Seven all-wheel-drive models were also new.

The total output of Freightliner Corporation were models over 26,000 pounds GVW.

White introduced a turbo-diesel model.

Diamond-T offered an Air-O-Steering power steering unit.

The American Trucking Associations stated that the trucking industry was unjustly taxed in the proposed financing of the national highway building program. William Bresnahan, assistant general manager of ATA, stated that a recent House-approved bill would tax a 5-axle truck $565 a year compared to $6.04 charged to a passenger car owner.

The American Trucking Associations and the Tire Manufacturers both endorsed a bill sponsored by Representative Hale Boggs (D.La) which proposed that the cost of financing the highway program be shared by all highway users.

Gas and diesel fuel taxes were raised 1 cent a gallon for the new federal road aid program. Additional excise taxes were levied on commercial vehicle operators. The new federal program emphasized "free" highways as opposed to toll roads.

Legislation was introduced in Congress to ban the sale of gasoline or motor fuel unless it was composed of at least 5 percent alcohol manufactured from grain.

New fuel injection systems were announced by American Bosch Arma Corporation and Thompson Products. Bendix introduced electrically controlled injection.

Southern Pacific Company entered agreements with American Airlines, Slick Airways, and United Air Lines to provide integrated truck air service between West Coast points and most principal United States cities.

ICC established stiffer regulations for braking systems on tractor trailers. A joint proposal had been made in 1955 by AMA and TTMA to require an auxiliary brake system on tractor trailers.

New York passed a compulsory safety inspection law which required yearly checks of all cars and trucks.

GMC Truck and Coach announced a new line of light and medium duty trucks, and added four-wheel drive as a factory-installed option on all its trucks.

The GM warranty policy offered repair of defects for 12,000 miles or one year (whichever came first) for trucks and cars.

Studebaker offered a locking differential as standard on its 1/2-ton truck.

The Small Business Administration pledged help to small truckers in their fight to get credit for financing new equipment.

The Interstate Commerce Commission charged that a nationwide safety check of private carrier vehicles showed that 90.1 percent had vehicular defects not in compliance with ICC safety regulations. The commission warned trucking companies and industrial truck owners that drastic official regulation would occur if regulations were not followed.

Mack acquired Brockway Motor Company.

The air force granted two large contracts to the truck industry.

Walter Motor Truck Company received a $9 million contract to build firetrucks.

Federal Motor Trucks, a division of Napco Industries, received a $2 million contract to build truck snow plows.

Mack acquired C. D. Beck and Company of Sydney, Ohio, a privately owned manufacturer of intercity buses.

Mack Trucks, Incorporated, established Mack Belgium S.A. to manufacture, assemble, and distribute Mack vehicles and diesel engines in Europe.

American Bantam stockholders approved plans to sell Bantam's property and buildings to Armco Steel Company and the remaining assets of American Bantam to Pressed Metals of America.

Copco Steel and Engineering Company announced the formation of a subsidiary, Copco Trailers, to produce a light-weight aluminum truck trailer.

Heil Company developed a one-piece molded plastic body for refrigerated trucks.

Mack received a $13 million army contract for three types of 10-ton trucks.

A new Allison transmission with retarder was offered by Chevrolet on the Powermatic transmission. The retarder improved safety on down grades for heavy duty trucks. It was put into effect by a pedal located in the normal location of a clutch pedal. Depression of the pedal flooded a transmission chamber, creating reverse hydraulic force against the engine-driven impeller.

Kingham Trailer Company introduced a trailer with blue anodized aluminum walls and gold aluminum extrusions. The undercarriage was spray-painted blue. Highway Trailer also introduced an anodized aluminum trailer in gold.

The Ohio Turnpike opened full length, and the last link of the Indiana Turnpike opened, completing the route from New York City to Chicago.

Plans were developed for an interstate highway of 41,000 miles.

Nine western states signed a reciprocity agreement.

The Fargo Division of Chrysler Corporation was awarded a $2 million army ordnance contract for 1 1/2- and 2-ton trucks.

Federal Motor Truck received a $1.5 million order for 200 Napco trucks.

Freuhauf received a $1.5 million contract for missile-loading truck trailers.

GMC Truck and Coach Division built the "Drake," a new giant amphibious vehicle for the army.

Ford revealed the design and engineering features of a passenger car-truck model to be called the "Ranchero," to be introduced early in 1957.

A major breakthrough allowed the tire industry to produce a tubeless tire for trucks. A new technique involved a 15-degree taper drop center one-piece rim which was pressure-sealed at the base of the bead.

Both car and truck production dropped from the record year of 1955; however, the decline in truck production was not as severe as the passenger car drop. Diesel truck sales were up approximately 9,000 units to a record 25,797.

Production in 1956 dropped slightly to 1,112,002 trucks and buses.

1957

Technology Explosion Emphasizes
Power, Maneuverability, Strength

Important engine and hauling improvements continued developing rapidly through continual research; new developments in all truck models were offered.

Chevrolet unveiled the Turbo-Titan experimental gas turbine truck. The Whirlfire turbine 200-horsepower engine was also an experimental unit. It was coupled to a conventional Chevrolet tandem-truck drive train and included a slightly modified power-matic transmission.

Chevrolet offered two new, 2-ton forward control multistop delivery models. The two new chassis featured greater maneuverability because of shorter lengths. They were engineered to use different manufacturer's cabs and bodies.

Diamond-T announced a new tilt-cab model, designated 430C and rated at 20,000 pounds. Emphasis was on strength and durability of chassis and engine. A twin hydraulic cylinder on each brake shoe was complemented by a Hydrovac booster.

Diamond-T offered a diesel-powered tractor, model 922, which used light metals to reduce weight. An average chassis, completely equipped, including trailer connections, weighed about 10,000 pounds for a single axle model and 12,000 pounds for a tandem model.

Diamond-T designed a model 730, specifically engineered for cement mixer use. The frame and bumper were extended eleven inches forward to accommodate a front-mounted power take-off which took the power from the engine crankshaft through a drive shaft with two universal joints.

The Spicer Thornton Power-Lok-Differential Kit was available for replacement on older trucks. The locking differential assured full power to the wheel having traction.

Ford introduced a Ranchero pickup model which featured passenger car styling and comfort, and increased load capacity.

Ford introduced "Transmatic Drive," a fully automatic transmission for heavy-duty trucks. The unit provided six forward speeds and a hydraulic retarder acting as a built-in brake.

Ford introduced a new tilt-cab series of six models from 181 horsepower to 212 horsepower. The new models were nine inches shorter than the cab-over-engine models offered last year.

Four Wheel Drive's "Teracruzer," built for the air force, was unveiled at the inaugural parade for President Eisenhower. The truck had eight-wheel drive with pillow tires called Terra Tires by Goodyear for off-highway use.

GMC Super E diesel engine featured four exhaust valves per cylinder and a hydraulic fan which operated only when needed.

International Harvester increased its all-wheel-drive line to twelve models with the addition of five 6-wheel and three 4-wheel drive models. The models featured a lower front chassis through the use of outrigger type spring mounting and a new design front drive axle.

International Harvester introduced a new automatic transmission, the Select-O-Matic for heavy-duty truck models. A shifting control button on the gearshift lever controlled the hydraulic clutch.

International Harvester celebrated its fiftieth anniversary of truck production. A new line of models called the Anniversary Line or A-Line was available in four-, six-, or all-wheel drive, and gasoline- and LPG-powered engines.

Western type cab-over-engine models, featuring hydraulically operated tilt cabs, were also introduced.

The new Dodge "stand-drive" model had a 95-inch wheelbase and measured only fourteen feet from bumper to bumper. Yet the load area was over 160-cubic feet.

Dodge introduced three power wagon models. All were four-wheel drive designed for off-highway use.

Reo's Super-V63 tractor measured sixty-three inches (from bumper to back of cab) and could pull a 35-foot trailer with a full-size sleeper bunk and remain well within legal limits in most states.

Studebaker introduced its Transtar line in 1/2- to 2-ton models.

White introduced Autocar and White highway series with gasoline or turbodiesel engines.

Willys added two FC-170 forward-control models to the Jeep line with nine feet of cargo space on pickup and stake bodies.

Fruehauf offered a unit for converting single axle tractors into tandem tractors. Called the "Tonnage Master," the unit was mounted on an all-steel frame and could be attached or detached by one man.

Freuhauf introduced a composite steel and aluminum Volume Van line of trailers. The vans were made in aluminum, stainless steel and high-tensile steel.

A special 14-ton aluminum truck trailer body by Gerstenslager Company expanded from each side to more than five times its on-the-road dimensions. At a touch of a button, the sides telescoped outward and aluminum floors dropped in place. While the trailer was eight feet wide in running position, expanded the width was increased to twenty-six feet.

A Hi-Cube furniture van with over 2,600-cubic feet of space, a low frame, and removable gooseneck was introduced by Dorsey.

Mack Trucks, Incorporated, introduced a forty-one-passenger cross-country luxury bus.

A new truck body by Thompson Trailer, called the Lo-Loader, could be raised to fifty-three inches, lowered to ground level, tilted rearward and to the side.

Available Truck Company was purchased by Crane Carrier.

Southern Pacific Railroad designed a flatcar specifically for hauling trucks and trailers.

Greyhound announced a joint air and bus shipping service. Sixteen airlines and two freight airlines joined Greyhound in providing the service for 6,000 communities.

Continental-Trailways introduced a luxury bus service between Pueblo and Denver, using an articulated German-bus, seating a total of sixty-four passengers. Service included hostesses, light meals, lavatory, and an excursion-type roof section.

Spicer introduced its air-shift 12-speed transmission and a heavy duty synchromesh transmission.

Greyhound initiated an express bus service between Chicago and New York. Six trips daily were made by "Scenicruiser" buses. The time for the 842-mile trip was seventeen hours thirty-five minutes.

New York City Transit Authority purchased 209 GM diesel buses, and the Indianapolis Transit Authority converted to all-diesel bus operations.

Seventy-five trucking firms signed with Slick Airways to operate air-road combination shipping.

New York's Fifth Avenue Coach Lines acquired the Third Avenue Transit Corporation to enlarge its operations to 2,200 buses and 6,000 employees.

White Motor Corporation purchased Reo Motors, Incorporated. Reo became a division of White.

Spector Freight System and Mid States Freight Lines merged to form Spector-Mid States with combined annual revenue of over $50 million.

Kaiser Aluminum developed an 8- to 10-yard capacity, all-welded aluminum dump box for General Machinery Company of Spokane, Washington. The weight savings amounted to nearly a ton and gave the dump truck an additional payload of 1,500 pounds.

Accessories for thwarting vehicle theft included safes which could be bolted to the floor, were locked by multiple tumblers, and had slots for collections. A decal on the side of the vehicle stated that the driver did not have a key for the safe.

Truckstell offered a third-axle suspension system, called Hydro-Trac for providing emergency traction and maximum tire-to-road contact.

Kenworth developed a CSE (cab-surrounding-engine) model which measured fifty-four inches BBC.

The Port of Houston opened a fishy-back operation for hauling trailers to Newark, New Jersey. Plans to extend the service to San Francisco were to be completed early in 1959. Pan Atlantic handled the operation and provided 10-acre parking at the docks.

P & H diesels featured injection plungers and timing means mounted in a 9 1/2-pound sealed unit with one adjustment for timing the engine. A "unitized" cylinder head and liner assembly, mushroom connecting rods, and completely immersed "wet" liners were also featured.

Gar Wood Company developed a load packer refuse body with "cyclomatic" loading and packing with a rotary panel in the hopper that exerted 81,000 pounds pressure for continuous loading.

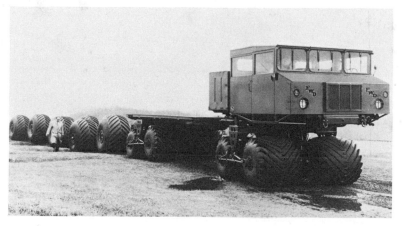

1955 FWD developed the "Teracruzer" personnel and cargo carrier for the army. Low-pressure pneumatic tire bags by Goodyear traveled easily over rough terrain.

1956 Diesel-powered, 6-wheel Brinks armored International Harvester model.

1955 Mack cab-forward D-model featured counterweighted door windows which could be raised or lowered without crank handles.

1957 This sleek Ford Ranchero featured passenger-car styling and comfort.

1957 White 3000 emphasized the ease of tilting the cab for instant engine accessibility.

1958 Chevrolet Apache panel delivery was powered by a 145-horsepower 6-cylinder engine. Heavy-duty automatic transmission and V-8 engine were optional.

1959 Modern Mack transit bus featured wrap-around windshield, dual headlights, lower entrance, and air-glide suspension.

Dodge offered a heavy-duty L series which featured the torqmatic automatic transmission.

GMC added an automatic transmission, the torqmatic, replacing the hydramatic in the 370 through 600 series.

Exide offered a "doughnut" battery hexagonally shaped.

Jimmy Hoffa succeeded Dave Beck in 1957 as head of the Teamsters' Union.

Gates Rubber Company introduced roll-on pulleys with V-belts to drive the dead axle on tandem-axle trucks. Called "Tandematic Drive," the device claimed greater traction, even tire wear, and reduced wheel hop.

Fuller introduced a new Roadranger R-35 transmission with seven forward speeds and one reverse.

RCA introduced a mobile 100-watt, 2-way radio called "Carfone."

The Spicer Synchro-Master 12-speed transmission featured synchronizers in all speeds, forward and reverse. The unit had six low speed range ratios in reverse, forced feed lubrication, oil filter, and spaced steps between ratios.

Johns-Manville Company color-coded brake blocks to indicate high (red), medium (yellow), and low (red) friction ranges.

Seventeen states and seven cities required vehicle inspection, with ten of the sixteen requiring inspection twice a year. Eleven other states were considering inspections. All but three states, Kansas, Massachusetts, and Nevada, required turn signals on some or all vehicles. Twenty-five states required either mud flaps or mud guards.

Fleet owners reported that flat tires, ignition problems and battery problems were the three major road-repair complaints.

New York State adopted highway traffic signs informing drivers of lower gear zones on seventy of the state's hills.

The concept of billboards on wheels grew as fleet owners used truck and trailer bodies for public relations advertising or they rented the space.

Autocar introduced a planetary-gear drive rear axle where the planetary reduction occurred at the outer end of the axle. The design reduced torque on the differential and axle shafts. Two off-highway models used the drive.

Dallas and St. Louis air-conditioned their bus fleets.

New York City bus lines showed a slight profit after seventeen years of losses.

Charged earlier with monopolistic practices by Attorney General Brownell, Greyhound Corporation reached an agreement with the government and agreed to break long-standing ties with General Motors and find new sources to supply its buses.

Production dropped again to 1,100,402 trucks and buses.

1958

"Heavies" Lose Weight

Progress in power, strength, maneuverability, and durability generated emphasis in increasing the use of light-weight materials like aluminum, fiberglass, and plastic. Every time a pound of weight was taken from a truck's structure, the vehicle could carry one more pound of cargo to hold down the cost of delivering products.

An aluminum flatbed trailer built by Williamsen Body and Equipment Company measured forty feet and could haul 50,000 pounds, yet weighed 2,000 to 4,000 pounds less than similar steel trailers and 1/2-ton less than shorter aluminum trailers.

Diamond-T introduced an all-aluminum tilt cab which was counterbalanced for manual operation with no disconnections necessary. The model offered a Hall-Scott 590 Spartan engine either gasoline or LPG fueled. The assembly of head, overhead camshaft, roller-type rocker arms, hardened valve seats and intake and exhaust valve assemblies was removable as a unit.

GMC introduced a light-weight highway tractor powered by the GM6-71 SE diesel. The GM diesel featured a device called the Economy Range Governor which operated in the top speed gears.

Dorsey Trailers introduced the Satellite series of aluminum trailers. The DALT-20 model had a 35-foot high capacity, 91-inch inside width, 90-inch inside height, and weighed only 8,750 pounds.

The GMC light-weight highway tractor model DR 862—displayed at the Chicago Auto Show—weighed only 11,000 pounds, complete with 100 gallons of fuel and a fifth wheel. Its unique air suspension eliminated road vibrations and shock and permitted the use of lighter materials.

A trailer was developed by Plasti-Glas, Incorporated, which was convertible from flat bed to van by slidable knockdown side-and-end sections. Tubular aluminum rods provided an upper mounting for a tarpaulin top.

A light-weight cast steel, low-mounted tandem unit by Reynolds Manufacturing Company, called the Reyco "30," featured a pre-assembled rubber bushed torque-arm assembly that required no adjustment and provided extended service life.

Mack exhibited an aluminum dump truck at the Chicago Auto Show which weighed twenty-seven tons with a capacity of 37 1/2-cubic yards. Powered by a 335-horsepower Cummins diesel, and with torquematic transmission with torque converter, the mammoth truck was thirty feet three inches long, twelve feet four inches wide, and eleven feet eleven inches high. Heil Company constructed the body with Alcoa aluminum.

Chevrolet announced three Fleetside pickup trucks featuring 6 1/2 and 8-foot boxes, double-wall side construction, extra-wide tailgate, and corrosion proof, nonshed hardwood floors.

Ford offered new grills, dual headlights, customized interiors, plus high horsepower and payload on its new line of trucks. More than 300 models were available with an automobile-inspired pickup design styling, a successful carryover, and now offering two-tone color combinations which matched custom-designed interiors.

Diamond-T announced the 923 model featuring Cummins HF-6-B diesel power and such a wide variety of options available that each truck was tailor-made to the buyer's needs.

Diamond-T developed an 8-wheel tilt-cab diesel with four axles and hauled 60,000 pounds in Pennsylvania coal mining operations. The unit weighed 20,600 pounds, including a 17-foot dump body with an 18 1/2-cubic yard capacity.

Ford introduced three new V-8 engines with horsepowers of 226, 260, and 277 at 7.5 to 1 compression ratios, designed specifically for heavy-duty trucks.

A FWD cab-over-engine transport tractor featured constant four-wheel drive, designed for pulling doubles in western states.

Kenworth tilt cabs were available in three cab-over-engine models. A double-acting hydraulic pump was operated by a detachable handle located at the rear of the cab. The pump operated two hydraulic rams which tilted the cab forward fifty-five degrees.

Reo offered a C-series tandem line with eight models, six gasoline and two diesel.

Freightliner introduced a 90-degree full-tilt cab.

The Mack cab-forward truck featured a wrap around windshield and extra-wide doors which enclosed the steps.

White introduced its "King of the Highway" model, a heavy-duty unit featuring operating economy. Its Cummins NH-180 diesel engine developed 180 horsepower operating at 2,100 rpm.

Hendrickson Manufacturing Company announced a new air-spring suspension for tandem axles. The series was interchangeable with all other Hendrickson suspensions.

A differential dual wheel was developed by the Anderson-Bolling Manufacturing Company. The wheel provided independent rotation of inner and outer wheels, giving positive braking on both wheels, dissipated heat more rapidly, and improved tire wear.

A frameless 21–23 foot dump trailer with the body hinged at the rear of the tandem frame was introduced by Trailmobile. All wheels remained on the ground when the body was elevated.

Dana Corporation introduced the Spicer Turbomatic automatic transmission.

A mobile weighing station was used by the California State Highway Patrol to supplement the regular scale installations. The unique mobile scale was a trailer carrying platform scales which could be raised and lowered hydraulically. Built by Locomotion Engineering, the trailer could be driven to any major highway at any time.

Hercules Motors acquired Hall-Scott Engine Division.

Four Wheel Drive Auto Company was bought by Paradynamics, Incorporated, of St. Louis.

Peterbilt was sold to Pacific Car and Foundry.

White Motor Company purchased the Diamond-T Motor Car Company which became Diamond-T Division of White.

The New York Central Railroad started a "piggy-back" service, loading semitrailers on flat cars for rail shipment. Piggyback services were offered by forty-three railroads by the end of 1958.

Goodyear Tire and Rubber Company introduced a double-chambered captive-air safety tire to avoid complete blow-outs.

An additional $1.8 billion was authorized in April to speed construction on the interstate highway system.

Matson offered "fishyback" services to Hawaii.

Road testing was started by the American Association of State Highway Officials (AASHO) late in the year. The testing was the largest highway research project in history. Two hundred different types of highway construction and 836 test sections were used. These tests continued until the fall of 1960, and the findings went to Congress in January, 1961.

Congress repealed the 3 percent excise tax on freight. The tax had been in effect since World War II and applied to all products hauled by common carriers.

Bartlett introduced the "Dock Walloper" highway trailer, which featured extra heavy-duty construction and weighed 1,000 pounds more than competitive models.

An automotive fifth-wheel lock, the Torre Safety Lock, provided use of a safety piston which locked the tractor to the trailer automatically each time the driver opened the air brake valve.

Production dropped drastically to 873,842 trucks and buses.

1959

Interstate Highways Speed the Long Haul

Construction of the federal highway system progressed rapidly. Opening freeways and thruways marked a high point in motor truck transportation.

Tests were made early in the year by six trucking companies, using eleven diesel engine tractors to determine the feasibility of using "double-bottom" tractor-trailer units over the 506 mile stretch of the New York thruway. The units were ninety-eight feet in length and hauled up to 130,000 pounds gross weight.

Approval was granted to operate tandem trailer double bottoms on both the New York and the Massachusetts thruway routes.

The 187-mile Illinois Tri-State Tollway system was completed, giving trucks a fast and economical route around Chicago. The route would eventually connect with the Indiana Toll Road.

The combination of compact, light-weight tractor and trailer gave tremendous gains in payload capacities. The added concept of double trailers complemented liberal length laws in many states.

Mack introduced a highway diesel Transport "G" series. The cab measured 51 inches BBC and 80 inches with an optional integral sleeper compartment. The cabs were all aluminum.

White featured a 50-inch BBC fiberglass cab on its 5000 transport tractor. The use of fiberglass was claimed to save over 200 pounds in weight as compared to a steel cab.

The White transport tractor featured light-weight construction with aluminum chassis parts and fiberglass fenders and engine cover. A light-weight diesel design used aluminum parts for an overall weight savings of 1,100 pounds.

Construction Manufacturing Company built a "Transcrete" all-aluminum transit concrete mixer on a Ford T-850 chassis. The model was only a third the weight of a steel mixer.

Aerobuilt Bodies offered an aluminum frameless trailer built on the aircraft "skin" design; the body itself was the load bearer. Weight saved was approximately one-third that of a regular trailer.

Trailmobile, Incorporated, announced the "J-Rail" model flatbed trailer which was quickly convertible to an open top trailer by attaching aluminum side panels. The task could be accomplished by one man. The main rails formed a "J" shape to eliminate weight.

Lodestar Corporation offered an aluminum frameless trailer. The unit was a full size dump trailer in 20- to 28-foot lengths.

Flynn Manufacturing built special light-weight, strong, corrosion-resistant aluminum containers, for "fishyback" operations on the Grace Line Seatainer Service.

Chevrolet offered an adjustable metal stake body called "Pak-Rak." Six side and six end post section rails, and corner posts of 14-gauge steel, provided bed widths from 45 3/8 to 76 1/4 inches, and lengths from 69 3/8 to 110 inches.

The GMC tractor with air springs and independent front suspension allowed a 3-inch lower trailer.

Watson Company offered an electrically powered conveyor pallet "Moto-Vator" for mounting on van and trailer floors.

Diamond-T introduced two diesel models, the 921 D and the 922 D. Both units featured the deluxe "D" cab with curved solex windshield, cowl, top, and window ventilators, roomy sleeper cab, and storage locker. Nine transmissions, eleven rear axles, and five diesel engines were available.

Dodge announced that it would install the latest Chrysler experimental gas turbine engine in one of its 14,000 GVW trucks for extensive tests under a research and development contract with the Detroit Ordnance District.

Dodge introduced a heavy-duty tandem tractor powered by the NM-220 Cummins diesel engine.

Detroit Diesel offered new compact V-line diesels, weighing less, taking less room, yet giving more power at the wheel.

A V-6 gasoline truck engine was developed by GMC Truck and Coach. The engine was said to give increased fuel economy, longer wear, and maximum torque at moderate engine speeds. A V-12 engine named the "Twin-Six" was also offered.

White introduced an air-suspension system on its 5400 TD model. The new suspension gave a soft ride for cargo and weighed less than conventional systems.

Another White newcomer was a pickup and delivery truck, the 3016 D, powered by a 6-cylinder diesel.

International Harvester's B-line models featured vertical dual headlights on conventional models, and horizontal dual headlights on compact models.

The Chevrolet "Task Force 59" featured four classes of commercial vehicles; heavy-duty Spartan, medium Viking, light-weight Apache and forward control trucks, and school buses.

Dodge "Sweptside" pickup was the glamour model of the line. Innovations included power brakes, concealed running board, suspended brake and clutch pedals, and hydraulically operated brakes.

Divco continued to emphasize its "passenger car ride" for cargo protection, ability to idle for long periods, and "squared up" body design for larger capacity.

Dart Truck Company merged with Kenworth Motor Company, a Division of Pacific Car and Truck. The new company, K-W Dart, built trucks under both names.

The El Camino led Chevrolet's entry into the prestige pickup field. It featured passenger car styling with truck utility.

The International "Sightliner" model had a 48-inch BBC and a dromedary van in addition to the regular semitrailer. Two windows were mounted below the regular windshield for added visibility.

Williams Research Company of Walled Lake, Michigan, reported the development of a low-cost, light-weight, medium-horsepower gas-turbine engine using a heat-exchange principle.

Diamond-T designed a 931 C diesel series with a manually operated tilt cab. A hand operated pump raised the cab to a 45-degree angle, its full open position. The cab was available with a 50-inch BBC as standard. A 25-inch sleeper cab or a 30-inch full-skirt sleeper were available. The cab was fully insulated and aluminum constructed.

Trans-Equipment Corporation introduced a reverse-steering "Saf-T-Trac" semitrailer. The undercarriage design placed the fixed axle near the center of the trailer, which pivoted around that point. The setup provided greater maneuverability because the off-tracking of the rear-steered axle was in a smaller path than the rear axle of the tractor.

Dodge offered a new rear suspension with saddle-mounted wide leaf springs in rubber bushings with one-piece tension shackles. The new design gave improved ride, quiet operation, and minimum maintenance.

Fruehauf offered two suspensions on its trailers, a safety air suspension and an S-2 leaf spring tandem suspension. A new line of column vans was available in steel or aluminum.

Two magnesium vans were built by Elder Trailer and Body for the United States Bureau of Standards for scientific field work. The units were built especially for air transport and had detachable running gear.

Despite advantages and success of tubeless tires, most new truck buyers purchased tubes for tires.

Firestone and Goodyear introduced wire-cord truck tires.

A V-6 diesel engine, the 6V-71, was introduced on the GMC DFR-8000 series highway tractor. Independent front-wheel drive, air suspension, and new aluminum fabricated frame were also highlighted in the new light-weight tractor.

The "Reo-Matic" automatic transmission featured a torque converter, constant mesh planetary gear-set, hydraulic control, hydraulic retarder, and converter-driven power take-off provisions.

Arrow Equipment introduced a steel I-beam platform trailer with carrying capacities up to 55,000 pounds.

Dorsey introduced a cargo hauling van which featured steel tie tracks mounted horizontally on sides of the trailer. These were for attaching web-straps, socket fittings, second deck beams, and shoring purposes. The adaptability of the van was directed toward hauling electronic and other sensitive cargoes.

GMC developed a modulated brake which reduced truck stopping distances to those of a passenger car. The braking effort at the rear wheels was adjusted automatically in proportion to the load.

Truck Equipment Company developed a dual front wheel assembly which allowed front axles to carry 18,000 pounds or more, and increased tire mileage more than 50 percent.

Cummins announced two light-weight, 4-cylinder turbodiesel engines, bringing their total engine line up to thirty models. Since

1952, Cummins had furnished over half the diesels used in new trucks.

The U.S. Supreme Court ruled that the Illinois law requiring contour rear fender splash guards on trucks and trailers was unconstitutional and a burden on interstate commerce.

White Motor Company acquired Montpelier Manufacturing Company, a truck body manufacturer.

White introduced the "Turnpike Cruiser" diesel tractor with a 50-inch BBC fiberglass cab mounted on a tandem axle trailer and powered by a Cummins NRTO-diesel engine.

Chevrolet developed Turbo-Titan II, a regenerative gas turbine truck, which used a Chevrolet heavy-duty, tandem-axle tractor chassis, and an economically improved Whirlfire GT-305 gas-turbine engine.

A 63-passenger bus, the "Super Golden Eagle," which operated between Denver and Colorado Springs, was assembled in Germany. It had side panels and wheels from America, and engines made in Great Britain. The superbus had a lounge, rest room, and hostess.

Delaware was the first state to issue license plates with both reflectorized numerals and background.

A special publication for the female members of the trucking industry was published by the American Trucking Associations, appropriately titled *The Spinning Wheel*. Editor was Jeanne Mueller of the ATA public relations staff.

United States Freight Company, which started a piggyback service last year, claimed that the time saving ratio of the service gave a 24 to 1 advantage.

Production up again: 1,124,096 trucks and buses.

The Sixties

1960

Piggyback Concept Grows

Piggybacking, or shipping highway trailers on railroad flatcars, continued its rapid growth. Service was handled by fifty of the major railroads. The total cars shipped in 1959 was 64 percent over the 1958 total and approached the half million mark.

Generally, there were four types of piggybacking: railroads moved trailers of motor carriers; railroads moved their own trailers; shippers used railroad flatcars with the shipper's own trailers; and shippers used their own flatcars and trailers while the railroads hauled them.

A fifth piggybacking plan was from railroad origins to destinations serviced by its motor carriers. Containers were made available for shipping household goods by Van-Pack of Des Moines, Iowa.

The ICC's annual report to Congress noted the following trends in the trucking industry: a move toward mass-produced highway trailers; cab-over-engine trucks with BBC measurements of fifty inches or less; reduction of tractor and trailer weight, the use of plastics, and light-weight metals and alloys; deeper frame sections; and a trend toward diesel power in household-moving van lines.

All trucks were required to have turn-signal systems to flash front and rear signals at the same time as a hazard warning by November 15. The signals could not be in combination with stop lamps.

The federal government was the largest fleet operator in the nation, operating 60,882 trucks, 15,129 wagons, ambulances, and buses. Over 15,000 trucks were 3 ton and over. Annual operating costs totaled $228 million or 11.88 cents per mile.

After a year of the 3-cent increase in the price of diesel fuel, many New York fuel dealers and truck stop operators reported a decline in diesel fuel sales. Fleet owners and drivers purchased their fuel in New Jersey or Pennsylvania or other nearby states.

A trial operation for the use of "double bottoms" over the Northern Indiana Toll Road and the Ohio Turnpike was authorized early in the year by both highway commissions.

Reflective markings on the backs of trucks and trailers reduced the danger of rear-end collisions.

Brockway offered a short, all-steel, sleeper cab. Welded sectional construction allowed easy repair and replacement of any section.

Chevrolet introduced a short, tilt-cab model with a 72-inch BBC dimension, 6 1/2-foot width, and independent front wheel torsion-spring suspension.

Diamond-T production was moved from Chicago to the Reo plant in Lansing, Michigan.

The Diamond-T 931 C tilt-cab model allowed walk-in accessibility for engine maintenance and repair. The large number of options provided custom design.

Diamond-T introduced a 990-series diesel with a 90-inch BBC. The unit gave the capability of hauling 40-foot trailers. A new 931 heavy-duty diesel was also introduced.

White introduced its model-1500 "Compact," a short wheelbase cab-over truck for short intercity runs. It was designed for PDQ (pick up-and-deliver-quickly) multistops with unitized body construction, fiberglass roof, and a removable power-dolly front end and power unit.

A pneumatically controlled discharge tank truck was developed by Delta Tank Manufacturing Company.

Aluminum Company of America developed aluminum-forged disc wheels for trucks.

Ford announced its P-100 compact parcel delivery model with a wheelbase of ninety-six inches.

Midland Ross developed an auxiliary control for trailer brakes.

Diamond-T offered fiberglass tilt cabs with manual actuation.

Dodge Cab-Forward models featured "Servi-Swing" fenders which swung out on piano hinges for access to the engine. A new heavy-duty heat-treated frame was made from Chrome-manganese steel.

Dodge offered its first sleeper cab on the new cab forward model.

Ford was awarded a contract for 3,482 pickup trucks for the air force and navy.

Ford introduced the Falcon Ranchero pickup truck with a new 90-horsepower, 6-cylinder engine. Front fenders bolted on for easy repair and fuel mileage was claimed to be thirty miles per gallon.

Ford offered 200 models in six series of light- and medium-duty trucks in GVW ratings from 4,600 to 21,000 pounds. Truck models offered by the company reached a record 480 models.

"Flexi Van" mail service began using the New York Central Railroad and highway coordination to carry mail and express between

Chicago and Detroit. Highway trailers were carried on the passenger trains to speed up mail delivery.

International offered a compact diesel tractor designated BC-225 D in four- or six-wheel design. The chassis featured a wide range of light-weight aluminum.

Fruehauf introduced the Warehouseman Van for professional movers. The van provided over 100-cubic feet more capacity than previous models. The customer had a choice of aluminum or steel body components.

American Body and Trailer designed a Possum Belly Cattleliner Trailer featuring extensive use of aluminum for weight reduction.

The Perfection Reefer trailer by Hupp used a unitized rigid insulation sandwich and fiberglass reinforced plastic skin. The new construction gave up to 1,500 pounds weight savings.

Goodyear developed a van tank made of rubberized fabric which inflated on any truck, railroad car, or ship to become a liquid-carrying conveyance.

A 2-kilocycle low frequency electro-magnetic device warned drivers when they were too close to edge of pavements. Developed by General Motors Electronics Instrumentation Laboratory, the device could be mounted on or in the pavement at low cost.

The Pennsylvania Turnpike limited all vehicles to a maximum of ten feet in width.

International designed a compact, 83-inch wheelbase highway tractor specifically for hauling mobile homes.

Mack added an "Aluminum-Light" six-wheel tractor series featuring extensive use of aluminum and other light alloys.

Reo introduced an "E" line diesel-powered series in the medium- and heavy-duty range.

Studebaker designed "The Champ" pickup truck with a passenger-car interior and truck strength with a reinforced frame.

White Motor Company purchased the half cab designs and tooling of Cook Brothers of Los Angeles. The half cab was an aluminum one-man cab located along the engine's left side. A set-back front axle gave a turning radius 3 to 5 feet shorter than regular trucks.

The White sleeper cab featured a separate heating system for the sleeper compartment; a new heating system was also available in the cab.

White added a series of diesel-powered, pusher-tandem tractors. The drive was on the furthermost rear axle, with either single or

dual-tire pusher axles and V-belt drive, for the dual-tire pusher.
A medium-duty White tandem tractor with flywheel power take-off was also introduced.

Brown Trailer Division of Clark Equipment offered a 2,600-cubic foot all-aluminum highway trailer built on a monoque design. The floor sills, and side and roof stiffeners formed a continuous circle around the trailer.

Consolidated Freightways devised a way to haul ten highway flatbed trailers on two flatbed double trailers.

Freightliner introduced its first top-mounted sleeper.

Cummins introduced a 250-horsepower diesel for heavy-duty use. The engine was designated the NH-250 and had an 855-cubic inch displacement. Fuel lines in the new engine were drilled in the cylinder head and insert injectors. Oil lines were also internal.

Trailmobile used curved-shell sections of extruded aluminum a unitized designed tank trailer. The design eliminated cross welding.

A torsion-bar suspension system for truck seats was introduced by Bostrom on its Viking model truck seat. An automatic shock absorber dampened severe shocks. The seat adjusted to a driver's weight by a ratchet mechanism.

First Fleet Maintenance Show opened in New York City.

The railways hauled 500,000 piggyback carloads in 1960, an increase of 35 percent over the 1959 total.

Truck production up again to 1,202,011 trucks and buses.

1961

Economy and Weight-Savings Featured

Despite a slight decline in production from 1960, this year again marked a 1-million plus year for the third year in succession. Truck production had dipped below 1 million units only once (1958) since 1950.

This year the economical 4-cylinder engine led the way in powering the new models. Light-weight structure continued to intrigue manufacturers.

Diamond-T featured a fiberglass tilt cab on its 738 CG and 838 CG models.

International diesel tractor DB 405 featured a 48-inch BBC and a forward-tilting hood and fender assembly of reinforced fiberglass.

Kenworth announced its S-900 series with a one-piece fiberglass front end that tilted forward for engine accessibility.

International Harvester offered three light-weight tandem rear axles with either spring-steel or rubber-cushion suspension, and aluminum-spring saddles and walking beam.

International Harvester introduced a C-line of low-profile, light-duty models available in two- and four-wheel-drive chassis. A new model, the Scout, was also available on a 100-inch wheelbase, and featured 4-wheel drive.

The American Association of State Highway Officials sponsored a highway research program designed to aid in development of future highways, evaluate existing highways, and to determine areas for further highway research.

Chevrolet introduced a 1/2-ton "Step-Van 7" model delivery van. The van had a wheelbase of 102 inches, an overall length of 167 inches and a 7-foot high walk-in-body. The model also featured independent front and coil-spring rear suspension.

Diamond-T made available its 5000 D model, a "snub-nose" tractor for use with 40-foot trailers.

Ford introduced its Econoline Van with double doors, both rear and curbside, 204.4-cubic feet cargo space, 4,000-mile oil change, and aluminized muffler. Power was by a Falcon 6-cylinder engine.

A 262-cubic inch "Big Six" engine was available on the heavy-duty 2-ton model. An added attraction was a printed wiring circuit on the Ford tilt-cab models.

General Motors' Diesel Engine Division unveiled twelve engines which ran on a range of fuels from gasoline to diesel fuel. In addition, the division developed conversion kits to change diesel engines to multifuel engines.

A 100,000-mile or 24-month warranty went with the Ford super duty V-8 gas engines.

The Mack front suspension system combined air-and-leaf springs. It was introduced on the model H cab-over-engine tractor.

Chevrolet offered a new heavy-duty chassis option for 2- and 2 1/2-ton models used in off-highway operations. It added heavier gauge rails, reinforcements, and strengthened cross members for torsional stresses.

Diamond-T introduced two gasoline-powered models, the "4000" two axle model and the "4300" six-wheeler model. Wet-sleeve engines were featured with short stroke and valve-in head design.

1960   "Doubles" (the hauling of two trailers) was one of the most significant developments in motor truck history.

1960 International logging truck model RDF-402. A fleet of twenty-nine vehicles logged 40 million board feet of lumber in 1959. Eighteen were International.

1960 GMC diesel powered tandem axle tank truck.

1960 Chevrolet light-duty panel, featured torsion-bar independent front suspension for improved ride and handling.

1960 Chevrolet forward-control step-van, designed for multistop delivery use.

1960   Jeep Panel delivery 4-wheel-drive provided a sturdy, economical utility vehicle for businesses.

1961   Street sweeper mounted on a Dodge D-400 chassis.

1961   International C-130 model featured a low-profile styling with a low-loading dump body and I-beam front suspension.

1961 Jeep commercial 4-wheel-drive fleetvan, designed for parcel deliveries.

1961 International bonus load pickup with front-wheel independent torsion-bar suspension.

1962 Condor motor home was made available through Ford dealers. Built on a modified Ford truck chassis, the unit had a complete kitchen, bathroom, dining and sleeping facilities for six people, and thermostatically controlled butane gas furnace.

1962 Divco D-300 door-to-door delivery used a Detroit Diesel engine.

White announced two "Payload Special" models with Super Mustang gasoline engines as standard equipment. A 145-horsepower engine powered the truck models. A 170-horsepower model powered the tractor model.

Dorsey refrigerated trailers featured a roller and track device to load and unload meat or other heavy hard-to-handle cargo. Rails and partitions moved by rollers on a track to any part of the body. A one-man loader allowed ground-level cargo handling.

A Dorsey gold-anodized aluminum trailer toured the nation with a message on the trailer in 20-inch letters, stating the amount of highway use taxes paid in each state.

Fruehauf developed a "cattle crusier" tri-level, double-drop frame trailer capable of handling forty-nine head.

Wells-Cargo, Incorporated, delivered thirty semitrailers by air to the air force. The 28-foot junior semi's were carried aboard C-124 cargo airplanes, two at a time. The trailers were used for exhibition displays providing information on nuclear attack.

Trailmobile designed a 40-wheel truck trailer for use in Iran. The body could be raised or lowered hydraulically for road conditions. Front and rear Mack tractors provided power. Two or more men operated steering engines above front and rear bodies. Telephones were used between front and rear operators.

A hydraulic fifth-wheel lift was developed by Bartlett Trailer Corporation. The lift extended to forty-eight inches and was raised by two 7-inch hydraulic cylinders.

Rockwell-Standard introduced its "Stopmaster" brake, which featured either air or hydraulic actuation by changing activator units.

Worthington Corporation developed an automatic refrigeration system for highway trailers. The unit provided heating, cooling, and automatic defrosting.

New models and product innovations in trucking included the Travelall, a 9-passenger, 4-door station wagon; and the Travelette, a 4-door, 6-passenger pickup truck. General Motors developed the first production models of a new line of intercity coaches powered by V-8 diesel engines. Willys Motor, Incorporated, introduced its Jeep Fleetvan, a 1/2-ton walk-in delivery vehicle.

Studebaker-Packard Corporation announced it would produce a line of medium-duty trucks and truck tractors with diesel engines.

Ford Motor Company purchased the Philco Corporation and two Electric Autolite Company plants. Studebaker-Packard purchased

Chemical Compounds, Incorporated, makers of STP, a motor oil additive, and bought Curtiss-Wright Corporation's South Bend plant. American Motors opened a new engineering and research unit in Kenosha, Wisconsin.

Goodyear Rubber Company announced production of Budene, a synthetic rubber expected to nearly double the life of tires.

An interstate motor freight common carrier operating coast-to-coast was required to have 136 identification items (plates, papers, etc.) for each truck and semitrailer combination operating in an eighteen state area.

Economy-type trucks, specifically 4-cylinder models in the form of vans and pickups, made a good first-year showing. Over 100,000 4-cylinder trucks were built. However, the production of 6-cylinder models far outdistanced 4- and 8-cylinder models.

Heavy-duty truck sales declined for a second consecutive year. *Production dropped slightly to 1,130,919 trucks and buses.*

1962

Recreation Vehicles Bring Fun and Travel

Manufacturers offered an expanded selection of motor homes, mobile homes, and campers for fun and travel as family recreation became more popular. The Champ, a multipurpose camper, was introduced by Studebaker. Special motor-home bodies were available for truck chassis by Chevrolet, Dodge, and Ford. Ford Division announced the Condor, a self-contained unit built on a modified Ford truck chassis. Traville Corporation of Detroit produced a self-powered deluxe travel home called the Traville, mounted on a one-ton Chevrolet chassis.

The Automobile Manufacturers Association (AMA) announced that, beginning with the 1963 model year, all United States motor vehicles would have amber-colored front turn signals as standard equipment. The move started in 1958 and culminated in an industry-wide project reevaluating all motor vehicle lighting-and-signaling components.

Chrysler tested its gas turbine engine in a 290-mile winter test run from Detroit to Chicago. The gas turbine engine was mounted in a Dodge "Turbo Power Giant" truck. Upon completion of the run, the experimental truck was exhibited at the Chicago Auto Show.

Piggybacking reached new heights in its amazing climb (approximately 25,000 trailers in use) and the use of double bottoms was beginning to grow.

Cryogenic liquid-or-injection vapor cooling in transit refrigeration was developing, as containerization and foamed-in insulation made instant cooling appealing.

Autocar offered the DCV heavy-duty series of over-the-road tractors. The light-weight Cummins V-8-265 diesel engine was standard.

Chevrolet offered series 53 diesel engines in its 15,000 to 25,000-pound GVW models in the 60, 60H, and 80 series.

Ford announced that a transistorized-ignition system would be available on its super-duty trucks in 1963.

FWD Corporation announced a new Tractioneer series, offering both rear-drive and multi-drive models. Featured was the Traction Lock driveline system where the driver controlled the electric, hydraulically actuated, locking device by flipping a dash switch.

Dodge offered an economical light-weight diesel engine for use in the short haul field. The engine was a Dodge-Perkins 6-cylinder, 4-cycle model with direct injection, and was capable of ten to fourteen miles per gallon in local service.

Dodge also announced a light-weight V-6 200 Cummins diesel engine on its chassis-cab and on its tractor cab-forward models C-800, C-900, CT-88, and CT 900.

International announced its "Loadstar" series of medium and light duty trucks. A new diesel engine, the D-354, had wide track front axle, a full-depth frame channel, optional wedge-type air brake, and a new 5-speed synchromesh transmission.

Mack introduced the F series, offering three cab-over-engine models. The F series cab featured an engine tunnel console with controls. A new "711" thermodyne engine was available.

Studebaker introduced its Transtar series in both heavy-duty and medium-duty models. A new diesel model was also announced, featuring a series 53 2-cycle engine manufactured by the General Motors Detroit Diesel Division.

White introduced its 7000 tilt-cab series with the cab constructed of fiberglass on an aluminum frame. Top and bottom radiator tanks were bolted to a radiator core for easy removal.

Brown Trailer Division and Van Rails, Incorporated, combined to develop a "Domelok" sliding bolster with an elevating truck-track which could transfer two 20-foot containers from a 40-foot line haul trailer chassis to a city truck chassis.

Dorsey Trailers offered interchangeable aluminum or steel parts on its new Golden series. Lights on the trailer were recessed in the upper rail. All wiring was accessible from outside.

Fruehauf offered a new "seal-temp" refrigerated van which was "sanifoam" insulated. It had a welded aluminum floor, special door seals, and latches, plus vent door to make the trailer as airtight and watertight as possible.

Fruehauf offered "walk-through" Twin-20's containers.

General Motors 6500 series featured a V-6 gasoline engine.

Willys Motors displayed a new series of four-wheel-drive trucks named the "Gladiator" line.

Studebaker featured a shorter diesel truck tractor in its E-45 line. The tractor could be combined with a 40-foot trailer and still meet legal length requirements in most states.

California enacted a law which required vehicles using air brakes to have either a device to prevent loss of air pressure, or a device to apply brakes upon loss of air pressure.

Apex Fiberglass Products developed a fiberglass diesel fuel tank with aluminum mounting brackets bonded to the tank body. The transparent tank permitted an instant check of the fuel level without using a gauge.

Caterpillar Tractor Company customized a display trailer to travel throughout the country to promote the diesel engine.

Continental Motors produced a new multifuel engine for the army called the Hypercycle LDS-427-2.

The Jacobs Manufacturing Company announced its model 25 Diesel Engine Brake for the Cummins NH-250 diesel engine. The retarder converted the engine into an air pump, which used 78 percent of the rated horsepower at 2,100 rpm to retard the driving wheels. One simple on-off switch activated the brake.

McCord Corporation developed stainless steel gaskets for cylinder heads and manifolds.

National Castings Company developed Trac Star, a load-equalizing, self-steering, self-contained, truck suspension. The front trailing axle related to the turning radius of the tractor to eliminate skidding and tire drag around curves.

The Truck Safety Equipment Institute was organized in Chicago by fifteen manufacturers of truck lighting and reflective equipment.

Production totals increased to 1,253,977 trucks and buses.

1963

Interstate Highway Systems Grow

As more industry moved near super highways, new terminal sites for trucking communities moved closer to freeways.

Throughout 1963, transportation interests awaited congressional action on President Kennedy's transportation program. Kennedy had recommended removing minimum rate regulation from all transportation of bulk, agricultural, and fishery commodities. The recommendation was in conjunction with the protection of the existing laws against monopolistic and predatory trade practices.

Autocar introduced a 4-axle truck with tandem axles in front and rear. The arrangement handled gross vehicle weights up to 60,000 pounds.

Ford introduced a new N-series short-BBC conventional truck with diesel or gasoline power. Measuring only 7 feet 5 inches from the bumper to the back of the cab, the model allowed a longer body and 500 pounds more payload.

Ford also announced a 300-horsepower prototype diesel designed for heavy-duty service. Called the 704 model, the engine relied on a turbo-compressor unit to supercharge the air. This reduced the size and weight of the engine because the necessity of handling more air was eliminated.

A Battronic battery-powered electric truck was announced by Battronic Truck Corporation of Philadelphia, jointly with Boyertown Auto Body Works. Operating economy, stamina, speed, pick-up were designed for stop-and start deliveries.

The "Roadranger" twin countershaft transmission was introduced by Fuller. The transmission opened the way for higher horsepower and increased torque engines.

Tandem axle diesel tractors were offered by GMC and Dodge. The Dodge standard equipment included Hendrickson suspension, Rockwell and Eaton rear axles, a 5-speed transmission and a Cummins NH-180 engine.

International Trucks introduced Fleetstar series in the 50,000 to 79,000 pound GVW.

A unique loading and unloading system operated by compressed air was installed in a prototype trailer by Clark Equipment Company's Brown Trailer Division. Called the air-in-floor system, aluminum floor planks served as air chambers. A gasoline-driven blower literally floated special pallets into place in the trailer body.

Dempster Brothers developed a hydraulic side-loader device for trucks to remove and place containers on rail cars and trailers.

Dorsey Trailers designed a cargo-lift trailer which could lift 40,000 pounds from four feet to twelve feet, providing easy loading-and-unloading of cargo from aircraft. Four hydraulic stablizing jacks took the load off the tires during lifting operations. Hydraulic powersteering was used in the rear axle.

Sliding bolsters with metal domes were used by "Mobilvan" on a hydraulic transfer frame for container transfer. The special frame could be mounted on a conventional chassis.

Trailmobile introduced a parallelogram tandem. A short rocker suspension, the system combined torque arm and radius rods in a unique linkage to form a parallelogram. This was said to check axle rotation and control tire hop during braking.

The use of rigid urethane foam for truck insulation continued to grow.

A new requirement in truck tires was reduced running noise. The most effective design technique for noise reduction was variable pitch tread elements. Adding sipes improved braking and traction, allowing a reduced number of tread groove to improve wear.

Sold as a component or as a complete assembly, Trac Star suspension by National Castings Company equalized load distribution to all trailer axles. It used a horizontal pivot design and self-steering front axle to track on any corner.

The new Stopmaster brakes by Rockwell Standard featured automatic brake adjustment.

Three new mobile homes were introduced during the year. International Harvester unveiled a family camper adaptation of its Scout utility vehicle. Clark Equipment Company introduced the Cortez, a mobile home that provided living and sleeping facilities for four adults. Stewart Coach Industries, of Bristol, Indiana, offered a 17-foot trailer that could be converted into a home on water.

Hendrickson tandem suspension featured four sets of two-stage rubber shear springs with aluminum beams and saddles. It had underslung equalizing beams and upper torque rods.

Bendix Westinghouse DD3 safety actuator provided an air brake system for parking, emergency, and service braking.

Production increased: 1,464,399 trucks and buses.

1964

Size and Weight Limits Eased

With nearly half of the 41,000-mile interstate highway system completed and open, the U.S. Department of Commerce recommended increasing weight and dimension limits for trucks using the interstate highways.

With prospects good for incentive-easing of length and weight restrictions on the super highways, the move to larger, more powerful trucks was under way.

The American Automobile Association reported to a House committee that highway users paid $12 billion annually in special taxes.

The restrictions of specialized hauling requirements and tariff rules and regulations were a growing concern of "For Hire" motor carriers services.

Ford offered three new heavy duty V-8 engines: the 330, 186 horsepower; the 361, 203 horsepower; and the 391, 235 horsepower.

The Ford 401, 477, and 534 super-duty V-8s were warranted for 10,000 miles or twenty-four months.

New Autocar Model AV-7064-T weight options saved over 1,000 pounds.

General Motors' experimental turbine-powered freight hauler, called the Bison, was shown at the New York World's Fair. The Bison was powered by a twin turbine engine, providing 1,000 horsepower, and was designed to carry containerized cargo. GM also displayed a turbine-powered bus, the Turbo Cruiser II.

Perkins-Engine, Incorporated, developed a "differential diesel engine" which combined automatic transmission with supercharging. When the engine speed fell, the differential gear linked to the supercharger increased the flow of air.

The Dodge Model L tilt cab was constructed of aluminum panels with a fiberglass skirt around the bottom. The combination provided strength along with light weight. The cabs featured a flexible chrome-manganese steel frame.

Mack introduced the U model with Commandcab, a cab built for visibility with a large wrap-around windshield, giving eight inches more viewing area than conventional models. The cab was offset eleven inches to the left, putting the driver on a line with the left front wheel.

Dodge announced a tilt-cab diesel tractor, a 4-axle unit, powered by a turbocharged Cummins.

GMC's new V-6 Toro-Flow diesels had a uniquely shaped configuration, or depression, in the top of the piston. This combined with a special intake port to swirl the incoming air in a three-way motion of air at fuel injection.

Containerization offered different approaches to freight handling and transportation. Even containers for handling frozen foods were available without the need for refrigeration. Ten such containers by Avcold Unireef could be carried on a flatbed semitrailer.

White Motor designed a tandem axle suspension which used natural rubber stressed in torsional shear instead of metal springs. The system isolated the frame from road shock.

Aero-Liner Company introduced a trailer which literally knelt at one end to permit ground level loading and unloading. Called "Kneeling Nellie," the trailer had three separate hydraulic cylinders to lower the front end where doors were opened for loading.

Diesel power gained popularity as a prime mover for transport refrigeration. Nitrogen as a refrigerant was also popular, although temperature control was important to proper operation.

Bartlett Trailer introduced the "snorkle," a high lift hydraulic fifth wheel which lifted the trailer fourteen feet eight inches above the fifth wheel. Another Bartlett innovation was a trailer elevator which lifted up to 4,000 pounds.

A 40-foot trailer filled with photographic material was hauled from New Jersey to Los Angeles (3,210 miles) by five driver-tractor teams in five days, two-and-a-half hours.

Navajo Freight Lines set a new transcontinental freight delivery record. A trip from Los Angeles to New York was made in just sixty one and one quarter hours.

Piggyback loading continued to increase. More than 602,549 cars were loaded with one or more trailers by midyear.

Hendrickson Manufacturing Company designed a tractor which weighed 55,000 pounds, had twelve wheels on six axles, and measured 12 feet wide and 12 feet high. A 525-horsepower diesel drove two sets of wheels. The huge tractor was built for Higgins and Sons of Buffalo, New York.

Rockwell Standard introduced a brake system where road traction created a reaction to front-brake traction. This sent a hydraulic pulse to rear-wheel brakes.

New developments in the trucking industry included the introduction of Dodge's new Camper Wagon; GMC Truck and Coach Division's Handi-Van, a light-duty truck; and Kaiser Jeep Corporation's Tuxedo Park IV, a sporty version of its Jeep Universal. GMC Truck and Bus Division introduced two forged I-Beam axles for front-wheel suspensions of light trucks.

Developments in the gas turbine field continued as Ford Motor Company introduced a 600-horsepower truck tractor.

Congress authorized incentive payments to states controlling outdoor advertising near new freeways.

The number of incidents of theft or unexplained shortages from trucks and trailers ranked second in total dollar-loss behind upset and collision.

Production totaled: 1,562,368.

1965

Containerization Joins Piggybacking

America continued to move toward a mixed-mode transportation system. Two outstanding concepts in goods shipments had occurred within the last decade. A dynamic rise of containerization, combined with the interchangeability and adaptability of trailers in highway, rail, and air transport, opened the way for intercontinental container transport.

Domestically, piggybacking and highways were still the major transportation news items, reflecting their booming prosperity.

Railcar trailer loadings reached the highest peak in history.

Union Pacific Railroad was the first major rail line to initiate piggybacking over its entire system. The Los Angeles to Chicago delivery run came close to matching the road time of most fleets and at bargain rates.

The increased use of double-bottoms (double trailer hauling) was extended to doubles in piggyback operations. However, as doubles use grew, the Truck and Trailer Manufacturers Association recommended: 4-foot cab from bumper to back of cab (BBC), 3 feet between trailers, and 2 feet between cab and first trailer, a 36-inch pin offset, and 10-inch radius corners on all trailers.

A slider device for fifth wheels was developed by Austin Products of Muskegon, Michigan. The unit permitted hauling different lengths of trailers, could be mounted on any tractor, and was adaptable to any fifth wheel.

The Bureau of Public Roads revised the price estimate of the interstate highway system upward by $5.8 billion to $46.8 billion, recommending that highway-user taxes be increased to meet a $3.1 billion deficit. Truck industries and many sectors quickly voiced their opposition to any increase.

Inequitable distribution of the highway tax was evident. Of the 19 million trucks using the highways, only about 2 million were heavy-duty trucks. Yet they paid 38.6 percent of the increase.

President Johnson signed into law a bill authorizing 2,300 miles of highways and 1,000 miles of access road in the eleven-state Appalachia Mountain area. The cost was $840 million.

International Harvester introduced its new multistop models called, "Metro," featured unitized construction on the smaller models, a choice of three body widths and eight lengths, and a wide choice of engines—4 cylinders, 6 cylinders, V-8s and diesels. A new series, CO-4000 cab-over-engine models, were also introduced in anticipation of increased legal weight allowances.

Brockway introduced a complete new line of fifty models called the 300 series. A back-mounted radiator shutter blocked incoming air and stopped heat loss behind the radiator. The engine temperature was controlled within a 5-degree variation.

Chrysler Corporation introduced a "drop-in" plan for engine replacement. New power plants, including accessories, could replace engines in older trucks in eight hours at a price comparable to overhauling an engine. The transfer included a new engine warranty.

Chevrolet introduced its 1966 short cab, measuring ninety-two inches BBC.

Ford offered a large number of optional items and accessories, and its customers had 250 models from which to choose.

Air-ride suspension was revived as operators who carried fragile cargo demanded soft rides.

White Motor Company shareholders approved changing the name to White Motor Corporation, reflecting its growth and diversification since 1919.

White Motor Corporation introduced a tandem-axle suspension, using natural rubber springs. Called "Velvet-Ride," the system was said to isolate road shock through the use of articulating beams.

Turbo Titan III, a truck of tomorrow, was introduced by Chevrolet. Called the "space age" truck, it was powered by a 280-horsepower gas-turbine engine and combined advanced styling and functional innovations, such as powered windows, retractable triple headlights, and dial steering.

Mack introduced a new R series with a measurement of 8 feet 7 inches (BBC). It also featured a tilt cab, fiberglass hood and fenders, adjustable steering wheel, extra wide doors and glass area, an air intake or exhaust cab ventilation system, and a snorkel tube engine air intake above the roof level for cooler, drier air.

KW-Dart Truck Company built a 65-ton end dump truck powered by a 700-horsepower diesel. The truck could turn in a 66-foot circle and had a truck capacity of 43-cubic yards and a heaped capacity of 55-cubic yards.

GMC introduced the "Magnum" series and the first V-8 diesel built by its division.

Autocar new models were designed as 6 × 6 in response to the demands for heavy-duty units capable of handling rough terrain.

Congress passed legislation to allow the Interstate Commerce Commission (ICC) and the states to cooperate in enforcing laws against illegal trucking.

President Johnson signed a bill which eliminated the 8 percent excise tax on rebuilt truck parts.

Air brake and other air pressure systems were inspected by an ultrasonic device, the Delcon Ultrasonic Translator Detector. The device responded to the flow of air molecules escaping through a leak, amplifying and translating the sound through a loud speaker.

Bostrom designed an air-suspension seat which automatically positioned the driver in the center of the ride zone.

An increased number of engine compression brakes were offered along with other brakes and speed reducers. This was designed to overcome the diesel's lack of retarding ability and the overrevving of gasoline engines, which could cause engine damage.

Production continued to rise: 1,802,603 trucks and buses.

1966

Federal Safety Bills Enacted

This year was seen as the biggest legislative year in transportation. There were forecasts of governmental deregulation, liberalization of sizes and weights, revamping of mail transportation to favor motor carriers, and formation of a Department of Transportation. Government research and development subsidies were expected for safer highway, driver facilities, and research for small entrepreneurs who were not in a position to finance research themselves.

President Johnson's State of the Union message urged Congress to establish a Department of Transportation. Its objectives would be to revise, strengthen, and coordinate national transportation and trucking policies, to further traffic, highway, and driver safety, to encourage new technology, to promote safety standards, to coordinate intermodal services, and to pull divergent interests together.

Congress passed, and the president signed, two safety bills: one for highways, the other for motor vehicles. The secretary of commerce was to set safety standards.

The Interstate Commerce Commission amended regulations for lamps and reflectors on trucks and tractors. Every truck eighty inches or more was required to have: two head lamps on front, an equal number at each side, two turn signals, two clearance lamps, one at each side, three identification lamps on the center line of the cab, and single lamp at the center of the cab.

As operating costs continued to go up, more carriers looked forward to "doubles." A trend even developed toward the use of three 27-foot trailers rather than two 40-foot trailers.

The full-service truck leasing industry showed continued growth as high interest and tight money found many firms going to short-term rentals or long-term full service leasing.

The automotive plastics industry recorded its greatest year to date with 13.5 billion pounds sold.

With added payload capacity, high speed highway travel, easier weight and length restrictions, many fleet operators investigated tandem axles to assure proper power usage.

The new Chevrolet tilt cab measured seventy-two inches BBC.

Diamond-T introduced a tilt-forward plastic hood and fender assembly, manually operated.

12 Passenger
8 Door
Aerobus

1963 The Checker 12 passenger Aerobus was available in 6 and 8 door models and included power brakes and power steering as standard.

1963 Built by International Harvester's Special Products Division, this giant was slated for service with the Gardner-Denver Company for oil field work.

1964 Containerization revolutionized the industry. This Twin-20' by Fruehauf could be transported and interchanged between rail, ship, and aircraft with minimum cargo handling.

1963   Crane Carrier Company custom concrete carrier mixed concrete en route to a construction site.

1964   This GM Bison Bullet experimental heavy-cargo hauler moved standardized containers at new peaks of efficiency with electronic loading and unloading equipment.

1964 One of the truck-and-trailer industry's challenges was to meet the demand for portable leisure homes.

1965 This rugged 8-ton mobile geological laboratory, built by GM Defense Research Labs for NASA, enabled simulated space-exploration missions.

1964 Ford gas-turbine experimental model was designed to operate on the multilane super highways.

1967 International Travelall rams a concrete wall while instruments measure results of impact barrier tests to meet federal safety standards.

Dodge added a tilt-cab truck in the medium-duty line with a 74.5-inch BBC. A variable rate suspension allowed the ride to remain constant whether the truck was loaded or empty.

Mack introduced its Maxidyne diesel engine with turbocharger.

Ford's truck line extended to almost 100 models. The latest addition was the W-series heavy duty tilt-cab tractor.

Freightliner built its first truck with gas turbine engine for long distance hauling.

International offered a full-width, all-welded aluminum cab. The development of the cab demonstrated the advances in industry techniques for accelerated test procedures.

The possible combinations available on one of International Harvester's heavy duty series was reported to be in the millions.

Kelsey-Hayes offered its "Hytrol," an antilock brake system for trailers.

Peterbilt used an air-assist device for raising and lowering its 90 degree tilt hood. A full door was located at the top of the hood for access to the radiator filler, dip stick, and oil filltube at the rear of the hood panel.

Reo introduced a 90 degree tilt cab series HC. Complementing the new compact light-weight diesel engines offered by many manufacturers were new turbochargers, which gave increased performance and maximum torque.

International Harvester built a truck weighing over 32,000 pounds to haul a combined weight of 180,000 pounds. The truck was 35-feet long, 9-feet by 10-inches wide, and 12-feet by 10-inches high.

Mack developed a series of high-powered, light-weight COE trucks to be produced by its Western Manufacturing Plant in California. The cab-over-engine series was designated the FL 700.

A 40-foot Trailmobile trailer was loaded and unloaded on a C-141 A Lockheed Starliner jet plane. The demonstration was to add emphasis to shipping truck and trailer by plane.

Cummins introduced two new compact diesel engines for "peddle haul" (frequent stop delivery) and "stop-and-go" operation: a V-6 140 horsepower and a V-8 185 horsepower, specifically for the medium-heavy-duty trucks.

An air-ride suspension was introduced by Dayton Tandem Manufacturing Company. It used a simplified multileaf spring design with air springs.

The advent of super highways stimulated the need for better brakes and brake components. The emphasis was on dependability, effectiveness, maintenance, and balance, especially on multiaxle trucks and trailers.

White Motor Corporation developed a heavy-duty truck engine which combined the advantages of both diesel and gasoline in a powerplant, using regular gasoline and weighing 40 percent less than a diesel engine.

White Motor Corporation truck's new 4000 and 9000 model series of heavy-duty trucks featured fiberglass, frame-mounted fenders easily removed for full engine accessibility.

Dodge offered an automotive dock leveler, a Hi-Lo hydraulic body lift mounted on a Dodge W-500 four-wheel-drive truck. The unit could be raised from ground level to forty-eight inches.

International Harvester exhibited a Scout 800 with Dreamer camper insert and a D-1000 Travelall with compact trailer.

Minibus, Incorporated, began supplying 19 to 23-passenger miniature buses to metropolitan areas for short-haul downtown service.

A special truck body, built by Affiliated Metals, routed engine exhaust through tubes under the floor of the body for heating.

White Motor Corporation announced purchase of the Hercules Engine Division of the Hupp Corporation.

Production recorded a drop but still a healthy 1,791,587.

1967

Safety Standards Challenge Truck Engineering

The Department of Transportation on December 26 announced twelve proposals for new motor-vehicle safety-performance standards. Eight of the proposed standards would affect vehicles manufactured after December, 1968, in addition to lighting and reflective-device standards announced December 14. The other four proposals would be effective on vehicles manufactured after December, 1969. Although the passenger car received most of the focus in the safety standards, motor trucks were also greatly affected.

Inflation posed new threats during the year, affecting highway construction first. Construction of the interstate highway system was cut by $700 million due to inflationary pressures. Government sources claimed that costs had risen 8 percent in 1966 while highway revenues increased only 4 percent. Although most of the proposed 41,000 miles of the highway network was open and in use, 23 percent still remained to be completed.

Ironically, the cutback followed a report by the Bureau of Roads citing the safety advantages of super highways.

The inflationary climate was reflected by a number of states increasing their fuel taxes.

Congress passed legislation for a research and development program involving electric cars for saving fuel. Studies concentrated primarily on the zinc-air battery and the hydrozine-air fuel cell.

Legislation was pending in many states to permit the use of studded tires in the winter.

The Bureau of Motor Vehicle Safety (ICC) became part of the Department of Transportation.

The use of stainless steel in over-the-road transport tankers continued to increase as users, especially chemical haulers, were impressed with the "wear-ability" and "clean-ability" of the stainless tanks.

The use of plastics in truck and trailer construction continued to show a steady increase. Lower costs, reduced weights, reduced maintenance costs, and longer service life complemented new molding techniques and smoother finishes.

The Mariner-5 spacecraft was transported from Pasadena, California, to Cape Kennedy by a Global Van Lines five-trailer fleet, equipped with air suspension. The vans underwent intensive tests to minimize road shock. Two-man driver teams were used on the nonstop trip. A convoy director monitored shock-and-vibration recorders.

New developments in refrigerated truck-and-trailer insulation featured panels of polyurethane foam, faced with a fiberglass reinforced plastic.

A liquid nitrogen truck stop, on the Chicago to New York run, was established in Ohio, mid-way on the route. A storage tank holding 1,300 gallons of nitrogen provided refrigeration for perishable cargo.

A swing-up axle, with adjustable air-ride suspension for trailers, was developed by LaCrosse Trailer Division. The unit could transform single axle trailers to tandems or tandems to triples.

White Motor Corporation introduced the "Western Star," designed for use in the West, and built a new plant at Kelowna, British Columbia, for its manufacture.

White Motor Corporation introduced two prototype models at the

ATA Chicago Convention, an "XRL" model for "extra reliability and long life" and the "LTL" model for "less than truck load."

FMC Corporation developed a "Terminal Tug" for spotting or moving semitrailers in truck terminals. The vehicle featured a "peek-a-boo" swivel cab that could swing ninety degrees to either side of the trailer for a view down the sides of the trailer.

International Harvester celebrated its sixtieth year of truck manufacturing. IH introduced the M-412-CBE for either highway or off-highway use. The truck was equipped with dual cylinder power steering, floatation tires, and a 16,000-pound front-driving axle with a 36-degree steering angle. Front suspension was by steel leaf springs.

Fruehauf Corporation earmarked $20 million for continuing research on future transportation needs. It predicted that, by 1970, trailers would have to be readily convertible to containers and back to trailers again. The prediction included a trend toward standardization for mass production to reduce trailer costs.

Frank Fitzsimmons replaced Jimmy Hoffa as president of the Teamsters' Union.

Kenworth light-weight model C-923 diesel transit concrete mixer featured tilting one-piece fiberglass hood, fender and radiator shell assembly, removable in minutes.

Mack manufactured an RL series, featuring light-weight components such as a unitized tilting fiberglass hood and fender assembly.

Mack merged with Signal Company.

Studebaker discontinued automobile and truck production.

Diamond-T and Reo, two of the oldest names in truck manufacturing, established a single dealer organization under the name of Diamond Reo Truck Division, White Motor Corporation. The new group comprised slightly fewer than 300 dealers throughout the United States.

Changes in motor vehicle size and weight limits were considered in twenty-five states. New legislation raised the allowable lengths on designated highways.

Ohio and Indiana Turnpike commissions approved toll road hauling of three trailers in tandem. The trailers were 27 feet in length and were hauled by Great Lakes Express of Saginaw, Michigan.

The Highway Beautification Program ended on July 1. However, government was pushing for a beautification-safety trust fund financed by automotive excise taxes.

The payloads of trucks gradually increased as the use of expressways and freeways expanded. Accompanying the larger capacity and longer hauls, was the use of third-axle suspensions. These gave greater weight distribution, traction, and less tire wear. *Production dropped again: 1,611,077 trucks and buses.*

1968
Industry Responds to Safety Standards

Safety standards continued to dominate the design and engineering talent of the industry as an increasing number of proposed standards came from the Department of Transportation (DOT). Many of the proposed standards lacked technical expertise and, in most instances, the unreasonable time limits for industry's comment posed great problems. The manufacturers were pressed to maintain their record production, accelerate research and development, and obtain the technical information necessary to develop practical safety standards.

Truck companies were hampered by size and weight restrictions which were twenty years old. Even use of the interstate highway system was denied many regular-route common carriers, despite the fact that they paid a large percentage of the highway-user taxes.

Another blow was the announcement by the secretary of transportation that the highway program would be cut to curb inflation.

American Coleman exhibited its "Space Star" prototype truck at the Trans/Expo. The new model featured four steerable drive wheels which turned 40 degrees.

Autocar introduced a half-cab model for construction use. The tilt cab featured a sliding aluminum door which locked open or closed. The engine was mounted to the right of the cab.

Brockway developed a 360 forward axle model and a 361 set back front axle model. Both featured chrome manganese steel rail frames, cabs with swing-out instrument panels, adjustable steering wheels, and drivers' seats.

Chevrolet offered an optional 427-cubic inch V-8 engine rated at 260 horsepower and operable on regular grade gasoline. All Chevrolet truck models included nylon cord tires and backup lights among standard equipment.

Crane Carrier Company introduced its DHT-14 model for on- and off-highway use.

Dodge emphasized horizontal lines in the front end, giving a low, wide appearance to medium- and heavy-duty models. The interiors featured passenger car appointments.

The Ford F-500 and F-600 models emphasized driver comfort. New upholstery materials, bucket type seats, padded instrument panel, and arm rests with door release, were several standard equipment items.

FWD introduced its ForWarD Mover model, the first FWD truck that did not feature all or four-wheel drive. The new ForWarD Mover was a conventional heavy-duty tractor with setback front axle and a 138-inch wheelbase.

International Harvester announced the Fleetstar-A and the Turbostar heavy-duty tractors. The Fleetstar cab was coil-spring mounted on a subframe. Wedge-type service brakes were standard on the air-brake chassis. The Turbostar was an experimental model powered by a gas-turbine engine developed by the IH Solar Division.

International announced that the Transtar CO-4070 would replace the CO-4000 as the company's premium tractor for heavy-duty transport.

KW Dart Truck Company introduced three diesel-electric, heavy-duty, off-highway trucks.

Bendix developed an antiskid device which used electronic circuits to control vehicle braking and eliminate lockup.

Jacobs Manufacturing developed an antiskid control. Its unit was mechanically controlled with an overriding flywheel which sensed deceleration, then released and applied the air brakes three to five times a second so they would not lock.

A spring emergency brake offered by Midland Ross was automatically applied when failure occurred anywhere in the brake system or when air pressure was lost in the emergency chamber.

Wagner Electric offered an air valve control to allow trucks with spring actuated emergency brakes to come to a controlled stop.

Fruehauf introduced an aluminum tank trailer model rated at 57,000 pounds with single or double bulkheads. It could be divided into five compartments.

Goodyear's Hi-Miller tire featured a separate raised panel for branding symbols or other identifying marks.

Allis-Chalmers introduced its city and country series diesel engines in 4 and 6 cylinders.

Ford Motor Company and Caterpillar Engines developed a medium heavy-duty V-8 diesel engine for stop-and-go delivery.

Mack Trucks introduced the END-475 short-haul Scania Vabis diesel engine. The engine block was cast integral with the upper half of the crankcase. A cold-start device, aluminum pistons, and aluminum air-inlet manifold were featured.

A frameless dump trailer was designed by Marion Metal Products. The trailer was available in 17-foot single-axle units or 20 to 26-foot tandem-axle units.

U.S. Steel Corporation exhibited an experimental all-wheel drive at the SAE show. The XM761 model was a 2 1/2-ton off-highway, military type truck. It was constructed of high-strength steel. All wheels were independently suspended.

Fiberglass reinforced plastics were used by trailer body and container manufacturers to reduce weight while retaining strength and flexibility.

Fiberglass was used by the Rudken-Wiley Corporation to develop its Airshield, a device for reducing aerodynamic drag. The Airshield was mounted at the back of the tractor cab roof. It diverted air up, over, or around the trailer.

White Motor Corporation purchased the Euclid rear and bottom dump business from General Motors, and established a new subsidiary, Euclid, Incorporated.

Trans/Expo 68, an outdoor truck and equipment show, was held in the 30-acre parking lot at Chicago's Soldiers Field. The Expo provided a chance to demonstrate trucks and equipment in operation.

The army evaluated an engine diagnostic computer system developed by Allen/UTI in California. The unit could be taken directly to the vehicle, hooked up, and interpreted by unskilled personnel.

A first in transcontinental transportation occurred when PIE (Pacific Intermountain Express) dispatched a tractor pulling a set of doubles from Boston to San Francisco. The final barrier to coast-to-coast doubles transport was cleared when New York and Massachusetts established rates for doubles on their thruways.

Piggybacking loadings increased for the fourteenth consecutive year and was approaching 1.5 million loadings.

Production gained to 1,971,790 trucks and buses.

1969

V-8 Engines Dominate Truck Field

Sales soared in 1969 as truck lines strained to meet consumer demand. As sales increased, development of new models kept pace with innovations to maintain sales momentum at a high level.

The use of V-8 truck engines increased so rapidly that by 1969, over two-thirds of all trucks were equipped with eight-cylinder gasoline power plants. This was 67 percent of the United States truck output, a 55 percent increase over the previous year.

Use of diesel engines continued to gain momentum. The diesel engine's high horsepower plants, designed for highspeed interstate highways, demonstrated an improved fuel consumption and an improved performance for longer engine life.

Truck cab air conditioning showed tremendous growth and was cited as an important contribution to safety and efficiency.

The National Highway Users Conference announced that bills were pending in seven state legislatures and Congress to divert highway revenues to mass transit and other purposes.

A federal use tax on highway vehicles was proposed on April 8. A hearing was held April 23. Revised weights became law on May 8, despite objections from truck interests.

Chevrolet entered the heavy-duty truck market with the introduction of its 90 series in twenty-two models, offering two GM Detroit diesel engines and one Cummins diesel engine, ranging from 218 to 335 horsepower. Of special interest was the ultra-modern interior of the aluminum tilt cab, combining highly efficient placement of controls and driver comfort.

Dodge offered two Power Giant V-8 engines as optional equipment on heavy-duty trucks. The engines, the 478 and the 549, gave 234 horsepower at 360 rpm and 256 horsepower at 3,400 rpm.

The Autocar 464 heavy-duty model was powered by a GM Detroit Diesel V-12 with 434 horsepower at 2,100 rpm's.

Brockway offered the Huskidrive automatic transmission on heavy-duty models.

Ford introduced its "Louisville Line" with 800, 900, and 8000 series. A cross-flow cooling system was featured to allow lower hood lines and better visibility. Radiator sight gauges and pressure radiator caps with levers were additional highlights.

1968   Chevrolet Turbo Titan III gas turbine truck of the future.

1968   The ForWard Mover COE model was introduced by FWD. Featured was the reverse-slope windshield which provided for optimum visibility and lower cab height.

1968   White model 1500 with drop frame and enclosed body.

1968 International Harvester Transtar premium-quality heavy-duty diesel designed after extensive interviews with drivers and maintenance men.

1968 International Harvester demonstrated its experimental "Turbostar" turbine truck by hauling triples at the company's proving grounds in Phoenix, Arizona.

1968   Warner and Swasey power shovel.

1968   White dump truck, designed to save hauling time in construction work.

GMC introduced the Astro 95 with an all-aluminum tilt cab that was partly welded and partly riveted for easy panel replacement. The electrical system was color-keyed, routed and mounted along the frame rail for easy servicing. The cab could be tilted 45 degrees for minor repairs or to a full vertical position for complete access to the engine.

Chevrolet introduced a light utility 4-WD *Blazer* in 587 models on forty-seven wheelbases.

Dodge introduced a new compact van where the engine was moved forward to provide a larger van interior than earlier compacts. Dual right-side opening doors provided easy cargo access.

GMC offered 6-speed Allison automatic transmissions in the 5500–6500 conventional-cab, gasoline engine models.

International Harvester announced a four-wheel-drive Unistar model C-O 7044A tractor to be produced early in 1970. The model could operate as a 4 × 4 or a 4 × 6 when a Jiffbox dolly was attached.

International added the "Transtar-400" series in five 6-cylinder and three V-8 engines.

The Kenworth K-100 emphasized lighter weight, offering an aluminum frame, cast aluminum radiator, top tank, aluminum front end casing, aluminum steering gear case, and a fiberglass fan shroud.

Mack announced a 50-ton off-highway dump truck, the M50AX, with a 165-inch wheelbase. Front axle suspension combined leaf spring and rubber supports for heavy loads. Body heating was achieved by exhaust through the hinge point of the body.

Peterbilt developed an air-suspension system with straight leaf springs in conjunction with lobe-type air springs. Two leveling valves controlled the height of the chassis, maintaining the same distance between the axle and the frame.

Allis-Chalmers introduced a series of V-8 and V-12 heavy-duty diesel engines with cooled unit injectors and differential-type nozzles for spray control.

A fire truck developed by Ansul Corporation of Marinette, Wisconsin, was capable of speeds up to 100 miles an hour, carrying 2,000 pounds of fire fighting chemicals.

Borg-Warner introduced truck skid-control systems for trucks with air brakes or hydraulic brakes. The system automatically adjusted brake pressure to load on the rear axle.

Cummins Engine Company announced production of diesel engine powerplants on its Cummins 903 series for cab-over-engine equipment, custom-rated at 280, 300, or 320 horsepower.

Cummins Engine Company and the Garrett Corporation joined forces to work on the development of gas turbine engines for highway trucks.

Detroit Diesel announced that its GT-309 gas turbine engine would be undergoing extensive field tests. It was scheduled for production in mid-1971.

Fuller Transmission introduced the RT-909 Roadranger 9-speed transmission and the AT-904 twin countershaft 4-speed auxiliary for use behind Fuller T 905 series twin countershaft transmission.

Diamond Reo featured diamond plate steel fenders and a butterfly-type steel hood as options for off-highway and forest trucks.

The Hope Truck Stabilizer manufactured by Hampshire Equipment Company was developed as an antijackknife device for tractor trailers. The stabilizer was similar to a disc brake mounted on the trailer's upper fifth-wheel plate and connected to the king pin. Upon application of the brakes, the disc dampened the motion between tractor and trailer.

An 800,000-pound capacity trailer was built by Peerless Trailer and Truck Service in Oregon for the Tennessee Valley Authority. The trailer was 133 feet long and had seventy-four tires. Cost of the trailer was $178,000.

Utility Trailer Company designed an expandible flat-bed trailer which could be extended from a 40-foot length to 60 feet.

A prototype Ford gas-turbine engine was installed in a Continental Trailways for engineering and road tests.

Oshkosh introduced a low-profile E series transporter for in-city delivery or line hauling.

White acquired Alco engine line from Studebaker-Worthington.

American Motors Corporation acquired Jeep.

Production continued to climb with 1,981,519 units.

The Seventies

1970

Air Pollution Problem a Challenge

Air-pollution control became government policy when, in mid-year, President Nixon created the Environmental Protection Agency (EPA). Control of engine emissions was one of the most complex problems the industry faced. On one hand, the Department of Transportation required new horsepower-to-weight ratios, calling for more powerful engines. Yet the addition of emission-control equipment would greatly affect engine efficiency. The most promising approach seemed to be catalytic mufflers or thermal reactor systems.

The diesel engine was viewed by the public as the worst offender, primarily because of smoke and the distinctive diesel odor.

No-lead gasoline became available. A new 91-octane low-lead gasoline was offered by the large refiners. Most 1971 models would be able to operate with either new no-lead or low-lead fuels.

Governor Ronald Reagan of California proposed a plan to convert 175 California fleet vehicles to a dual fuel system which used natural gas. A six-point program was designed to encourage smog-free motor vehicles in California.

The Federal Highway Administration required installation and use of seat belts in trucks, tractors, and buses by July 1, 1972.

Vehicles with sleeper berths had to be equipped with a sleeper berth restraint system.

New safety standards coming out of Washington were called second-generation standards by the engineers. The first regulations involved areas that the industry had been working in. The new proposed standards on power, brakes, and emissions required new technology and time to develop that technology.

The U.S. Department of Transportation's Bureau of Motor Carrier Safety published new driver safety regulations to include more stringent physical requirements, plus strict written and road tests. A companion proposal banning the use of alcohol and drugs was also under consideration.

Automatic and adaptive brake control systems received increasing attention as proposed regulations seemed imminent.

Bendix-Westinghouse introduced an adaptive air-brake system. Wheel speeds were sensed electronically and regulated through a controller and modulator that regulated air pressure when a wheel was about to lock.

North American Rockwell introduced an automatic antiskid brake system called "Skid-Trol." A single computer in the cab monitored itself and all other components. When a malfunction occurred, the vehicle brakes automatically reverted to standard operation.

The New Jersey Department of Transportation, New Jersey Turnpike Authority, and the Port of New York Authority combined to form the State Transportation Commission to apply for federal funds to finance exclusive bus lanes.

Autocar introduced a 12,400-pound tractor with computer-controlled brakes, electronic speedometer and tachometer, air conditioner, sound-proof cab, and over-size radiator.

Chevrolet introduced a 1-ton series in its light van line and increased the model count to thirty-six. Vans were available in two body styles, the commercial Chevy-Van and the dual-purpose Sportvan wagon. The Beauville, a luxury Sportvan, was also available.

Dodge developed the Tradesman and the Sportsman compact vans. The Sportsman was a camper type model. Forward axle and engine placement provided good engine accessibility.

Ford offered over 650 medium through heavy-duty models in its Louisville line with a choice of ten gasoline and twenty diesel engines. Each air-line system in the truck was color-coded for easier servicing.

Freightliner announced a truck chassis with a detachable container incorporating a sliding fifth wheel. The landing gear of the container folded into the floor when the container moved to load position. The rear truck frame was locked to the undercarriage of the container.

GMC 1971 light-duty van series offered thirty-six different models in two basic body styles, the Vandura Commercial vehicle and the dual-purpose Rally wagon.

The International Transtar model provided sealed electrical junction boxes for headlight and tail-light connectors. Flexible hoses were used for fluid systems rather than piping.

International Harvester introduced its "Cargostar" cab-over-engine models with a 70-inch BBC cab. These featured panoramic windshield, U-jointed steering column, gearshift lever on console and low-entry doors.

International Harvester introduced an air-suspension axle. An antiskid system for hydraulic brakes was available on light trucks.

Kenworth introduced its PD-200 series in the medium-duty range. Three models were offered, with Cummins diesel engines.

Mack introduced a 325-horsepower Maxidyne V-8 diesel and 5- and 6-speed Maxitorque transmissions. The Maxidyne was an over-square engine and featured a constant horsepower technique.

Mack trucks installed aluminum bumpers as standard equipment.

Mercedes-Benz of North America joined the B. E. Olson Corporation of New York to produce a city-delivery van, the 508D, powered by an OM diesel engine.

Oshkosh introduced its "E" series highway and city tractor, featuring a fiberglass front service panel across the cab for service maintenance.

Peterbilt and Kenworth introduced new heavy-duty city tractors built in Canada and available with Detroit Diesel or Cummins diesel engines for Peterbilt. The model was the first offered under a GVW of 33,000 pounds.

White introduced the Xpeditor multipurpose truck for city delivery. A welcomed driver feature was an 18-inch step for easy access.

Interest continued to mount in the gas-turbine engine.

Reflecting an advanced-design, two-way attack on pollution not previously encountered, the GMC Turbo-Cruiser III continued public appearances. It emphasized its low exhaust emissions, noise control, and lack of vibrations.

Freightliner Corporation tested a Detroit Diesel gas-turbine engine in a test fleet on a test run from Portland to Pamona, California.

Continental Trailways used a Ford turbine engine in its Silver-Eagle coach for the New York to Los Angeles run.

Dallas Transit Company received a $300,000 contract with the Department of Transportation. It was to develop, in conjunction with LTV Aerospace Corporation, an external combustion Freon engine for buses. The design for the freon engine was purchased from its inventor, Wallace Minto, of Sarasota, Florida.

Hertz truck rental ordered from International Harvester 2,300 medium-duty Loadstar 1600 models with V-304 V-8 engines.

Transcon Lines of Los Angeles ordered 330 White-Freightliner heavy-duty COE sleeper tractors powered by Cummins NHCT 270 engines.

General Motors paid $50 million for the production and sales rights to the Wankel rotary engine.

United Parcel Service used specially designed trailers developed by the Illinois Institute of Technology Research to improve loading and unloading efficiency and reduce labor costs.

Kelsey-Hayes introduced its electronic-controlled antiskid system to eliminate brake locking. KH had purchased rights to such a system from Hydro-Aire Division of Crane Company which had used such a system on aircraft and had developed one as early as 1958.

Fruehauf developed an intermodal, universal tank container for road, rail, and sea transport. A 5,000-gallon-capacity tank of stainless steel, carbon steel, or aluminum was fastened to a frame structure 20 feet in length.

Highway Products, Incorporated, makers of Twin Coach buses, offered a full line of Twin Coach "bare" shells in 24- and 28-foot lengths for anyone wishing to build his own bus.

California received over $1 billion from highway user taxes. Total revenue for highway taxes in the United States amounted to over $8.5 billion. In California, the trucking industry paid one-third of the total.

The National Automobile Dealers Association reported that, from 1963 to 1969, car and truck leasing increased 160 percent.

Bendix-Westinghouse dual air-brake system combined three unique valves to control the service and emergency braking.

Eaton developed a Selecto-Torq tandem axle. It combined an auxiliary transmission with a driving axle to give both highway and off-highway axle ratios, high speed, and high torque capabilities.

Bendix-Westinghouse introduced an air-dryer for solving moisture and dirt problems in air-brake systems. The unit was an absorptive dryer.

A driver alertness-aid, OWL, was developed by Life Technology, Incorporated, to alert drivers with a buzzer and warning light. The "Road Buddy," as the unit was popularly called, electronically measured and stored the driver's back-and-forth movement of the steering wheel. If the steering pattern deviated from the driver's regular pattern, he was warned by the OWL.

A radar collision detector was developed for truck application by Bentley Associates of Massachusetts, called the "Autostop."

Ryan Aeronautical Corporation developed a remote control for army Jeeps used as mine detectors.

Warner Gear and Motive Division of Borg Warner developed a four-wheel-drive system for off-road and highway use. The system consisted of a locking differential with a chain-drive transfer unit.

Firestone Tire and Rubber announced a new steel-belted tire and a manufacturing process of liquid molded tires.

Highway engineers expressed concern over the use of studded snow tires.

Budd Company introduced a "Ledge-Weld" steel disc wheel to accommodate the use of radial ply and wire cord tubeless tires.

Safety radiator cap, the Lev-R-Vent, was introduced by Stant Manufacturing. A lever had to be lifted on the cap before opening so that hot steam was exhausted through the overflow tube.

DOT indicated that it would consider a standard requiring two hood latches to eliminate hoods opening accidentally.

Portable preventive maintenance trucks were used by fleets on the West Coast to service widely scattered fleets. "Fuelers," as they were commonly called, carried about 500 gallons of diesel fuel, 200 gallons of gasoline, plus engine oil, air, water and gas filters.

Total production for 1970 dipped to 1,733,821 trucks and buses.

1971

Truck Production Tops Two Million

A milestone in truck output was reached in 1971 when production went over the 2 million mark.

Much of the truck industry's research and development emphasis in 1971 focused on meeting government regulations in brake safety and emission control.

The Department of Transportation issued an air brake standard establishing requirements for service brakes and parking brakes.

The Bureau of Motor Carrier Safety initiated new rules involving driver qualifications.

Breakaway sign posts were mandatory on the federal interstate highway system.

The National Highway Safety Bureau changed its name to the National Highway Traffic Safety Administration.

Truck thefts and hijacking were expected to exceed $1 billion, with New York, Los Angeles, Chicago, and St. Louis as the primary targets. Organized-crime developed a firm stronghold, prompting new security measures by the trucking industry.

Triple bottoms—three trailers hauled by a highway tractor—were allowed on the New York State Thruway during winter months.

Larger engines with more power were being installed by most manufacturers in both gas and diesel models. Turbocharging was increasing, gas-turbine engines highlighted the year.

General Motors Detroit Diesel Division developed a rugged and versatile 280-horsepower gas turbine known as GT-309.

Interest in spring brakes continued. Both diaphragm and piston type spring-brake manufacturers agreed that spring brakes were inexpensive, durable, and offered excellent performance.

Automatic lubricating system use increased as simplicity of the new units, and reduction in maintenance time, appealed to most trucking firms.

Brockway developed an air brake system in which the air brake was separate from other accessory uses. It had a constant 60 psi, despite failure of any other accessory.

Brockway truck and tractor cabs were custom padded for noise reduction as well as impact protection.

Brockway introduced the Huskiteer, its all-purpose heavy-duty model designed for gross weights up to 80,000 pounds.

GMC introduced a customer's direct-to-factory communications system to answer service and maintenance questions.

International Harvester introduced the Scout II, the "second generation" of its Scout sports-utility vehicles on a 100-inch wheel base.

International Harvester offered glider kits for CO and COF-4070 models and DF and FCF-400 models.

The International Fleetstar Cab was mounted on a subframe of steel rails with a coil spring shock absorber support.

The GMC Vari-rate rear leaf-springs adjusted automatically to load conditions. The bottom leaf served as a radius rod to help control braking and driving thrusts.

White displayed a new Freightliner with the Cummins NTC-290 engine at the American Trucking Associations Convention. The model featured a solid state tachometer, plastic tubing for fluid systems mounted high on the frame, self-tightening steering linkage, and a frontal air intake which also served as a nameplate.

Cummins introduced a new heavy-duty V-555 diesel engine rated at 225 horsepower at 3,300 rpm.

Mather Company introduced a jackknife-control unit which replaced the king pin on a fifth wheel.

The Mack model F tilt cab featured four-point mounting and hydraulic operation of the tilt cab which could be stopped at any point up to 90 degrees.

The Mack Interstater model a deluxe cab with padded interior and wrap-around console, year-round climate control, and a fold down rider's seat. The tilt cab opened to a full 90 degrees and was operated by a hydraulic pump for one-man operation.

Mack introduced an "Extended Service Interval" of 16,000 miles or 300-engine hours as standard on its 6-cylinder diesel engines.

A pneumatic bellows was used to elevate the fifth wheel raising-and-lowering device produced by the Holland Hitch Company. Compressed air for the bellows was controlled from the cab.

Consolidated Freightways conducted a 30-day safety test by driving all of its trucks with lights on in the daytime. In three previous tests, the lights-on program improved company safety records.

Union Oil continued adding to its large system of auto truck stops with the introduction of a huge ultra-modern rest and service complex in Albuquerque, New Mexico.

White Motor Company announced the sale of Diamond Reo to F. L. Cappaert, an industrialist from Vicksburg, Mississippi.

Daimler Benz of Germany set up the Mercedes Benz of North America to market heavy-duty trucks.

Dorsey Trailers, Incorporated, agreed to purchase Trailco Manufacturing and Sales Company.

The American Trucking Associations held its thirty-eighth convention in Washington late in October.

The American Truck Historical Society was organized with headquarters in Dearborn, Michigan. Staffed by volunteers, the society's goal was to preserve United States and Canadian truck history.

1971 production topped the 2 million mark: 2,088,001 units. The dollar value of trucks and buses this year increased to almost $6 billion.

I972

Safety and Emission Control Emphasized

Emission control and safety requirements for heavy trucks continued to absorb engineering efforts. Emission regulations were to become effective in 1974.

The National Highway Traffic Safety Administration (NHTSA) amended Standard 121, Air Brake Systems for Trucks, Trailers, and Buses. It established a new effective date of September 1, 1974, to allow additional fleet testing.

The Federal Highway Administration announced standardization of color combinations for new highway signs and symbols to be used by 1975. The signs relied on symbols and shape, rather than words, to give warning and information to drivers.

Legislation was proposed to convert the highway trust fund into a national transportation fund. Strong objection to such legislation was voiced by the truck industry.

Four-wheel drive was reported to be increasing in the heavy-duty field. Both 4 × 4 and 6 × 6 units were developed for highway use.

Larger engines to provide greater power highlighted the heavy-duty models for 1972.

Tubeless-tire use on heavy trucks continued to increase. Tire manufacturers predicted that the next big development would be to steel-cord tires.

The Detroit Diesel offered on Chevrolet heavy-duty models was the largest engine ever used by Chevrolet. The 12-V-71 model provided up to 400 horsepower.

Dodge low-cab forward models were changed to accept larger engines. Diesel engines were added on its short conventional heavy models.

Fabco Division of Kelsey-Hayes introduced a heavy-duty utility truck featuring an 8-foot wide tilt cab. It was constructed of fiberglass, with steel inserts and reinforcement at the front for an impact belt.

Ford introduced a 50,000-pound tandem and 18,000-pound front axle on its LTS-9000 model.

GMC expanded the Cummins diesels, offered in some 9500 series, and the Astro 95 tilt-cab models with the 320-horsepower V-903 diesel.

Ford Motor Company and GM Chevrolet Division started selling

import compact pickup trucks in March: Ford Courier and Chevy
LUV. Retail sales in 1972 were: Ford Courier, 26,000 and Chevy
LUV, 21,098.

International introduced its Paystar 5000 series for construction
work. The new diesel models featured a full-length straight steel
frame with optional capacity rails, a cooling de-aeration built into a
radiator top tank, two-stage air cleaners, a fiberglass insulated steel
cab, and a fiberglass tilt hood and fender assembly on the tilt-cab
model.

International Transtar models offered gross combination weight
ratings up to 130,000 pounds with large diesel engines.

Kenworth introduced its new "Brute" model designed for construction work. The front axle was set back 64 inches for a short
turning radius. The turning angle was 37 degrees.

Marmon-Herrington added a one-man cab heavy-duty truck line
for special hauling, off-road, and mountain situations. Marmon
converted Chevrolet, Dodge, Ford, GMC, and International chassis to all-wheel drive for heavy-duty applications.

White introduced a new model, the Road Commander, which was
aerodynamically designed.

Fruehauf developed a 23-cubic-yard, vertical side bottom hopper
dump trailer with 66 × 88-inch gates, which were air operated.

Flex-Truc spotter tractors featured power steering, automatic
transmission, and hydraulic fifth wheel.

A new control system, where large power-shift transmissions could
be fully automatic, was shown by Detroit Diesel. The development
made automatic shifting for off-highway vehicles practicable.

The Automobile Manufacturers Association changed its name to
the Motor Vehicle Manufacturers Association (MVMA). The
MVMA stated that the new name would more accurately reflect the
make-up of the association to include trucks and other vehicles.

MVMA recommended that uniform motor vehicle noise standards
be established at the national level.

International Harvester formed a new truck company in conjunction with Van Doornes Automobile Company in Europe. The
company was DAF and would produce medium and heavy trucks,
buses, and military vehicles for world markets.

Ford used a deep-dip electrocoat primer paint process that electrically bonded the primer to the metal, giving excellent protection
for longer cab life.

Mack trucks approved a $1 million contribution to establish an

American Truck Historical Museum in Allentown, Pennsylvania. *Truck and bus production continued to climb: 2,482,503 units.*

1973

Truck Sales over 3 Million

This year was the most successful year in truck history. Over 3 million trucks were sold, an increase of over half a million from the previous year.

Significant areas of research included development of adaptive brake controls, or antiskid systems, to meet federal motor vehicle safety standard 121.

Bendix introduced its adaptive braking system to control lock up. The antiskid system automatically released air pressure through a device controlled by a wheel-mounted sensor.

A triple action skid control unit was offered by Goodrich. Speed sensors and exciter rings were located on each wheel. As each wheel turned, a signal was sent to axle relay valves, which dropped brake pressure enough to eliminate a skid.

Wagner skid control featured wheel-mounted sensors, modulator valve, and a solid-state control box.

A fuel shortage, which began in late 1972, continued as cold weather created shortages of gasoline and diesel fuel, especially in New England. Many carriers were faced with increased prices or refusal by oil companies to renew contracts. Late in the year, President Nixon requested that states adopt a 50-mile per hour speed limit for cars and a 55-mile per hour limit for trucks and buses.

A number of cities and states had, or were enacting, restrictive noise laws. Many trucks were cited for noise violations. California required an 86-decibel (db) level for this year, and an-80-db rating by 1978.

A critical energy crisis developed from fuel shortages, brought on by oil embargoes from the Mid-East, prompted Secretary of Transportation Brock Adams to encourage a joint industry-government Voluntary Truck and Bus Fuel Economy Improvement Program.

The new Rockwell-International Skid-Trol system included wheel sensors, relay pneumatic valves at each axle with logic modules and solid state computers (a small digital chip). The computer-monitored wheel deceleration and air pressures some 50 times a second, according to Rockwell.

1970   The interstate highway is the lifeline by which trucks can serve the nation with unparalleled delivery speed.

1970   International Co-Loadstar truck combined with special Cargomatic 14-foot vans. The container was hydraulically lifted into or out of galley sleeves on the aircraft.

1973 International Paystar model F-5070. A 6×6 construction truck, diesel-powered with all-wheel traction drive can pull the heaviest allowable loads on off-highway terrain.

1973 A fun-and-travel GMC motor home had 15 floor-plan variations and was 23 or 26 feet long.

1972   The Chevrolet Luv (top photo) and the Ford Courier pickup trucks introduced a move to subcompact models and a new concept of "captive imports." Both trucks were made in Japan; the Luv was built by Isuzu, and the Courier by Toyo Kogo.

1973   The Dodge LT1000 featured an all-aluminum cab.

1974   Diamond Reo C-119 diesel tractor with twin stacks.

1974   Autocar heavy-duty tractor and a long, light-weight dump trailer to handle a heavy load with ease.

1974   The heavy-duty Autocar roll-on container eased the task of waste removal.

1974 A welcome sight to the motorist in distress was the durable Dodge D-300. The new heavy wrecker featured easy accessibility of equipment and a club cab which provided space for additional tools and personnel.

1974 Two Chevrolet pickups—the C-30 Crew Cab and C-10 Utility Body—light but tough no-nonsense vehicles.

1974 Chevrolet Vega panel express.

Chevrolet Titan 90 single axle highway tractor weighed less than 9,875 pounds. The cab was constructed of light-weight aluminum with steel doors and had six layers of insulation for noise reduction.

Chevrolet offered the Turbine N-6 diesel on its new models with Cerametalix clutches and 4- and 5-speed Allison automatic transmissions.

Diamond Reo installed a gas turbine engine in a construction truck to test the economics of the gas turbines in off-highway situations. The gas turbine tested was a Detroit Diesel Allison Division model.

Dodge trucks introduced electronic ignition as standard.

Dodge introduced the Bighorn Long Conventional Model equipped with either Cummins or Detroit Diesels, extra large 1,500 square inch radiator, tilt hood, tilt-away steering, fold-down dash with bi-torque gauges, foam-insulated cab, and automatic reset circuit breakers mounted below the dash.

The Ford Louisville 9000 series featured heavy-duty truck-type power steering, adjustable steering column, tilting fiberglass front end, crossflow radiator, removable Air Pac (including hand or air controls, pressure gauges, tubing and connections), double-channel frames, two-stage air cleaners, and automatic circuit breakers.

GMC introduced a new Series 379 with 432-C V-6 gasoline engines complementing the regular line of straight 6's and V-8 gasoline models and the V-6 DH-478 diesel engine.

GMC also introduced the Pedd-A-Liner tilt-cab tractor designed for delivery or short-haul situations.

International introduced the F-5070 6 × 6 construction model, designed for mixer or dump truck use.

International developed a Neoprene-sealed king pin on the front axles of its medium- and heavy-duty trucks.

Kenworth featured forged aluminum hubs, oil-lubricated wheel bearings, and brake drums mounted outboard for ease of maintenance.

Mack announced its 300 Series Maxidyne 6-cylinder diesel, which was turbocharged. It introduced air-to-air aftercooling through two heat exchangers on top of the engine.

Marmon Motor Company introduced a diesel road tractor in cab lengths from 60 to 86 inches. The high, wide cab featured a flat, sloping, frontal area.

Peterbilt also introduced all-wheel drive 6 × 6 and 8 × 6 mixer dump trucks. These had set back front axles, dual power steering, and were powered by a Cummins V-555 diesel.

Walter Motor Truck offered the Junior Model snow plow truck in three models with weights of 28,000, 33,000, and 36,000 pounds. A full-time center differential highlighted the all-wheel drive.

White introduced the "Road Boss" tractor, featuring a wider hood with larger radiator on most models, greater stability for fuel tanks, closer location to frame rails, and factory-installed stationary or sliding fifth wheels, pre-engineered with the frame-rail combinations. A sturdier more comfortable cab stressed noise reduction.

Fruehauf introduced a new platform trailer series. Beam-type 4-inch high cross members were welded to side and main member, and extended the width of the trailer. The exceptionally strong trailers featured carrying capacities up to 60,000 pounds.

Oshkosh featured a 4-point tandem rear suspension on its F-Model 6 × 6 concrete mixer trucks. Four wide-frame attachment points, for support brackets, and four variable-rate leaf springs, were combined with triangular walking beams to negate the typical mixer lean so common when heavy concrete shifted in the mixer drum. The model replaced the long nose model-C, which was phased out because FMVSS-121 did not permit feasible weight reduction with a front axle set back so far.

The 359 Peterbilt offered a new cab featuring extensive use of aluminum in construction, hinged instrument panel, larger tinted windshield, dual-controlled air-operated windshield wipers, improved driver comfort, and increased noise control insulation. Another model, the 346 was available in 6 × 6 and 8 × 6 versions.

Arrow Manufacturing Company introduced a new Wrangler tractor 152-inches long with a 98-inch wheel base for terminal operations. A removable cab and tilt engine hood for servicing were also featured.

Spicer developed a semi-automatic transmission which used an electric clutch, electric brake, air controls, and electric components to provide automatic shifting while retaining driver control. The driver used the main clutch only for speeds under 3 miles per hour and then shifted a single lever.

A fuel injector for diesel engines, which delayed fuel input according to the top-dead-center position of the pistons, was introduced by Detroit Diesel Allison Division of GM. The C-type injector reduced nitrogen oxides by about 25 percent.

A jackknife-control system was developed by Herbert Trucking Company. The system tightened a stainless-steel control cable connected to the tractor from the air brake cable reel on the trailer. Tension was maintained, and increased angle between the tractor and trailer was prevented to eliminate jackknifing.

Fabco introduced a Yard Hustler with dual controls, especially designed for handling containers.

The Ottawa Commando yard tractor was introduced by Daybrook-Ottawa. It featured an air-suspension tilt cab and elevating fifth wheel.

Firestone designed a smooth rim truck wheel specifically for radial tubeless tires.

Wayne Corporation introduced its Lifeguard bus. It featured one-piece body section guard rails extending the full length of the body on sides and top. Inside, all edges were shielded, protrusions eliminated, and foam padding used throughout.

Mini-trailers for use with pickup trucks were introduced by Clark Equipment. The trailers included a 22-foot dual axle flatbed trailer, a 30-foot tri-axle and two aluminum wall van trailers.

Broken windows had plagued the transit industry for years. DuPont found a potential solution with the introduction of Abcite, a new acrylic glass substitute.

Detroit Diesel announced an optional Leece-Neville alternator on its 8-V-71 series engines. The alternator was driven directly off of the engine blower drive gear and eliminated drive belts.

Results of the experimental steam bus tests, initiated in California, December, 1968, and funded by $1.6 million from DOT's Urban Mass Transportation Administration, revealed that steam-powered buses reduced nitrogen oxides and hydrocarbons substantially, and were acceptable in road performance, acceleration, and noise control. However, the excessive fuel consumption in comparison to diesel engines pointed to the need for additional research and development.

A Ford 395-horsepower gas-turbine engine was mounted in a fire truck by Sutphen Fire Equipment Company of Columbus, Ohio.

A triangular warning device for breakdown was required by MVSS-125, effective January 1, 1974.

U.S. truck-trailer production set a record in 1973 with 175,000 units valued at about $886 million.

California Bank of America maintained a fleet of eight mobile banks for use where there were no permanent banks. The units were built by Condor Coach on Ford M-500 truck chassis.

The National Institute for Automotive Service Excellence (NIASE) conducted certification tests for heavy-duty truck and bus mechanics.
Production of trucks and buses for 1973: 3,014,361.

1974

Energy Crisis Surfaces

The truck industry of 1974 was challenged as never before to solve intricate problems for long-term fuel economy. Reduction of speed limits from 70 to 55 miles per hour because of fuel shortages and Mid-East oil embargoes was one solution.

Many trucks could show fuel savings with the 55 miles-per-hour limit. But heavy-duty line-haul diesels built since 1966 were designed with power trains (engine, transmission, axles) to deliver maximum efficiency at 60 or more miles per hour for new interstate highways.

To maximize fuel saving yet minimize heavy-duty truck problems and production backlogs, various alternatives were considered: Extra trucks to deliver goods (which cancelled fuel savings); increased or heavier payloads with less fuel economy but eliminating one truck out of four or five for overall fuel saving; regearing the rear-axle gears, very costly procedures with such gears in short supply; expansion of intermodal piggyback truck-rail transport.

The National Science Foundation funded research projects for developing streamline devices to reduce truck and trailer air drag and wind resistance.

Fuel shortages and high fuel prices resulted in many fuel-saving devices: engine-cooling fans with temperature controls, lighter fan blades, special fan clutches.

Hyland Manufacturing Company designed the Air-Trol fiberglass nosepiece for trucks and trailers to reduce air resistance.

Alternative power plants also received much attention, and research was devoted to electric power: AM General received a $2 million contract for 350 1/4-ton electric delivery trucks for the U.S. Postal Service. The electric system was manufactured by Gould Electric and placed in the same body as the AM General gasoline postal truck. Battronic Truck Corporation introduced the Goliath electric van for multistop delivery purposes. Otis Elevator Company announced production of an electric delivery van for short-haul operations.

Transit bus development also became an area of research because of the energy crisis.

AM General introduced a transit bus with unitized body and frame of special low-allow steel body structure and aluminum side panels. The bus was available in four models and powered by two Detroit Diesel engines. Air suspension was of the bellows type.

The Urban Mass Transit Administration performed tests on three prototype transit buses in the Arizona desert. The buses tested were manufactured by GMC, Rohr, and AM General, and were evaluated on performance, in service tests, endurance, and barrier crashes.

Greyhound exhibited the Americruiser Turbine VII gas-turbine bus at the International Gas-Turbine Show in Zurich, Switzerland. The Americruiser was based on the MC-8 bus built by Motor Coach Industries, Incorporated.

GM adapted its multipurpose chassis and body from a motor home vehicle to a commercial, medical, and a general transportation vehicle.

Dodge introduced the Ramcharger, a four-wheel-drive utility vehicle powered by a 318-cubic inch V-8 gas engine, wheelbase of 160 inches and overall length of 184.6 inches.

The Dodge medium-duty truck featured electronic ignition, cellular-tubular cooling with radiator cores up to 600 square inches, and options, such as new process automatic transmission and power steering.

Ford offered a full-time, four-wheel-drive option on its F-100 and F-250 series pickup trucks.

Ford offered a Super Cab light-duty pickup, with an optional full-width rear seat which folded down for cargo space.

Diamond Reo introduced its Royale II cab-over-engine model with design changes in performance, safety, comfort, and appearance.

A low-profile urban truck model CF-60 called the "Rogue" was offered by Diamond Reo. The durable, yet lightweight cab featured a steel-frame roll bar and 20-gauge exterior panels welded to the frame.

Diamond Reo used a novel means of demonstrating its new model, the "Raider." The company advertised in truck periodicals and truck stops listing the dates that the "Raider" would be displayed at various Union 76 truck-stops from coast to coast.

FWD announced a light-weight special 6 × 6 model with aluminum hood and shroud; radiator and fuel tanks plus radiator shutters were also aluminum. The radiator shell was constructed of fiberglass.

Transtar II cab-over-engine model by International featured a weight-saving chassis, aluminum components, 60-gallon fuel tank, 1,200-square inch radiator, dual-brake system, large slow-cooling fan, windshield wipers top mounted, and dual-stage air-intake system. International also introduced a V-800 turbocharged diesel engine with four valves per cylinder, multi-orifice injectors, intake manifolds cast integral with each cylinder head, improved cooling, and overall light-weight construction.

International also introduced the CONCO short hood model with a 66-inch BBC. The conventional cab-over-engine model had an offset cab favoring the driver's compartment with the engine mounted under the cab. The hood extended only 16 inches beyond the windshield.

Continued testing of 20 DAF tractors from the Netherlands to determine the adaptability of the tractors to U.S. highways was announced by International.

Kenworth introduced two new COE models, a 90-inch BBC, offset cab model, and a "project blue" model with two sleeper bunks. The 90-inch BBC featured a sloping hood and a 1,500-square inch cross-flow radiator with a 4 1/2-inch core and dual hydraulic-driven fans for better cooling. The "project-blue" had a double deck for sleeper berths and a 11 1/2-foot high cab with a two-level feature which served as a limited type of wind deflector.

The V.I.T. conventional tractor was announced by Kenworth with an extra-wide walk-in sleeper compartment. Access was by a 28 × 54-inch passage between the seats.

Freightliner introduced its "Power Liner" model and also the lightest in its class light-weight conventional model.

Peterbilt adapted its 300 short-haul tractor to fire trucks.

Plymouth introduced a 4 × 4 utility vehicle and the Voyager compact van wagon.

White announced the Road Xpeditor, a low profile tilt-cab model which stressed chassis-component standardization with other road models. A larger, 1030-square inch radiator was standard with the larger Cummins and Detroit Diesel engines.

Volvo introduced the F-86 US heavy-duty model for sale on the American market. The low-profile model used many U.S.-manufactured components. The diesel engine, transmission, and rear axle were built in Sweden.

Delco Remy introduced a maintenance-free heavy-duty battery for trucks.

Perkins Engines developed a squish-lip design for diesel engines to reduce exhaust emissions and noise levels by about 50 percent.

Disc brakes for heavy-duty trucks and buses were available from Kelsey-Hayes and B. F. Goodrich.

Millco Services in Texas featured a specially built tractor with a car carrier above the cab for moving-van service. Family cars could be transported along with household goods.

Rockwell Standard developed Skid-Trol for trailers. Hubcap wheel sensors sent signals to a sensor on the axle then to a digital computer.

Bendix and Eaton announced a joint agreement: Bendix would supply the heavy-duty aftermarket with Eaton's skid-control.

Berg-Fiat antiskid brake control featured inboard and outboard sensors, a controlling air logic modulator (CALM) valve, and a computer which maintained wheel rotations.

Kysor Industrial introduced an electronic instrument system with digital display read outs, audible alarms, and paper tape trip reports.

Federal noise-control regulations were set to a maximum limit of 90 decibels (db-A) at the driver's seat. The effective date was October 1, 1974, for new vehicles and April 1, 1975, for others.

The National Safety Council reported that energy-crisis lower speeds helped reduce traffic fatalities by 25 percent.

The National Women's Trucking Association held its first annual convention in Charleston, South Carolina. The association membership totaled 200 and included drivers, clerical employees, and drivers' wives.

In a complete reversal of form, the National Highway Traffic Safety Administration proposed a delay in the effective date of FMVSS-121 "in light of the magnitude of the cost of complying with it."

The Transportation Safety Act of 1974 removed the authority for controlling and regulating hazardous commodities from the existing regulatory board to the secretary of transportation.

In the final hours of the 93rd Congress, new limits for truck weights on interstate highways were passed. Single axles were permitted up to 20,000 pounds and tandem axles up to 34,000 pounds.

1974   production of trucks and buses dropped: 2,746,538 units.

1975

Controversial Brake Standard 121
Takes Effect—Business Recedes

The controversial government antiskid safety performance standard for air brakes, known as the Federal Motor Vehicle Safety Standard 121, became effective for buses, trucks, and trailers. The act required vehicles to stop in shorter distances with wheels that do not lock uncontrollably when stopping. Antilock designs were aimed to minimize skidding. The standard also required a "split system" for separate brake lines to front and rear brakes, so that a failure would not result in a catastrophic loss of all vehicle brakes.

Looming on the horizon was an accompanying triple-faceted standard for brake safety (FMVSS-105), referring to hydraulic footbrake stopping. The standard required: a parking brake that would hold on a 30 percent grade; a warning light to indicate failures of hydraulic brakes; and a system designated to provide residual braking in case of failure of the service.

Monitoring the progress and evaluating the performance of manufactured systems to meet Federal Motor Vehicle Safety Standard (usually noted as FMVSS followed by a number) was under the jurisdiction of the National Highway Traffic Safety Administration (NHTSA) part of the Department of Transportation (DOT).

Despite last-minute attempts to delay the controversial antiskid air-brake performance standard, FMVSS-121, it went into effect on January 1 for trailers and March 1 for trucks and buses.

Drastic effects of a business recession coincided with the effective date of standard 121. International Harvester closed its San Leandro heavy-duty truck plant; Mack announced the closing of its Hayward plant for several weeks; Peterbilt shutdown its Newark heavy-duty truck plant for several weeks; Freightliner cut production and closed several plants during March; and White closed two plants in April for several weeks, after its Cleveland plant shutdown in March.

Paccar, Incorporated (Peterbilt and Kenworth) initiated legal action in federal court to force a review of the relevant safety data used by the National Highway Traffic Safety Administration in establishing FMVSS-121, the air-brake antiskid law.

Dodge announced that it would discontinue production of heavy-duty tractors, citing the complexity of producing heavy-duty trucks under the ambiguity surrounding brake and noise standards. The company stated that it would continue production of light and medium trucks.

The costs of motor vehicle regulations continued to escalate, and the industry predicted overwhelming costs in equipment and labor if proposed retrofit regulations went into effect. The cost of new equipment for antilock brake systems and noise reduction would vary somewhere between $1,000 and $1,800 per vehicle.

All segments of the trucking industry were asked to contact their representatives in Washington to amend unreasonable standards which were not practicable. Many states were actively enforcing noise levels on highways.

With shortages of ethylene-glycol antifreeze and rising prices, many truck fleets were searching for ways to extend the life of the antifreeze without the danger of harming heavy-duty engines.

White introduced the "Road Commander 2" cab-over, first of its completely redesigned new family of trucks, featuring interchangeable commonality of parts and design.

The Electrobus Division of Otis Elevator Company provided a twenty-passenger 35-mile-an-hour electric bus for tests in San Francisco by the Municipal Railway. The bus had a range of 60 miles and a five-to-six-hour capacity before recharging.

Ford introduced a longer Louisville linehaul model, the LTL-9000, with an 118.3-inch BBC, plus 36-inch sleeper. Equipped with a 12,000-pound front axle, a 38,000-pound rear axle, and dual 100-gallon aluminum fuel tanks, the LTL-9000 also offered custom paint colors, trim designs, factory-installed CB radio, and stereo radio-tape deck.

Eaton introduced a 23,000-pound driver-controlled traction differential. It only limited the differential rather than locking it.

As a continuation of the bus evaluation tests by DOT's Urban Mass Transportation Administration, the three prototype transit coaches (GMC, Rohr, and AM General) were subjected to "public testing," in-service tests in various large cities.

GMC transbus was a gas-turbine model with 4-speed automatic transmission and a fluid coupling.

AM General Bus used a Caterpillar turbocharged diesel engine and a 2-speed Spicer automatic transmission with a torque converter. The converter served as a retarder during braking. The final drive setup was unusual—the transverse rear engine diesel and transmission directed the final drive forward at the extreme right of the bus to tandem rear-driving axles.

Rohr Industries transbus featured twin front-steering axles, Allison 3-speed automatic transmission, air suspension on four axles with trailing arm tied to a DeDion tube at the rear, and independent upper and lower control arms at the front.

Autocar introduced a shortnose heavy-duty truck for construction use with an elevated cab offset 6 inches to the left and fuel tank, muffler, and air filter at the extreme right side of the cab.

Dodge announced two new Kary Vans (one medium- and one light-duty model) and a Tradesman Van.

Ford introduced a new parcel van with a 14-foot body, 8 feet wide, giving a capacity of 10,725 GVW. Side doors were either sliding or opened flat against the sides of the body. Roll-up doors were available as an option.

Fontaine Truck Equipment Company offered a five-year warranty for maintenance on their 5000 series fifth wheels.

International announced the Transtar EEV (Energy Efficient Vehicle) with a fuel-savings package. It included a Cummins 290 engine with turbocharger. A new heavy-duty model, the Eagle, designed for owner/operators was also introduced.

Oshkosh Truck Corporation announced a B-series cement mixer truck with a center-mounted low-profile cab and rear-engine drive for forward placement of the mixer.

GM Research and GMC Truck and Coach jointly developed the "Dragfoiler" air deflector which reduced aerodynamic drag by 35 percent.

Xentex division of Exxon developed truck and trailer body panels made from a composite of structural foam reinforced with fiberglass.

Uniroyal guaranteed a 10 percent fuel improvement with the use of its new tear-drop-shaped air deflector.

Tesco Company offered an illuminated air deflector called the "Nose Cone" for mounting on the nose of semitrailers. Decals could be placed on the deflector for identification or advertising and could be illuminated by lights located behind the Nose Cone.

With the expiration of the Highway Trust Fund in October, 1977, a number of proposals were made to change the fund by diverting a portion of the fuel taxes at the federal and state levels.

Jimmy Hoffa, controversial expresident of the Teamsters' Union, disappeared mysteriously on July 30, 1975.

Brockway received a $22.6 million order from Iran for 575 trucks. The bulk of the order was for dump trucks.

Caterpillar introduced a semi-automatic transmission, model 7155, with heavy-duty diesels. The clutch was eliminated, and shifts were air controlled by one lever in a straight line shift pattern.

The recreational vehicle manufacturers, set back by the energy-crisis, welcomed a burgeoning demand and experienced a sales "boom" in four-wheel-drive sports vehicles.

Production dropped for the second consecutive year: 476,976 units.

1976

Air Brake Standard Skids in Courts

A formal motion to stop enforcement of the FMVSS-121 was filed by Paccar (Peterbilt and Kenworth). The American Trucking Associations and the Truck Equipment and Body Distributors Associations filed an "intervenor" brief to support the suit. Freightliner and International Harvester joined the suit. San Francisco's Ninth Circuit Court of Appeals in mid-January halted compliance with standard 121 by granting a 60-day suspension.

NHTSA modified the controversial air brake standard FMVSS-121, so that only one air pressure valve and logic module were required to brake two axles. Sensors need not be placed on all axles.

The Motor Vehicle Manufacturers Association appealed to the Senate Finance Committee for repeal of the 10 percent federal excise tax on medium- and heavy-duty trucks.

Brockway introduced the "776," a conventional model with a constant depth frame rail for snow plow and dump truck use.

Ford developed a dual-displacement engine changable from 6-cylinder power to 3 cylinders when cruising at highway speeds.

Chevrolet introduced the Bison heavy-duty conventional model in either 108-inch or 116-inch BBC models. The frame was matched to customer's need and loads by computer. Both steel and aluminum frames were available in various rail designs.

Dodge accessory equipment on its truck models this year included electronic warning devices, fluid-level sensors and overheating sensors for automatic transmissions, windshield-washer nozzle located on wiper arm, and glide-out spare-tire carriers.

Forward Incorporated of Huron, South Dakota, entered the truck field with a 6 × 6 rear-engined "Chuting Star" front-discharge mixer. The new model was powered by a Cummins diesel.

Freightliner introduced its LGF model, a low cab-forward truck with a set back front axle, 63-inch BBC cab, vertical exhaust, 90 percent tilt cab, and a 34-inch or 40-inch sleeper box, complete with swivel dome lights.

GMC introduced the General Series with an all-aluminum alloy cab and tilting fiberglass two-piece hood. The cab and frame were extensively corrosion-proofed. Stainless steel and aluminum trim were used on cab, hood, and fenders.

Hendrickson developed a terminal switching tractor, called Dockmaster. The enclosed one-man tilt cab was rubber mounted.

International Harvester designed a seven-man cab on its Transtar II chassis for use by Caterpillar Tractor Company to demonstrate its 3406 diesel engine.

International introduced two new models, the Scout Terra, a compact pickup truck, and the Traveler, a utility station wagon. The Scout Terra featured a 118-inch wheelbase, 184-inch overall length, 70-inch width, with a 6-foot pickup box and 2,400-pound capacity. The model was offered with two- or four-wheel drive.

International's Transtar II featured an aluminum front axle which reduced weight by 140 pounds and required lubrication at 60,000 miles rather than 12,000. Aluminum was used for the radiator, radiator supports, and the transmission shift tower. A new light-weight V-800 diesel was also featured.

Kenworth offered a unique cab door with door jambs providing reinforcement of the cab structure. The cab was constructed of riveted aluminum for easy maintenance. The frame was cut and drilled to the customer's specifications.

Mack produced an economy 300-plus diesel engine with six cylinders in-line and air-to-air intercooler, a turbocharger with new blade configuration, new injection pump, and temperature-controlled self-feathering flexible stainless-steel cooling fan.

Oshkosh Truck Corporation offered an eight-wheel-drive fire truck pumper capable of dispensing 48,000 gallons of fire-fighting foam in 150 seconds. The truck measured 45 feet in length, 10 feet in width, and was 14 feet high. Each pair of tandem axles was driven by its own diesel engine. The truck weighed 125,000 pounds with 6,000 gallons of water.

Warner and Swasey offered a fire truck chassis with a five-man service cab, only 89 inches in height. The chassis was designed for use with aerial equipment and had seven bolted cross members and rigid frame to withstand the weight of the aerial ladders.

White introduced the Road Xpeditor 2, a low cab-forward truck tractor, designed for freight hauling, city pickup and delivery, and refuse collection.

AM General reported that it would build 234 articulated buses for ten California transit authorities.

GMC transit bus RTS (rapid transit series) featured independent air-suspended front wheels, an optional "kneeling system" which lowered the bus at the door by about five inches, extensive use of stainless steel alloy in corrosion areas, and a body constructed of eight 5-foot modular sections welded together.

The Argosy short route bus was introduced by Airstream on a Chevrolet forward-control chassis with Chevrolet engine and transmission. The bus was designed for downtown shuttle and light passenger-load situations. It was available with either 15, 19, or 23 passenger seating arrangements.

The electric vehicle reappeared as Congress established the Energy Research and Development Administration (ERDA) and recommended $160 million for electric-vehicle research.

Eltra Corporation was awarded a grant by ERDA for research study on batteries for electric vehicles.

Dart Truck introduced two mechanical-drive off-highway trucks: model 3100 truck and model 4150 coal hauler.

Flxible, a division of Rohr Industries, introduced the model 870 transit, built by modular construction with sidewalls, roof, and floor built separately.

Billings Energy Research Corporation tested an experimental hydrogen-powered bus, using a Dodge truck engine in a converted Winnebago 19-passenger minibus.

Wind deflectors continued to be a primary fuel-economy item.

Cab top air-deflector was developed by ADV Industries.

A transparent vortex stabilizer to be used with the Airshield wind deflector was announced by Rudkin-Wiley Corporation. Called the Gap-Sealer, the device was a retractable flexible baffle. It connected to the back of the tractor cab and sealed the air space between cab and trailer.

Trailmobile introduced the AirVane wind deflector.

A National Science Foundation study to determine the effectiveness of truck-and-trailer-mounted air deflectors was conducted by the University of Maryland. Three International Harvester tractor trailers (two with air deflectors) were used in the testing. One vehicle recorded a 12 percent fuel savings, while the other recorded a 6 percent savings.

Rights to manufacture and market the Terrapin air deflector were acquired by Airshield Division of Rudkin-Wiley Corporation.

Prime Manufacturing offered fiberglass air deflectors. A 32-inch model for high cabs and a 42-inch model for low cabs were snowplow shaped and claimed to save 10 percent in fuel.

Aeroboost Products designed a concave perforated air deflector, the Aeroboost III.

GM "Dragfoiler" air deflector claimed 21.65 percent better mileage with selective fuel-economy components.

Airodyne air deflector built by Plastic Products claimed a 27 percent fuel savings at 70 miles per hour and a 10 percent savings at 50 miles per hour.

Ottawa Commando yard tractor featured a Reverse-N-Drive that allowed a combination seat and steering assembly to rotate 180 degrees, so that the driver could easily steer and control the tractor in reverse.

Linehauler introduced the Yardmaster terminal tractor.

A dump trailer by Alaskan Western was manually or hydraulically adjustable to extend over a total of 22 feet and could take advantage of extended wheelbase weight laws.

AC Spark Plug introduced a low tire-pressure alarm system which flashed a warning light on the instrument panel; and a signal displayed on the tire itself.

Bendix developed a "Sure Stroke" automatic slack adjuster for S-cam air brakes.

Fruehauf announced the "Long Ranger" with a five-year warranty on all new trailers, new trucks, equipment, and other components for the original purchaser if serviced and maintained properly.

1975 International milk tanker on a Paystar 5000-gallon 6×6 chassis.

1975 A second glance is needed to spot the driver's compartment in this tractor-trailer combination. The new concept introduced by Strick Trailers provided greatly increased payload capacity.

1975 RTS (Rapid Transit Series) bus by GMC.

1976   Jeep Cherokee Chief.

1975   AM General electric postal delivery truck.

1975 GMC Gentleman Jim limited-edition pickup with passenger-car features.

1976 Newcomer to the Ford pickup line, F-150 4×4, featuring a 6,050 pound gross weight rating and 133-inch wheelbase.

1976 GMC Sprint Classic pickup, popular for family service needs.

1976 GMC crew cab and trailer.

1977 The customized pickup Warlock from Dodge provided real oak sideboards, fancy wheels, and gold tape stripe accents.

1977 Chevrolet Suburban, a flexible family-size multipurpose vehicle with the utility of a light truck and the comfort to serve family and recreational needs.

1977 GMC introduced a roof-mounted air-drag reduction device on the Astro 95 highway tractor.

1977   Peterbilt model 387 for off-highway use was diesel powered and available in a range from 350 to 450 gross horsepower.

1977   This unique vehicle was operated by the University of Michigan's Highway Safety Research Institute to test truck tire performance. International Harvester donated the tractor, and the automotive industry provided the funds for test-unit development.

At the International Trucking Show three manufacturers, Dayton-Walther Corporation, B. F. Goodrich, and Kelsey-Hayes, displayed prototype direct air-disc brake systems.

Delco Moraine developed a hydraulic-over-hydraulic Hy-Power brake system for trucks and school buses up to 42,000 pounds GVW.

International developed two new engines, an oversquare big bore V-8 gasoline model V-537 and a midrange diesel called the Express, a 180-horsepower version of the DT-466 engine.

Rockwell International introduced a new 17-N X-Tra Life universal joint with positive lubricant metering system and antidrain back design to the bearings and thrust washers for 50 percent more service life and fewer lubrications.

Williams Air Controls developed a sliding gate diesel engine compression brake for 4-cycle diesel engines.

Heil Company designed a one-man refuse collector called the Colecto-Cub. It was equipped with a Ford engine and automatic transmission.

A trend to automatic lubrication (oil or grease) resurfaced. Although automatic lub systems were not new, these emphasized precise cycle time and measurement of the lubricant. Oil-level monitor systems and replacement systems were also developed so that time lost and higher costs of on-the-road oil changes could be eliminated.

Use of spin-on filters continued to increase.

Diamond Reo's equipment and property were sold at auction.

Motor Vehicle Manufacturers Association announced that forty-one new and continuing research programs would be funded at twenty-one independent laboratories and universities during the next twelve months.

The Eaton DS0380 tandem axle featured a positive force-flow lubrication system, 16 1/2-inch spiral level gear, and two helical gear power dividers with solid input shaft. Two planetary double reduction tandem axles were also announced.

Trailmobile designed the Petro-80, a top- or bottom-loading petroleum tank trailer, with a one-piece A-shaped rail which served as an integral trough for vapor recovery systems.

Jeep Corporation scaled new heights in 4-WD sports-utility sales, 45 percent higher than its previous year's best-selling record.

White Motor Corporation sold its White Superior Division to

Cooper Industries and its Alco operation to GEC of England.

Van and pickup sales soared to a new record. Three out of every four new trucks were pickups or vans. Van sales soared 49 percent above 1975, with domestic-make pickups 23 percent over 1975, and import pickups from Japan up 3 percent.

Combined federal and state highway user taxes paid by truck owners approached $8 billion in 1976. California alone collected nearly $700 million for highway users revenues.

This was a record year with total truck sales soaring to 3,181,254 units. Of that total, 7 percent were imported trucks.

Total production for 1976: 299,703 trucks and buses.

1977

Rising Energy Prices Fuel Inflation

The truck industry continued to concentrate on fuel economy and grappled with meeting mandatory vehicle safety standards. The search for lighter materials, more economical engines, more fuel-efficient performance was increasingly difficult with spiraling inflation. In addition, the worst winter weather in 100 years played havoc with schedules and created greater fuel shortages.

Truck theft rate continued to be one of the more serious problems facing the industry. High-crime areas were reported on Connecticut, New Jersey, New York, and Pennsylvania highways.

AM General received a contract for tactical vehicles to be supplied to marines, air force, and four foreign countries. Value of the contract totaled $29 million.

Autocar Division of White developed a front tandem axle construction truck.

Brockway entered the glider kit field. Glider kit models included frame, cab, hood and front fenders, radiator, front axles and brakes. **GM** introduced its first factory-built glider kit in the Astro 95, 54, and 86-inch BBC models.

Dodge added standard and optional luxury items for all models and design changes in the medium line. Light-duty models offered new exterior trim options, new exterior colors, and dress-up packages.

Dodge Warlock pickup trucks used oak sideboards on the pickup bed. The sideboards were preserved with a water-repellent substance and clear urethane finish.

Ford light-duty trucks emphasized fuel economy and increased use of precoated steel and plastics. The Ranchero featured passenger car styling, electronic ignition, and choice of three V-8 engines. The F series featured longer lubrication intervals, plastic fender shields above the tires, and heavier duty engines.

Econoline Van and Club Wagon offered a 2.75 to 1 rear-axle ratio with a wide ratio 3-speed manual transmission with the standard 6-cylinder 300-cubic inch engine.

The Courier was built by Toyo Kogyo for Ford and featured a longer and wider cab and a 5-speed overdrive manual transmission.

GMC introduced a 26-foot Kingsley motor home.

International introduced the S series, with seven basic models in the line.

International introduced a COF 5370 truck, a special purpose model using a Cargostar cab on a Paystar chassis with a high-strength steel heavy-duty frame. The unit was powered by a Cummins NTC-250 diesel.

Mack Trucks announced that Solargen Electronics Limited signed a letter of intent to purchase Brockway. However, it was disclosed later that negotiations with Solargen had failed and Mack would liquidate Brockway Division after 65 years of operation.

Road Boss 2 by White Motor featured a truck air center (TAC) module and a truck electrical center (TEC) module for centralized diagnostic tests on both systems. The TEC module was mounted on a sliding track inside the cab and centralized electrical circuits in three plug-in connectors. The TAC system was mounted directly under the cab and centralized all air-system components. Both units could be connected to an off-board mini-computer and tests of the systems completed in minutes.

The Volvo F-86 tractor was powered by two 205-horsepower diesels with an 8-speed range transmission.

Volvo introduced a new medium-duty model to the American market. The model F-613 was designed for intercity delivery. The F-613 was powered by the TD 60 Volvo diesel engine.

Toyota of the United States introduced an SR-5 sports pickup to its line of imports bringing the number of pickup models to five.

Fan clutches were offered by Motor Components Division, Facet Enterprises and Harton Industries for Cummins engines.

Caterpillar announced a 200-horsepower midrange diesel, which used exhaust gas recirculation to divert part of the exhaust gas back into the intake manifold at low engine load. The result was low emission levels capable of meeting California's 1977 regulations.

Detroit Diesel reported that oil changes for intercity highway trucks and buses could be extended to 100,000-mile intervals if the lubricant and fuel oils were those recommended for Detroit Diesel. The extension of the interval applied to the 53, 71, and 92 series engines. The company also announced that warranties on the 71 and 92 series engines were extended to 200,000 miles.

Continental Trailways invested $2 million in Eagle International in Texas to help restructure the company and to assure a continuation of Silver Eagle buses to Trailways.

Strick Corporation introduced a "cab-under" prototype model in which the tractor fitted under the trailer.

Duplex Truck became a division of the Nolan Company, purchaser of Warner and Swasey Company.

A dump conversion for pickup trucks was developed by Uni Corporation in Dallas. Called the Uni-Hoist, the conversion was a bolt-on design and featured electric-hydraulic operation.

Contractor Cargo of California transported the 153-foot long Earth Orbiter model spacecraft 36 miles. The weight of the load was 220,000 pounds.

Airstream announced a delivery van, the A/Van, an all-aluminum multistop truck built on Chevrolet, Ford, GMC, or IHC chassis.

Fruehauf developed a new trailer, the "Mighty Mouse" featuring the largest rear cargo door-opening in the industry and an all-riveted sealed roof assembly.

A radar detector with visual and audible signals was offered by Applied Marketing Corporation of Ann Arbor, Michigan. The device which was mounted on the front panel plugged into the vehicle's cigarette lighter.

Ohio Body Company introduced its open-top trailer of fiberglass-reinforced plastic. The color-impregnated body did not require painting and provided smooth interior and exterior walls.

New flexible cooling fans were also offered by a number of manufacturers. Flex-a-lite Corporation offered two stainless steel models with flexible changing axle blades and Fan Clutch Incorporated offered five and seven blade flexible fans.

The Motor Vehicle Manufacturers Association announced that Paccar, Incorporated, makers of Peterbilt and Kenworth, had become a member of the association.

Federal taxes on all highway vehicles were reported to be 4 cents per gallon on fuel, 10 cents per pound on tires and tubes, and 6 cents per gallon on lubricating oil.

Gerard Incorporated introduced a wrecker truck with dual hydraulically actuated booms which swiveled on the take-up pulley to balance the load.

Hemco Corporation offered fiberglass fenders for tandem truck axles. The 26-inch wide fenders featured wide side flanges to reduce spray.

Visual display signs were located on Interstate 90 at intervals of 78 miles to inform truckers and motorists traveling over Snogualmie Pass in Washington when chains or traction devices were needed.

The Presidential Medal of Honor was awarded to a civilian for only the fourth time in history. Armand E. Aubin, Jr., of Providence, Rhode Island, a Sun Oil truck driver, was cited for rescuing a fellow driver from a burning tractor-tank trailer. Aubin waded through a 2-inch pool of burning asphalt to rescue the driver.

Farr Company introduced a light-weight disposable air cleaner.

On May 19, 1977, the United States Transportation Department required all local transit agencies, using federal funds, to purchase the Transbus (the DOT $27 million bus developed over six years and featuring a low-floor, large-doors, and a low ramp for wheelchair entry) after September 30, 1979.

Exotic super materials, carbon or graphite fibers used to reinforce plastic, were under development. The advanced composites were claimed to be extremely strong, light, and corrosion proof.

International Harvester introduced the 2200, 2500, and 2600 S-series models.

In 1977 there were three times as many private fleets with over 1,000 vehicles as there were common carriers. Of the total 18,388,000 light trucks in use, about 6.5 million were used as recreational vehicles.

At the first International Electric Vehicle Exposition and Congress held at Chicago's McCormick Place in April, there were over 100 exhibitors, indicating the renewed emphasis placed on electric vehicles and components.

An electric retarder brake for gas and diesel vehicles was developed by Jacobs Manufacturing Company.

Bendix announced a "second generation" antiskid brake system.

The system was based on a new controller (electronic) and modulator (mechanical).

The National Highway Traffic Safety Administration was urged by a Senate Consumer Committee to develop standards to prevent underride in rear-end collisions.

Kelsey-Hayes introduced air-operated disc brakes for heavy-duty applications.

Bendix introduced an air-operated fan clutch.

Rovac Corporation developed an air-conditioning system using a closed loop rotary air circulator rather than a freon or other fluorocarbon compressor.

Kenworth offered a high-roof option called the Aerodyne which offered increased headroom to 6 feet 10 inches. It also served as a built-in wind deflector.

White Motor Corporation sold its Hercules operation to a private company and Euclid, Incorporated, to Daimler Benz, AG of West Germany.

On December 7, the U.S. marketing agreement covering White Freightliner trucks terminated and the U.S. White Motor organization no longer offered that nameplate.

The increase in truck sales continued and soared to 3,675,439. That figure included import truck sales, 8.8 percent of the market. *Total production in 1977 topped the 3 million mark: 3,489,128 trucks and buses.*

1978

Truck Sales Soar above 4 Million—
Fuel Savings Still Challenge Industry

In 1978, while fuel savings dominated the truck industry's interests, new sales soared, setting records in all truck categories.

One in four new motor vehicles sold in the nation was a truck. Motor Vehicle Manufacturers Association said the increase in truck sales reflected a prosperous national economy, with trucks—from light delivery vans to heavy-duty freight haulers—serving the needs of business, industry, and individuals.

Light trucks under 14,000 gross vehicle weight became popular in recreation as well as work and accounted for more than 90 percent of the truck market, totaling sales of 3.5 million units.

Four-wheel-drive trucks were the fastest growing segment of the light truck market. Sales reached nearly 1 million units, a 150 percent increase since 1974 when just over 396,600 were sold.

Suburban growth was an important factor in heavy-duty truck demand, particularly in areas not served by rail. Sales of heavy-duty trucks also set a record in 1978 with more than 201,000 units sold.

The ambitious totally voluntary 5-year program of 1973 climaxed in successfully saving 1.5 billion gallons of fuel in the "greatest domestic challenge our nation will face in our lifetime." More than 200 trucking organizations and governmental agencies had joined the United States Department of Transportation (DOT) in a Voluntary Truck and Bus Economy Improvement Program during the past five years.

President of the Motor Vehicle Manufacturers Association, V. James Adduci, cited five widely accepted fuel-saving options that heavy-truck and bus manufacturers voluntarily researched, developed, and aggressively marketed since 1973 to achieve the voluntary fuel savings: *Variable fan drives* which disconnected the cooling fans of large trucks—the fan being needed only 5 percent of the time—saving more than 380 million gallons of fuel; *high-efficiency diesels* which provided high-torque, low-speed turbocharged diesels on new heavy-duty trucks—saving over 699 million gallons of fuel; *small diesel engines* instead of gasoline engines—diesel used 35 percent less fuel—saving 100 million gallons of fuel; *aerodynamic drag-reducing devices* on truck cab roofs—saving more than 83 million gallons of fuel; and *radial ply tires*—saving nearly 201 million gallons of fuel.

MVMA also stated that truck manufacturers voluntarily increased ongoing research and developmental programs, searching for new breakthroughs in fuel economy. The key improvements which added to fuel savings were: Redesigned drive-lines which consumed less fuel in transmitting power from engine to wheels; wheels and bearings modified to reduce friction; new "slippery" lubricants which reduced maintenance frequency and friction; and new truck designs which reduced wind drag over the entire vehicle.

Transportation Secretary Brock Adams complimented the truck industry for its fuel savings and stated that if the current trend continued in the industry, the fuel savings would amount to 18 billion gallons by 1990—an amount equivalent to that used by all trucks in the United States during 1975 alone.

Some companies established driver training programs to be fuel-economy minded and reported early success.

The dramatic voluntary fuel savings were overshadowed by inadequate "lead time" needed to meet future fuel economy standards as mandated by the National Highway Traffic Safety Administration.

The stringent fuel-economy standards for 1980–81 models were potentially dangerous to the national economy. MVMA cautioned that inadequate time to develop ways of meeting the mandated standards *could cost jobs, hurt the economy and consumer choices, and still not provide the added fuel savings sought.*

DOT acknowledged that by the date specified a significant portion of light-duty trucks and vans, both two- and four-wheel drive, could not meet the proposed standards and that reductions in miles per gallons for two- and four-wheel-drive vehicles would be changed to be more favorable for allowing the needed technology to be developed. DOT also acknowledged that it underestimated the retail price hikes and manufacturing costs involved for repowering light-duty trucks and vans to diesel powerplants in order to meet the higher-fuel economy standards by the date DOT specified.

DOT doubled the maximum allowable headlight intensity for automobiles and trucks to 150,000 candlepower per vehicle. The new standard would allow the use of halogen headlamps.

The Bureau of Motor Carrier Safety announced that the levels of toxic gases in truck cabs would be studied.

The National Highway Traffic Safety Administration and the Bureau of Motor Carrier Safety jointly issued an "Advance Notice of Proposed Rulemaking," requesting comments on upgrading truck bumper regulations "to prevent the underriding of vehicles," although several standards were already established.

The United States Ninth Circuit Court of Appeals in San Francisco declared antiskid airbrake safety standard FMVSS-121 to be invalid. The controversial regulation was set aside after years of debate.

Michigan imposed a sixteen-hour ban (between 6 A.M. and 10 P.M.) on double-bottom tankers in densely populated areas.

The GMC Brigadier model featured weight-and-fuel savings with a new molded fiberglass tilt cab, newly designed optional Dragfoiler air deflector, larger crossflow radiator, hydraulically controlled variable speed cooling fan, and choice of Cummins, Detroit Diesel, or Caterpillar engines.

Fruehauf developed a fuel-saving nose cone to disperse air over the top and around the sides of trailers for reducing air drag.

Schwitzer Company introduced a viscous fan clutch with a 250,000-mile warranty.

Goodrich heavy-duty disc brakes were installed on thirteen tandem-axle Budd trailers.

White introduced its Autocar Construcktor-2 for on-and-off highway duty. The frame was of the variable drop section with a rail depth of 14 3/4 inches for increased durability. The cab was primed by electro-deposition before painting to prevent rust erosion.

White introduced a redesigned top of the line Western Star, the first cab-over for this nameplate. Mural-type western scenes were painted on introductory models.

Freightliner introduced an on-and-off highway tractor for use in logging. Heavy-duty cab, reinforced radiator, steel suspension cross members with 1/4-inch steel gussets, steel C-channel cross members and other special supports for components were noted. Hendrickson RT or RS suspensions were mandatory.

Chevrolet's rugged medium truck line was available in eleven wheelbases with five engines and fifteen transmission choices.

Ford announced its CL-9000 highway linehaul COE series, designed to be a pace setter in styling, performance, driver comfort, and economy for tough heavy-duty reliability. It culminated seven years of research for innovative development. A 20 percent lower operating cost and reduced maintenance for less downtime was achieved, plus improved component accessibility, sealed lub-for-life front spring batteries, simplified electrical and coolant systems, and multispeed transmissions.

Leisure Time products reintroduced the Flx Van, formerly built by Flxible Southern. Based on Ford components and marketed through Ford dealers, the van was designed for multistop use and featured full-width opening side doors, roll-up rear door, paneled and insulated cargo area, and pedestal tilt seat.

Kenworth introduced a low-cab-forward model 700 with a cab step-plate and foot-wiper bar only 22 inches from the ground.

Mack introduced a new generation of cab-over-engine models, series MC for city delivery and MR for construction and refuse purposes.

Mercedes Benz of North America introduced an L1418 model in the 32,800-pound range which featured a five-cylinder diesel engine, five-speed synchronized transmission, air-assisted hydraulic brakes, and a driver's seat adjustable fore and aft and side to side.

The Peterbilt low-cab-forward model 310 also featured fiberglass and aluminum cab construction and heavy-duty alloy steel frame and cross members which were custom drilled.

A special cargo truck developed by Sky Chefs for meal catering featured the same rear and front design and was powered by a Detroit Diesel, mounted amidships and driving the rear axle.

White designed a prototype in its Road Boss 2 model with a 7- by 3-foot bunk area built integrally in a cab with a BBC of 151 inches.

The Cam-Master "Q" brake by Rockwell could be disassembled and reassembled by hand without tools.

The International S-series replaced the Loadstar line in the medium-duty range. Standardization cut the total number of parts in the series by 30 percent and allowed most of the parts in the twenty-one models offered to be interchanged.

Detroit Diesel developed a Flexi-Spec engine which could be set to the operator's specific requirements, and then changed by the dealer to meet new conditions.

Industrial Turbines International (ITI), a partnership set up by Mack Trucks, Garrett Corporation, and Klocher Humboldt-Deutz developed the GT-601 recuperated cycle, free-power turbine engine.

The Magirus diesel medium-duty truck was introduced to the American market by IVECO Trucks of North America. Four models were offered and equipped with Fiat diesels. The IVECO Corporation was a holding company of Fiat, Lancia, OM, Unic, and Magirus-Deutz.

Rockwell announced a center-point front-steering axle design and a trailer axle.

A wiper for truck mirrors was offered by Farbyn Industries in California. Called Airwipe, the device blew air across the outside mirror to remove water in two or three seconds.

Digital displays for instrument panels were built with flashing lights that automatically actuated at danger levels. The gauges were offered by Precision Digital Gauges.

The first Diamond Reo Giant truck rolled off the Osterlund Incorporated production line in Harrisburg, Pennsylvania.

1978 An AM General articulated transit bus.

1978 This high profile Freightliner tilt-cab model was designated the Powerliner. The range of 350 to 600 horsepower provided ample power for specialized hauling.

1978 Oshkosh forward placement concrete carrier can pour mixed concrete directly into framed construction forms.

1978   White Road Boss 2 was used in the successful fuel-efficiency test sponsored by DOT and SAE.

1978   Ford CL-9000 cab-over linehaul diesel truck offering advanced engineering concepts for control, fuel-efficiency, driver comforts, and conveniences.

1979 Kenworth Aerodyne cab-over model with raised rear cab section for more headroom and for use as an aerodynamic airshield to maximize fuel efficiency.

1979 In only one minute International F-5070 Paystar 6 × 6 can load five stacks of hay weighing a total of 30,000 pounds.

1979 Chevrolet Bison with diesel engine for heavy work featured lightweight aluminum cab and fiberglass sheet-molded compound construction.

1979 Peterbilt and similar big rigs aptly demonstrated their power and flexibility in the growth and revitalization of America's cities.

1979   This special vehicle designed by Walters Motors not only removes snow from northern highways, but also services airport runways to keep the transportation system running in winter months.

1979   Duplex fire-service truck provided a 7 × 11 foot four-door cab capable of seating seven. The versatile model could serve as a rescue vehicle, pumper, or mobile command unit.

1979   GMC Vandura van can be fitted with a wide range of traveling or camping equipment.

1979   Ford Econoline van with trendsetting "youth options."

1979   Ford Bronco with 4-wheel drive.

DuPont introduced metallic colors to its line of IMRON hard-glass polyurethane enamels, giving an extremely durable wet look for truck-trailer bodies.

The Regular Common Carrier Conference and ATA Services Incorporated developed a new computerized system to match carriers and loads through a computer terminal. The system was designated as the Computer Interchange Substituted Service (CISS).

American Motors Corporation, despite success in the transit bus market, announced that its AM General subsidiary would suspend transit bus production because of governmental delays and indecisions concerning standards and regulations.

Grumman Buses of California used Dodge components in their twelve-passenger airporter bus with single seats along each side at a 45-degree angle.

Grumman acquired Flxible Company from Rohr Industries.

Freightliner Corporation and the Nolan Company manufacturers of heavy-duty and custom truck chassis joined the Motor Vehicle Manufacturers Association.

Metro-Transit Company announced a sixteen-passenger prototype bus with air conditioning, automatic transmission, electromagnetic retarder brake, and hydraulically powered steplift ramp.

Wayne Corporation introduced the Lifeguard schoolbus constructed of full-length panels, heavier steel structural material and frame. The bus met or exceeded all federal requirements.

Greyhound introduced a small transit bus called the "Citycruiser" which was 30 feet long and seated thirty-two passengers. A Detroit Diesel 6-cylinder engine powered the new model.

Trailways installed a movie screen in its Golden Eagle bus for the Los Angeles to San Diego run.

The United States Defense Department ordered 10,820 vehicles from five firms of the Federal Republic of Germany. The value of the order was estimated at $120 million. The Pentagon stated that the life-cycle cost of the vehicles was cheaper from Germany.

Total production for trucks and buses for 1978 was 4,110,335.

1979

Deregulation Becomes National Issue

The record-setting truck sales upsurge of 1978 brought momentum and optimism to 1979.

This year's models were more fuel efficient, met strict safety and emission standards, and still performed the diverse transportation demands of the American consumer.

Travel-loving Americans demonstrated a strong desire for the mobility provided by recreational vehicles which allowed vacationers to travel at their own pace, while "staying in their own place." As a result, recreational vehicles evidenced spectacular growth.

Continuing pressures from governmental regulations was a major concern for manufacturers, making these the most challenging as well as difficult times in the industry's history.

The emphasis on reduced weight became the most important key to fuel economy. The rule-of-thumb proved that there was a gain of one mile-per-gallon in fuel economy for every 400 pounds removed from a vehicle.

Aluminum, plastics, high-strength steel, thinner glass, and composite materials were being combined with new engineering designs for vehicle weight reduction.

For 1979, several manufacturers offered fuel-saving diesel engines as options in their light trucks. Many announced extensive weight-reduction programs for future models.

Light-duty trucks met fuel-economy standards for the first time.

Heavy-duty truck manufacturers accelerated fuel-saving improvements through aerodynamic spoilers, more fuel-efficient diesels, variable fan drives, and radial tires.

A Federal Energy Administration study showed that proper regulation of traffic lights to smooth traffic flow would mean significant fuel savings. Computer-controlled systems could adjust the lights to accommodate the varying traffic flow.

Deregulation was a major topic of conversation throughout the truck industry in 1979. Deregulation involved removal of shipping rates and services, route limitations, commodity limitations, and other commerce controls.

The Carter administration continued to emphasize its belief that deregulation was in the best interest of the nation and also contributory to combating inflation. President Carter indicated that either full or partial deregulation was under consideration.

Truck fuel-saving options and the 55 mile-per-hour speed limit continued to benefit the energy crisis and assumed even greater significance with the cessation of oil imports from Iran.

The 55-mph speed limit came under fire in the western states, particularly in Wyoming where legislation was proposed to return to the 65 miles-per-hour limit.

International Harvester introduced its new fuel-economy 9-liter V-8 diesel engines, designed for its S-series medium-duty trucks, school bus chassis, and Cargostar models.

Chevrolet's new tough linehauler, called the Pappa Bear Bruin, offered five series of diesel engines with quick response to power demands.

Dodge introduced its efficiency-size pickup designed for sporty performance in play or work.

Duplex offered a four-door cab on its fire truck pumper chassis. The seating could be arranged to handle seven persons.

Ford offered three luxurious cab types on its tough pickup trucks: the Regular Cab with full width front seat, the Super Cab with full width front and optional bench, and the Crew Cab, a four-door pickup which could seat six. A new deluxe Ranger series included the Lariat, the ultimate in style and prestige, and the XLT luxury models.

GMC Astro "SS" highway-hauler package included an assortment of engineering innovations with fuel efficiency high on the list.

Ford received an order for 700 CL-9000 cab-over trucks—the largest single linehaul diesel truck order in its history—with an option for an additional 150 units in 1980. The order totaled $40 million and was placed by East Texas Motor Freight of Dallas.

Kenworth introduced the Aerodyne 86, featuring Airglide suspension, Hi-Rise aerodynamic cab with dual-sleeper bunks, tinted Vista windows, air-sliding fifth wheel, and polished aluminum wheels.

Mack and GMC built prototype trucks for United Parcel Service which met 75 db (A) noise levels.

Mercedes-Benz reported that a new truck assembly plant was under construction in Hampton, Virginia. Production was to begin in 1980 with a first-year goal of 4,000 units.

An extruded aluminum interlocking panel trailer was announced by International Truck Body Company. The panels offered greater strength and durability plus the advantage of easy replacement.

Freightliner agreed to market Volvo diesel trucks in America.

Heil Company developed a hydraulic cylinder, using an inertia welding technique that eliminated costly foundry procedures, yet retained quality and strength.

Federal-Mogul developed two new engine bearing alloys: A-250, an aluminum alloy, and H-166, a copper-lead alloy. Both were specifically designed for heavy-duty engines.

A vehicle speed limiter (VSL) was developed by Lemar Industries. The system reduced fuel flow automatically to maintain pre-set speeds.

An aluminum truck trailer with steel-flanged wheels and standard rubber-tired wheels was developed by Bi-Modal Corporation in Connecticut. The concept would provide for trailer transport on highways or on rails without the need for flat cars.

In late April, General Motors informed the secretary of transportation that it would withdraw from the federal Transbus Program. GM was the last of three companies involved in building transbuses. Flxible Division of Grumman Corporation withdrew from the program in March and AM General Corporation in June, 1978.

White introduced the new Air Brake Proportioning (ABP) system which automatically balanced the air input of the brakes either in loaded or trailerless situations. The system allowed for greater stability and control in normal and panic stop situations, and could meet the stringent stopping distance initially required by FMVSS 121 without the complexity of electronics. Ease of maintenance and low cost were also cited.

Pioneers

The brief biographical sketches of the motor truck pioneers cited are a small representation of the numerous pioneers who inspired, nurtured, and refined an emerging industry which has become a vital and integral part of our everyday lives.

Many automotive giants have been associated with the truck industry at one time or another. They, too, could stand among the pioneers in trucking. Dynamic pioneers such as Duryea, Olds, Dodge, Buick, Chrysler, Leland, Kettering, Franklin, Durant, Chevrolet, Bendix, Briscoe, Studebaker, the Fisher brothers, the Stanley brothers are but a few. Their stories are told in a companion volume, *Automobiles of America* (published by Wayne State University Press).

Motor Trucks of America presents the highlights of truck pioneers. Their efforts made possible the growth of the motor truck industry as we know it today.

BUDD, EDWARD GOWEN (1870–1946)
Innovator of Steel Technologies for Trucks and Wheels
Born in the iron center of Smyrna, Delaware, Budd was apprenticed at an early age as a machinist with Smyrna Iron Works. His arrival on the industrial scene was at a time when iron in America was being replaced by steel.

Demand for essentials like wheel barrows, shovels, wheel hubs, and numerous metal forms for the railroad industry provided the stage for the young Budd. He was first employed in 1890 by the American Pulley Company to produce pressed steel pulleys, and subsequently worked for Hale and Kilburn in 1902, developing steel replacement parts for the Pullman Company.

Budd quickly assumed management of Hale and Kilburn. However, when the firm was sold, he resigned and opened his own firm in 1912, the Budd Manufacturing Company in Philadelphia. His company produced truck bodies and also built a coal truck for a local business. He pioneered the construction of elaborate jigs and methods of fusing and shaping metals.

In 1912, working with Emil Nelson of Hupmobile, Budd devised a means of forming and welding panels to desired shapes for an all-steel passenger-car body. That same year the Budd Company received its first order for a Buick body. After tooling for an order of 2,000 Oakland bodies, Oakland went into receivership, and as a result, Budd's Detroit property was closed in late 1913. The Philadelphia factory, however, remained operational with truck body orders from Packard and Peerless.

In 1916, Budd formed the Budd Wheel Corporation, producing the steel-disc wheel which replaced the wooden wheel. From 1916 to 1923, he modified the steel-disc wheel for vehicular use. He introduced stainless steel into his lines to minimize rusting, initially in stainless streamlined trains, but eventually into trucks as well.

In 1946, Edward Gowen Budd died at the age of 76. The company became the Budd Corporation, a name which lives on as a major automotive supplier. His staffs were proud of being with Budd.

CHRISTIE, JOHN WALTER (1886–1944)
First Active Proponent for Front-Wheel Drive

A brilliant engineer and the first active builder of a front-wheel drive in America, John Walter Christie's numerous ventures in front-drive race cars, taxicabs, and passenger cars proved the soundness of his engineering concepts and made him a favorite with the automotive press.

As early as 1909, he conceived the idea of a front-drive tractor. From 1911 to 1916, his endeavors climaxed into successful front-drive tractor-conversion units for fire equipment companies. More than 600 tractor-conversion units driven by 90-horsepower gasoline engines were built for New York's fire department by Christie's Front Drive Motor Company in Hoboken, New Jersey. It updated and motorized New York's out-dated horse-drawn pumpers and ladder wagons. The fame of Christie's innovative achievements in New York was quickly recognized in cities around the world.

During World War I, Christie was recruited by the War Department where his engineering genius was directed toward developing rugged armoured tanks and vehicles. He became the world's foremost expert builder of tanks. His innovative designs were known the world over. In World War II, he again played a dominant role in tank construction.

CLARKE, LOUIS S. (1867–1975)
Father of Autocar Trucks and Automobiles

In 1908 after 10 years of innovative experimentation and manufacturing of passenger cars, Louis Clarke turned exclusively to manufacturing commercial vehicles.

Twelve years earlier, Clarke introduced America to its first shaft-driven vehicle with the production of his motorized three-wheeler. Its success led to the production of a four-wheel passenger car in 1897 with the establishment of the Pittsburgh Motor Vehicle Company—the fulfillment of Clarke's dream since 1890. The company's name was changed to the Autocar Company in 1899, and its capitalization was increased from $30,000 to $1,000,000.

Other hand-made innovations credited to Clarke were porcelain spark plugs, the first circulating oil lubrication system, a double-reduction gear axle drive, and the disc-type clutch. Consistently far ahead of his time, and contrary to the trend of that era, Clarke advocated left-hand drive, believing that it would better road vision.

In 1907, he introduced his first truck, Model XVII, a two tonner. It was an immediate success; one of the most efficient of the period. It was noted for its high maneuverability, light-weight but rugged construction, and economy of operation requiring a minimum of maintenance.

From 1908 to 1920, over 30,000 two-cylinder XXI models were built, featuring a 97-inch short wheel-base and the engine mounted under the driver's seat. Again ahead of his time, Clarke devised a novel arrangement of hinging the driver's seat so it swung out of the way to make the engine accessible for repairs.

As engine lines and truck capacities increased over the years, Clarke's short wheelbase Autocar trucks survived with almost exclusive markets. Whereas the start of worldwide-trade interests in 1929 brought an end to many truck manufacturers, world trade merely heightened a constant flow of forward progress for Autocar Trucks.

Prophetically, in succeeding years as more and more states placed restrictions on overall lengths and widths on trucks, the Louis Clarke concept of cab-over-engine soon dominated the modern commercial vehicles.

Eventually Autocar became a division of the White Motor Corporation, offering a wide range of vehicles.

CUMMINS, CLESSIE L. (1888–1968)
Engineered Diesel Power into American Trucks and Buses
A staunch supporter of the diesel engine for American transportation, Clessie Cummins developed, roadtested, and demonstrated the first high-speed, light-weight diesel-engine vehicles in the early 1930s.

The diesel engine is credited with revolutionizing the highway-transportation industry by adapting the cumbersome marine diesel engine for truck use. Cummins demonstrated the automotive capabilities of diesel by installing a 4-cylinder marine diesel engine in a Packard automobile chassis in 1930 and driving it from Indianapolis to New York. In 1931, one of Cummins diesel-powered trucks was driven from New York to Los Angeles.

Cummins founded the Cummins Engine Company in 1931, the largest manufacturer of diesel engines in the United States. He served as its president and chairman of the board until 1956.

Cummins's confidence and belief in diesel engines as the future power source for commercial vehicles is clearly evident today, as almost all heavy-duty trucks use diesel engines.

The name Cummins is synonymous with diesel engines in America. He spearheaded the use of the revolutionary power concept invented by Rudolph Diesel in 1897.

DANA, CHARLES A. (1881–1975)
Developed an International Industrial Giant
Born into a New England family which traced its forebearers to the Revolutionary War and included famous financiers, authors, and politicians, Charles Dana added several more distinctions to the

family name, those of renowned industrialist and philanthropist.

Charles Dana graduated from Columbia University with a master's degree in international law. Within five years after graduation, he assumed the presidency of two water companies, served as a legislator in New York state, and gained stature as a corporation lawyer.

In 1914, he purchased controlling interest in the Spicer Universal Joint Manufacturing Company which was in serious financial difficulty. A short time later, the foundation for an industrial empire was set and Charles Dana began adding companies and products to the Spicer organization to meet a growing industry's needs.

Spicer Manufacturing Company in 1946 officially changed its name to the Dana Corporation, thus honoring the man who had recognized the need for Spicer products and developed the company into an international industrial giant.

FAGEOL, FRANK AND W. B.
Originators of Wide Tread, Trendsetter Safety Coach Buses

Early pioneers in the automotive field, the Fageol brothers built their first gasoline-driven automobile in Iowa in 1899. Although successful in the automotive field, the designing and engineering talents of the brothers were most evident in bus transportation.

In 1921, the twin brothers designed what was probably the first bus built specifically for rural and intercity service. The Fageol Safety Coach with its unique low center-of-gravity construction, full-height doors, and worm axle was a trendsetter in the industry. Many manufacturers adopted its design. The coach was a distinct change from prior buses which used a truck chassis upon which was added a passenger bus body. The Fageol Safety Coach was an immediate success. It marked the real beginning of the intercity motor coach industry as we know it today.

In 1923, the Fageol Company moved to Kent, Ohio, where the company was sold in 1926 to American Car and Foundry.

In 1927, Frank Fageol designed and built two models under a new company name, Twin Coach. The numerous innovative bus developments, such as riding comfort, smooth engine performance, economical operation, and safety emphasis, justify Frank Fageol's designation as "the father of the modern bus industry."

FORD, HENRY (1863–1947)
A Giant in Transportation History

Decades ahead of his time, Henry Ford even as a youngster recognized how important trucks and tractors could be to farmers in saving time and getting farm products to market more quickly. He constantly dreamed of "ways to take the work off men's backs and lay it on steel and motor... so as to lighten the chores of farming... that men might have time for a better life." Even when there were no roads, Ford envisioned trucks moving farm products between cities over highways around the world. "It was an era of change for the country and from early youth Henry was determined to be right in the middle of it," his sister said.

A farm boy who loved to tinker with moving parts and who at an early age developed "a surgeon's touch" with machinery, Ford constructed a steam engine when he was only fifteen. At age sixteen he worked at various jobs from watch to engine repairing, and eventually he became chief engineer for the Edison Illuminating Company in Detroit.

In 1893, Ford worked on a 2-cycle gasoline engine, testing it on the kitchen sink. By 1896, he built his own quadricycle.

Henry Ford II, stated that his grandfather "believed so deeply in the utility truck, that the first vehicle he built for sale was a panel delivery truck. That was in 1900, three years before the Ford Motor Company was founded." The sale of that delivery truck was the beginning of a dream to manufacture utility trucks. That dream became reality, as almost 22 million trucks have been manufactured with the world-famous Ford signature through 1978, its seventy-fifth anniversary.

Ford wanted the benefits available to all people not merely to a luxuried few; but policy conflicts to create low-price vehicles brought his first company to a halt in 1900. In 1901, undaunted in his dream to build at a low price "a better car the public could afford," Ford began forming another company. Incorporation papers for The Ford Motor Company were filed June, 1903. One month later, Ford's first Model-A was sold for $850. Sales shot up within a month, and his company was on its way.

Today, Henry Ford's pioneering achievements are legend: the moving assembly line, $5-a-day wage, 8-hour work day, 40-hour week, profit sharing, and rebate plans were each revolutionary in their day. Those concepts have literally changed the world. Although most of Ford's fame is in automobiles, he has also achieved many milestones in trucks:

In 1904, Ford's first regularly produced delivery wagon, the Model E, was announced and produced until 1911.

In 1908, Ford designed his famous Model-T which saw extensive duty as a commercial vehicle and power source on farms.

By 1914, trucks from the Ford Model-T chassis were built by numerous truck manufacturers.

By 1916, Ford designed his first Fordson truck, a 1-ton vehicle, featuring a stronger frame, 2-foot greater wheelbase, a rugged worm drive, selling less than $600. It was efficiency at a reasonable price. The Fordson was introduced in 1917.

In 1916, tractor-making was to a large extent hand tailored. Ford foresaw beyond this expensive process and focused on mass producing for a low price.

In 1927, Ford launched a 1 1/2-ton truck.

In 1927, Ford added a 2-ton truck besides the 2 1/2 ton, both models featuring now a V-8 plant with 60–85 horsepower.

By 1935, Ford had produced 3 million trucks.

During World War II, Ford increased truck power to 95 horsepower and built the 1/4-ton reconnaissance trucks, including an amphibious version, followed by a 3-ton payload with 145 horsepower after the war.

From the beginning Ford was a leader in training dealers in accounting and the significance of profits and banking. Ford dealers usually led the way in small communities.

Few realize that Ford never collected royalties on any patent he held, despite an impressive, distinguished record of pioneering with innovations that are still used worldwide.

Henry Ford was active in management of the Ford Motor Company until 1945 when his grandson, Henry Ford II, was named president. Henry Ford II, as dynamic as his grandfather, began a new era of great Ford leadership.

FRUEHAUF, AUGUST C. (1868–1930)
From Horseshoer to World's Leading Trailer Manufacturer

In 1903, a blacksmith shop was opened at 1384 Gratiot Avenue in Detroit, Michigan. The masthead of that enterprising firm read "August C. Fruehauf, Practical Horseshoer." Within a decade, the firm moved across the street to new and larger quarters, and the sign was changed to read "August C. Fruehauf, Manufacturer of Trucks and Wagons."

In 1914, the thriving truck manufacturer was contacted by Frederick Sibley, a Detroit lumberman, to build a wagon for hauling a boat. The wagon was to be attached to Sibley's Model-T Ford Roadster. The result was the first Fruehauf semitrailer. It was a two-wheeler which used a pole for the tongue and also the brake. Subsequent trailers were bought by the Sibley Lumber Company, and by 1916, the Fruehauf Company had become renowned for building platform trailers.

Always innovative and a staunch believer in quality and craftsmanship, August Fruehauf introduced a number of important trailer developments, such as the automatic semitrailer, the refrigerated trailer, and drop frame tank semitrailer for hauling gasoline and oil.

August Fruehauf served as president and chairman of the board of directors for his company. His brother, Roy Fruehauf, a cofounder, was a former chairman of the board. In 1929, August passed the presidency on to his son Harvey Fruehauf.

August C. Fruehauf died the following year in Grosse Pointe Park, Michigan, knowing that his fledgling blacksmith enterprise had become one of the world's leading trailer manufacturers.

GRABOWSKY, MAX (1874–1946)
Early Detroit Pioneer of Gasoline Trucks

One of Detroit's earliest truck pioneers, Max Grabowsky experimented with motor trucks in his small machine shop at Woodward and Winder streets just before the end of the century.

In 1900, he sold his first truck to Detroit's American Garment Cleaning Company. That 1-cylinder model with the engine placed horizontally and the rear-wheel driven by chains was among the first gasoline-powered delivery trucks on Detroit streets. Other models, equipped with double opposed gasoline engines, followed quickly.

Under the guidance of Grabowsky, Rapid Motor Vehicle Company was formed in 1902. Approximately seventy-five trucks were built in the next three years. In 1904, the company incorporated. Needing more space, a factory was built in Pontiac, Michigan, supposedly the first plant in the country built exclusively for the manufacture of gasoline motor trucks. It offered twenty types of commercial vehicles.

In 1909, Rapid Motor Vehicle Company joined General Motors and was later merged with the Reliance Motor Truck Company. From that consolidation came the GMC truck. After the sale of his Rapid Motor Company, Max Grabowsky continued to build trucks under his own name.

GRAHAM, RAY A. (1887–1932), ROBERT C. (1885–1967), and JOSEPH B. (1883–1971)
A Triumvirate Teamed to Build Trucks and Buses

In 1900, with machines invented by Joseph Graham, the Graham brothers teamed up to manufacture glass in Indiana. The Graham Glass Company successfully manufactured bottles and was merged with the Owens Bottle Company of Toledo, Ohio. In 1916, it became Libby-Owens and Ray Graham became its president.

Ray, while managing a 5,000-acre family farm in Indiana, became interested in developing light-weight trucks to expedite farming activities, as well as bottle delivery. Joseph, known as a mechanical genius, and Ray combined their talents to invent a spliced frame rear axle where a Ford chassis could be converted into a truck.

A cab and body were developed, and a factory was acquired in Evansville, Indiana, to build trucks. The brothers sold to Detroit the first 140 buses used to augment trolley service.

In 1916, the Graham Brothers Truck Company built cabs and bodies for Dodge trucks. They entered a contract with the Dodge brothers, John and Horace. Graham Brothers agreed to build trucks and buses under their own nameplate but exclusively used Dodge engines, power plants, transmissions, and parts, and marketed their products only through the Dodge dealer system. Six months later Dodge bought a major interest in Graham Brothers. Shortly after, Dodge acquired the remaining stock.

In 1925, the Graham brothers became managing and manufacturing executives for the Dodge organization in Detroit. Their management of Dodge Brothers, Incorporated, lasted until 1927 when they bought and reorganized Paige-Detroit, forming Graham-Paige Motors Corporation. They made an initial investment of $4,000,000 in Graham-Paige, with plans to expend an additional $4,000,000 for improvements, expansion, and development.

HAYNES, FREDERICK J. (1871–1940)
At the Helm of Dodge Brothers' Success
Frederick J. Haynes guided the establishment of Dodge Brothers as one of the most successful and largest automotive companies in the United States.

After working for H. H. Franklin Automobile Company as assistant superintendent, John F. Dodge persuaded Haynes in 1912 to join him and his brother Horace in producing parts for Ford cars.

In late 1914, the three men established Dodge Brothers Automobile Company to manufacture their own cars. They sold over 50,000 models in their first year. Production climbed and success continued in succeeding years. Suddenly, in 1920 John and Horace Dodge died within months of one another, and the board of directors elected Frederick Haynes president and general manager.

In 1926, the company was purchased for $126 million by Dillon Read and Company. Fred Haynes was retained as president.

HEIL, JULIUS P. (1876–1949)
A Pioneer in Tank Truck Construction
In 1901 at age 25, Heil founded the Heil Rail Joint Welding Company in Milwaukee; the name was later changed to the Heil Company. Heil pioneered the development of tank trucks, and trailers, dump bodies and hoists, and a number of highly specialized units for airplane loading, garbage collection, and other heavy tasks. His development of the Hopper Hi-Lift featured an enclosed rear section for hauling coal loads from 4 to 6 tons.

In 1907, Heil built a rivet-constructed tank trailer with a 200-gallon capacity for carrying petroleum. His frameless 5,600-gallon

"Trailerized" petroleum tank featured an all-welded, smooth-skin exterior with the welds ingeniously inside, and typical of all his equipment, designed as an integral unit.

Heil's innovative tandem units centered rocker bearing arms to transmit the load through center bearings, with special torque tube between the axles for brake torque distribution.

Julius Heil served as president and chairman of the board of directors of the Heil Company until 1946 when the presidency was passed on to his son, Joseph Heil.

During his active presidency of the Heil Company, Julius Heil also served as Republican governor of the State of Wisconsin for two terms from 1939 to 1943.

HENDRICKSON, MAGNUS (1864–1944)
Designer of Tandem Axle Suspensions

In 1887, Magnus Hendrickson immigrated from Sweden to Chicago. After detouring for twelve years to Wisconsin and Michigan manufacturing bicycles independently, he returned to Chicago.

He built his first motor truck in 1900. It had wagon-type wooden spoke wheels with steel bands for tires.

In 1902, he built a 1-cylinder passenger car and sold it to a doctor. Every piece was designed and machined by-hand in his own machine shop. The following year, he designed a clutch which is still in use. In the same year he joined J. Lauth to produce by-hand custom-made motor trucks and cars.

In 1906, Hendrickson invented a hollow-spoke steel wheel. Similar hollow-spoke wheels are still in use on most heavy-duty trucks.

For the next six years, from 1907 to 1913, Hendrickson was chief engineer and designer for Lauth-Juergens, the company which first manufactured tilt-cab models in 1911.

Two years later in 1913, Hendrickson with sons George, Carl, and Bob organized the Hendrickson Motor Truck Company of Chicago. The firm prospered in manufacturing custom motor trucks and patented truck hoists.

They supplemented their custom-truck business by designing a tandem axle with an equalizing beam in 1926. The success of that now-famous system provided extra work necessary to maintain their work force despite the crash of 1929.

In 1933, an exclusive contract was signed with International Harvester Tractor to provide tandem suspensions. Hendrickson's product line was expanded to include power dividers and experimental diesel engines. So successful was Hendrickson in supplying the parts to truck manufacturers that two out of every three six-wheel trucks manufactured in America are equipped with Hendrickson's tandem suspensions.

Although Hendrickson's continues to make custom trucks and a complete line of crane carriers, the Tandem Division is a most significant contribution to the trucking industry.

HERRINGTON, ARTHUR W. (1891–1970)
Designed Four-Wheel-Drive Conversion Units
Designer, manufacturer, and automotive engineering authority, Arthur Herrington served as a transport officer in World War I and became determined to design the best off-road vehicles available.

After the war, Herrington became a consulting engineer for several automobile companies and the U.S. marine corps.

Recognizing the need for four-wheel-drive trucks, he designed and manufactured four-wheel-drive conversion. Then he joined Walter Marmon in forming the Marmon-Herrington Company. The company manufactured specialized vehicles based on Herrington's designs.

The combination of Marmon's business talents and Herrington's engineering skills developed the Marmon-Herrington Company into one of the largest truck and specialized-vehicle manufacturers in the world. Herrington was president of the Society of Automotive Engineers in 1942.

HERTZ, JOHN (1880–1961)
Taxi King and Pioneer of Motor-Rental Concepts
Austrian-born John Hertz became America's taxi king in the early days of public transportation in the 1920s. He was also a pioneer of today's rent-a-car, rent-a-truck, and fleet-leasing concepts.

His early innovative employee-benefit programs of free dental, medical, legal, and life insurance services for his employees and their families complemented a 20 percent company-earnings profit-sharing plan. Such concepts provided the most competent workforce possible in the Hertz $100-million empire which included firms such as the Yellow Cab Motor Company, Yellow Truck and Coach Manufacturing Company, Fifth Avenue Coach Company, Chicago Motor Coach Company, and New York Transportation Company.

Hertz was a vital force in public transportation in the 1920s.

JAMES, LELAND (1892–1964)
Founder of Maximum-Payload Freightliner

In 1913, Leland James converted a Packard into a small freight truck. With a team of his own designers in Salt Lake City, Utah, he formed a company to deliver sand and gravel.

As president of his company in 1929, James created the Consolidated Truck lines to fill an unavailable transport need. He offered a versatile all-purpose service, individually designed to the specifications of each shipper: "You pay for it, we'll haul it," whether it be dry freight, liquid tanks, livestock, cartage, or household goods.

Convinced that long-haul service in the West required a new approach, he delivered light-weight trucks to haul larger payloads within legal limits and with greater maximum traction. Daring to risk tooling-and-engineering costs, Leland James established the Freightliner Corporation, a subsidiary to Consolidated Freightways.

In 1939, Freightliner Corporation built its first light-weight high-gross truck tractor and became one of America's leading haulers. Large light trucks were built to high standards, often custom crafted, introducing a wide range of new concepts to the trucking industry.

In 1951, James allied with The White Motor Company in an agreement whereby White would handle sales and service of Freightliners under the name White Freightliner. The agreement lasted until 1977. Today Freightliner builds maximum payload, efficient COE, and conventional trucks plus tractors, designed for highway and long-haul operations.

JEFFERY, THOMAS B. (1845–1910)
Developed the Famous Jeffery Quad

In 1879, Thomas Jeffery began to manufacture bicycles under the tradename "Rambler," the second bicycle manufacturing firm in the United States.

As early as 1891, Jeffery began experimenting with motor vehicles, saying that he "built the same car over and over until 1901 until it came up to his ideal of a machine he could offer to the public." In 1900, he successfully produced a motor vehicle. The same year he sold his bicycle business and purchased a factory in Kenosha, Wisconsin. He began to manufacture G&C cars, later known as Rambler cars, in 1902.

The 1905 Rambler line consisted of eight models with its metal parts produced entirely in the Rambler plant. In his day, Jeffery was one of the strong opponents of the Selden patent.

Jeffery remained president of the company until his death in 1910. Six years later, the Rambler Company was reorganized as the Nash Motor Company where his son, Charles, served in key positions.

In 1913, the Rambler Quad drove, steered, and braked on all four wheels in a 3/4- to 1-ton truck which sold for $1,325. The Rambler Quad had a phenomenal first year record in which 5,578 were produced. In 1914, the name was changed to the Jeffery Quad, available as a 2 tonner and powered by a 21.4 horsepower four-in-line engine.

LaFRANCE, TRUCKSON (d.1895)
Steam Patents Led to Fire Engine Developments

The world-famous name LaFrance has been associated with American fire engine development since the industry's very beginnings.

As American refugees of Huguenot, France, the Hyenveux family settled in Pennsylvania where iron workers had such difficulties in pronouncing the family name that it was changed to LaFrance.

In 1860, Truckson LaFrance worked for the Elmira Union Iron Works where his interest in steam engines led to several patents on rotary steam-engine improvements. With John Visher, he developed a small fire engine business. Local interests in 1873 purchased the operation, and the firm became known as LaFrance

Manufacturing Company. Truckson LaFrance was the chief mechanic of the new organization, and his brother, Asa, joined the firm later as a representative.

Success with the initial rotary steam fire engines and later piston-type engines complemented other fire-apparatus businesses which had been acquired.

Truckson LaFrance died in 1895, and the reigns of the company were taken over by his brother Asa.

In 1903, the LaFrance Manufacturing Company merged with a reorganized International Fire Engine Company. The new organization became the world famous American LaFrance Fire Engine Company.

McCORMICK, CYRUS HALL (1809–1884) and CYRUS H. (1859–1936)

World's Greatest Farm Laborsaver: International Harvester

In less than a century, the McCormicks not only mechanized American agriculture, but also became the major producers of both motor trucks and farm equipment.

In 1831 at age twenty-two in his father's blacksmith shop, Cyrus succeeded in inventing—then demonstrating to a group of skeptical farmers—his reaper, a machine to cut grain in the fields. In half a day, it reaped several acres of grain, as much as four men could cut by-hand in the same time. He constantly improved the reaper. By 1884 it was selling briskly in eight states.

As he traveled, the broad expanse of fertile prairies in western states challenged his imagination until in 1847 Cyrus moved his McCormick Reaper Works from Virginia to Chicago. His brothers joined him to expand production; and he employed men of genius for product development, thus setting the pattern for today's engineering research. This company became the foremost manufacturer of labor-saving food-producing devices of that day.

By 1884, McCormick Reaper Works grew to an output of 54,841 machines, possibly the largest manufacturer in the world. 1884 was also the year of his death. His eldest son Cyrus H. McCormick succeeded him as president. Under his son's management, vigorous company activities and manufacturing continued uninterrupted.

In 1902, a merger occurred between the McCormick Company Deering, Plano, Milwaukee, plus Warder, Bushnell and Glessner, all agricultural equipment manufacturers. Their combined valuation totaled $60 million, enabling research and foreign expansion.

The new organization was called International Harvester (IH). Alert that horse-and-cart agricultural transportation needed updating, IH aimed to keep pace with vehicle developments to suit farmers' needs. The first elected president of International Harvester was Cyrus H. McCormick, son of the inventor of the reaper.

Under Cyrus H. McCormick's product development program in 1893, an engineer installed a gas engine in a wagon chassis and drove it successfully between home and the McCormick factory. From this vehicle in 1905, International Harvester's *Auto-Buggy* was developed. It was fitted with a twin-cylinder air-cooled engine mounted on a high-wheeled chassis.

In 1907, the first International motor truck was built, the Auto Wagon, which was designed for hauling farm produce. In 1910, the name Auto Wagon was changed to International. U.S. army truck requirements in World War I boosted truck production to 92,000 by 1918. Truck production continued to leap as IH concentrated design efforts on powerful lines of heavy-duty trucks.

Employing the newest technological concepts available into a wide variety of dynamic Scout S-series, Transtar and Paystar models, International trucks are built not only in the U.S., but in Australia, Mexico, Canada, Great Britain, New Zealand, South Africa, Uraguay, and the Philippines.

MACK, WILLIAM C. (1859–1953), JOSEPH S. (1871–1953), JOHN M. (1864–1924), AUGUST F. (1873–?), and CHARLES W. (1859–?)

The World's Largest Manufacturers of Rugged Heavy Trucks
The motor truck industry had just begun at the turn of the century when the five Mack brothers joined forces to manufacture sightseeing buses and then heavy-duty motor trucks. John Mack had the mechanical genius, Gus the design talent, while William had a sense for business success, all of which propelled the Mack name into the ranks of America's honored truck pioneers.

In 1893, this trio purchased and reorganized the Falleson Carriage Company. It immediately developed a reputation for quality work, strength, and durability.

Intrigued by motor vehicles, the brothers experimented with steam and electric until Jack experienced his first ride in a Winton touring car where he realized the potential for a gasoline sightseeing bus.

Gus designed the bus similar to a large touring car with rear entrance tonneau to complement an exceptionally strong and well-built chassis with a gasoline-powered 4-cylinder-opposed engine.

Their first commercial vehicle, a 20-passenger bus, rolled out of their wagon shop in Brooklyn in 1900. In 1903, their sightseeing bus, called the Manhattan, was great for trips around Brooklyn's Prospect Park. It was powered by a vertical 4-cylinder L-head gasoline engine which developed 60 horsepower and had a cone clutch and 3-speed transmission.

In 1905, another brother, Joseph, suggested a large factory site in Allentown, Pennsylvania. The inventive minds of Jack and Gus combined with the business acumen of Willie and Joe. In 1906, their first seat-over-engine was launched, a forerunner of the current C.O.E. engine. It featured a 5-ton capacity and 60 horsepower. In 1909, the company branched out into producing fire trucks and hook-and-ladder fire apparatus.

In 1910, Charles finally joined his brothers, the same year in which the name Manhattan was replaced by the Mack trademark, the Bulldog crest.

Mack Brothers Motor Car Company was one of the world's largest manufacturers of heavy-duty trucks by 1911. With Mack Brothers turning out 3 vehicles a day, ranging from 1 to 7 ton, a merger occurred between the Mack Brothers, American Sauer, and Hewitt Motor companies, forming the International Motor Company. Expansion led to another name change to Mack Trucks, Incorporated. Mack acquired Brockway Trucks in 1956; and merged with Signal Companies in 1967.

Throughout the years, the Mack organization has had a profound effect upon the technological progress of the industry. Numerous

Mack engineering developments have become industry "standards." Today, Mack is one of the most highly integrated truck manufacturers in the industry. Because of this, it has attained a high degree of interchangeability which allows production of a wide variety of chassis types.

As a part of the trucking industry, the Mack bulldog symbolizes, the world over, excellent quality, strength, and power in heavy-duty trucks, fire apparatus, and off-highway equipment.

MARTIN, CHARLES (1868–1953)
Inventor of the Rocking Fifth Wheel
Charles Martin entered the automotive industry in 1900 as a motorcycle traveler. In 1901, Martin built a small car for the Springfield Cornice Works which sold 16 additional models.

In 1903 soon after joining the Knox Automobile Company, Martin developed a 1-ton commercial vehicle—the forerunner of the waterless Knox Truck, winner of the famous 1903 Motor Truck Test Trials. The most significant contribution by Martin, however, was his patented rocking fifth wheel for coupling tractor to trailer.

The introduction of truck-tractors and intersupporting trailers opened new vistas in the infant truck industry. Martin broadened those vistas with the most popular and one of the earliest coupling devices for locking tractor to trailer, the Martin Rocking Fifth Wheel. It was an invention of profound significance to the truck industry and used by almost every truck manufacturer. The ease of connecting and disconnecting tractor from trailer with the fifth wheel no longer subjected trucks to long waits for loading and unloading.

MORRIS, HENRY G. (1840–1915) and SALOM, PEDRO (1856–?)
Pioneers of New York's First Electric Hansom Fleets
The partnership of pioneers Morris and Salom heralded the introduction of electric vehicles to public transportation in New York City and Philadelphia.

Henry Morris was a renowned mechanical and electrical engineer, a director of the Pennsylvania Steel Company, and an early advocate of the Bessemer process. After designing some machinery, he became interested in electrical storage batteries.

Pedro Salom was a chemical engineer and served as assistant as-
sayer of the United States Mint in Philadelphia and as president of
the Standard Steel Casting Company. For nine years, he devoted
himself to the development of a storage-battery business and took
out several patents.

Although both men were highly successful in other business affairs,
they joined talents to improve and develop storage batteries for
the transportation business. Together, they constructed the first of
many electric vehicles in 1894, and were prominent in motor
vehicle demonstrations at early events, such as the *Times Herald*
Race in 1895 where they were awarded a gold medal for excellence of design.

In 1896, Morris and Salom founded the Electric Carriage and
Wagon Company. Fleets of their electric cabs were operating in
Philadelphia by 1896 and in New York City by 1897. These electric vehicles were probably the first horseless carriages in operation
seen by large numbers of the general public.

NASH, CHARLES W. (1864–1948)
Builder of Great Organizations
Nash's career in vehicles started in 1884 at age twenty, working as a
trimmer in a buggy factory for $1 a day. He worked up through the
ranks to manager then vice-president of a firm that grew into the
Durant-Dort Carriage Company. Here he created the highly productive straight-line conveyor-belt system, a standard item in today's auto assembly plants. Under his management, the company
turned out an unprecedented 56,000 units and gave employment to
600 men in 1906.

When his employer Durant bought the controlling interest in
Buick, he took Nash with him. Nash moved up fast to general
manager by creating productivity out of manufacturing chaos. This
was a time of the new automobile "boom." By 1910, Nash was
president of Buick.

Buick so prospered under Nash's leadership that Buick was merged
with General Motors in 1912. In 1913, Nash became president of
General Motors. As president he led General Motors to treble
production with a sixfold increase in annual profits: from 43,000
units a year to 132,000 a year, from $7,460,000 in 1913 to

$29,150,000 in 1916. Nash held the position of president at General Motors until 1916 when he purchased the Thomas B. Jeffery Company.

By 1918, Nash delivered an amazing volume of 11,494 units of the Quad truck to the U.S. army and Allied forces. Known initially as Rambler Quad, the vehicle had been first unveiled in 1913 by the Thomas B. Jeffery Company. The company was subsequently named Nash Motors and today is American Motors Corporation.

RIKER, ANDREW (1868–1930)
Pioneer of Electric, Gasoline, and Steam Propulsion
Inventor, designer, engineer, Andrew Riker worked in all three areas of vehicle propulsion: electric, steam, and gasoline. Riker built his first automotive vehicle, an electric tricycle, in 1884 at age sixteen, each rear wheel driven by a separate battery. "Not too practical, but it ran," he claimed. He was president of his own electric company by 1888 at age twenty.

In 1899, he formed a company to produce a full line of electric passenger and commercial vehicles at Elizabeth, New Jersey. He produced what was proclaimed to be the world's largest truck for that day—an electric, with 2 1/2 horsepower.

One year later, he added a 5-ton electric truck, supplementing his original 1-ton electric delivery vehicles which had been an instant success with New York department stores.

In 1902, Riker joined the Locomobile Company to design their first gasoline vehicles. At Locomobile, Riker designed the Riker Worm Drive Truck. He served as vice-president and chief engineer until 1921.

Famous also as the first president of the Society of Automotive Engineers, Riker served in this SAE office during its important formative organization phase.

SPICER, CLARENCE WINFRED (1875–1939)
Father of the Enclosed Metal Universal Joint
Intrigued with eliminating the troublesome chain-drives of early cars, Clarence Spicer invented an improved universal joint which made possible the shaft-driven car. To test his patented theory, Spicer built an experimental automobile in 1903. Soon after, he

started making universal joints in a "converted corner" of a printing-press plant in South Plainfield, New Jersey.

With phenomenal success, orders poured in. Ten leading auto and truck manufacturers were ordering Spicer Universal Joints by April, 1904. The first year's business was $16,000. With a corps of associates, Spicer was responsible for developing the class "B" Liberty truck for the army during World War I.

His first manufacturing company, organized in 1905, became the Spicer Manufacturing Company of Toledo. It manufactured Spicer universal joints, Brown-Lipe clutches and transmissions, Salisbury front and rear axles, Parish frames, and other motor vehicle equipment. The oldest Spicer customer was the Diamond-T Motor Company of Chicago, a customer since 1907. Spicer universal joints and shafts are used in 90 percent of the motor vehicles built in England.

Spicer's enterprise became a corporation in 1916, and in 1946, it became a major division—the Spicer Manufacturing Division—of the Dana Corporation of Ohio. Dana is now a worldwide designer and manufacturer of transmissions and power systems.

STERNBERG, WILLIAM M. (1847–1929)
Founder of Sterling Motor Trucks

Sternberg built motor trucks as an extension of his machine shop where he manufactured agricultural implements. In 1907, in association with his sons, Ernst and William, Jr., and R. G. Hayssen, he formed the Sternberg Manufacturing Company in West Allis, Wisconsin, to build trucks.

Sternberg's first truck featured a wood-lined chassis frame with solid oak pressed into the chassis side. It was equipped with double-cone-and-disc drive providing two speeds forward and one reverse.

His second truck featured a friction-drive system giving a variable number of speeds. Both trucks had 2-cylinder engines, each with 20 horsepower driving the rear wheels through chains.

Cab-over-engine highway tractors were the company's specialty. But in 1914, it introduced its first conventional layout truck. The company name was changed to the Sterling Motor Truck Company in 1915, and new models succeeded the cab-over-engine featuring worm-type rear drive. Truck lines later included heavies with either chain or worm drive. Orders for army trucks poured in during World War I. After Sternberg's death, the company name was changed in 1933 to Sterling Motor Corporation. Sterling was among the first to offer the oil engine as an alternative power plant. An innovative Sterling feature was the chain-driven four-wheel bogie for tandem trucks.

World War II production involved a wide variety of heavy-duty trucks for the Armed Forces, including dual-chain-drive rear bogie for 20-ton semitrailers.

In 1951, Sterling was sold to The White Motor Company and was integrated as a division to produce custom-built trucks. The Sterling nameplate was subsequently phased out.

TILT, CHARLES ARTHUR (1877–1956)
Truck Pioneer of Quality Diamond-T Fame

Starting with shoe manufacturing and expanding to transportation, the Diamond-T trademark was emblematic of a diamond's quality with the "T" standing for the family name Tilt.

It is probable that no other automotive executive, with the possible exception of Henry Ford, equaled Charles Tilt's uninterrupted record of fifty years as president and general manager or chairman of the board of directors of the Diamond-T Motor Car Company.

Tilt's first business experience was with his father's shoe manufacturing company, the J. B. Tilt Shoe Company, whose top line of shoes was called the Diamond T.

In 1905, Charles Tilt formed the Diamond-T Motor Car Company of Chicago. During the first six years, custom-built passenger cars were manufactured by hand in the rear of a small one-story garage.

Diamond-T switched exclusively to building motor trucks, discontinuing its entire passenger-car lines in 1911. His truck production prospered beyond belief. In the late twenties, with a desire for increased truck speed, Charles Tilt started streamlining the trucks. He regeared the trucks by replacing the slow speed with the faster speed 6-cylinder engines and air-cushioned pneumatic tires. Simultaneously, Tilt marketed nationwide and later worldwide through a dealer-distributing organization, an innovation at that time. These dealerships led to company growth as exemplified by the production of more than 50,000 heavy-duty military vehicles for our armies in World War II.

Diamond-T was responsible for many advancements in truck design. These included the fin-and tube radiator, the adoption of 7-bearing 6-cylinder truck engines, four-wheel hydraulic brakes, fully enclosed deluxe cabs, and hydraulic shock absorbers as standard equipment for heavy-duty trucks. In 1958, Diamond-T was purchased by White Motor Corporation and became a division of White. It continues to be a leader in truck design.

TIMKEN, HENRY H. (1868–1940)
Developed Precision Bearings, Axles, and Suspension Parts
The Timken name was well known in vehicle circles as early as the 1880s when the St. Louis carriage shops of Henry Timken produced vehicles with roller-bearing equipped axles.

It was in 1898 in the family carriage plant that Henry Timken developed the tapered roller bearings that would be in use on 90 percent of the motor vehicles produced in 1926. Demand by carriage builders grew rapidly.

Although trained as an attorney, H. H. Timken preferred the challenges of the family business. With his brother, W. R. Timken, he guided and expanded the firm to recognition as one of the largest and most respected automotive parts manufacturers. Timken bearings, axles, and suspension parts continue to serve the auto industry and industrial communities of the world. The name Timken is synonomous with antifriction and precision.

WALTER, WILLIAM (1863–1945)
Pioneer of Specialized Fire Fighters and Snow Plows
One of America's oldest names in the motor truck industry is Walter. With a history of continuous production since 1898, Walter produced heavy vehicles for fire fighting or snow plowing.

William Walter's first contribution to the industry was the Walter Car in 1898, manufactured in a Manhattan factory on West 65 Street in New York. By 1905, the Walter-designed cars were enjoying such great popularity, their production rate was 300 a year. His Manhattan factory housed complete facilities for manufacturing engines, transmissions, axles, frames, radiators, and bodies.

One year later, he formed the Walter Auto Company of New Jersey where the famous Mercer car was later produced.

Intrigued with the potential and future demand for trucks, William Walter founded the Walter Motor Company in 1911 and concentrated his energy on the heavy-duty truck market.

In 1957, the company moved from a factory in Queens, Long Island, to the New York State Capital District, where it has continued to produce fire fighters, snow fighters, and special vehicles.

WHITE, WINDSOR (1866–1958), ROLLIN (1872–1962), and WALTER (1876–1929)
Giants of the Famous White Motor Truck Complex

In 1900, the entrance of a sewing machine company into the automotive world extended the White name into the world of transportation.

With inventor Rollin handling the manufacturing, Walter as president doing executive legal work, Windsor in charge of marketing, each brother contributed technological expertise. This trio provided the groundwork by which White gained high honors and grew as a truck manufacturer.

The brothers joined their father's business about the time when four-wheel vehicles were emerging. The changes from sewing machines to transportation products came by degrees: from roller skates to bicycles, then autos and trucks, from steam to gasoline.

A truck chassis emerged early in their initial plans to develop transportation vehicles: The first truck was a White steam-powered light delivery truck, introduced in 1900. In 1905, Rollin White was awarded a gold medal at the St. Louis Fair for conspicuous, inventive skill in developing a steam truck. A larger company had to be formed to accommodate their growing business volume. The White Company was incorporated in 1906, separate from The White Sewing Machine Company.

Although their original success was with steam vehicles, in 1910 the first White gasoline truck, a 3-ton model, was shown in the New York Auto Show. Additional truck models and improvements followed, and by 1915, the continued growth required reorganization of The White Company into The White Motor Company, with a new starting capitalization of $16 million. White purchased: Freightliner and Sterling in 1951, Autocar in 1953, Superior Diesel in 1955, the Reo Corporation in 1957, and Diamond-T in 1958.

Today, engineering developments in heavy-duty truck lines by White Motor Corporation are in an innovative "family" concept. Most parts have interchangeable commonality of design among family models, ranging from basic to luxury options.

WOOD, GARFIELD ARTHUR (1880–1971)
Contributed the Labor Saving Hydraulic Hoists
Bodies by Wood were made in St. Paul, Minnesota, as early as 1909. Success in the specialized truck body field quickly followed and the Gar Wood invention of a power-operated hydraulic hoist for dump truck bodies was one of the great labor-saving devices of its time. His plants in St. Paul, Detroit, Ontario, England, and France were a tribute to his business acumen.

A large segment of people throughout the world are more familiar with Gar Wood through his daring as the most successful American race driver in international speed boat racing.

ZACHOW, OTTO (1862–1942) and BESSERDICH, WILLIAM A.
Succeeded in Powering Front-Wheel Drive
In 1908 two inventive friends, Otto Zachow and William Besserdich, blacksmiths and brothers-in-law, patented an idea for applying power to front wheels as well as rear wheels.

Zachow and Besserdich designed a front axle "ball-and-socket joint" with a universal housing that permitted normal steering, yet could transmit power to the wheels. Their first working model was machined out of brass castings made from their own hand-fitted wooden patterns at Zachow's Clintonville Machine Company.

In 1908, they produced a vehicle which incorporated the four-wheel-drive principle. Its only failure was in its power plant—a cross-compound steam engine. Correcting this with a 45-horsepower gasoline engine, their second vehicle gained fame as "the Battleship." Severe tests on hills, mud, and deeply rutted sandy roads proved the superiority of four-wheel drive.

With financial help from an attorney, Walter Olen, a manufacturing company, called the Four Wheel Drive Company, was established in 1910.

They produced their first four-wheel-drive truck and test drove it in 1912 for the United States Army. The test run from Washington, D.C., to Indiana proved that it was the only truck that could successfully complete the run. Their FWD truck was the direct cause of replacing the army's traditional horse-and-cart transportation mode with motorized trucks.

In 1917, William Besserdich joined B. A. Mosling and founded the Oshkosh Truck Corporation. Besserdich became president of Oshkosh trucks which have become a symbol of quality in larger capacity models for snow removal, heavy-duty hauling, and highway construction.

The first Oshkosh vehicle was produced in 1918, promoting advanced engineering achievements with "an automatic positive locking center differential which considerably increased the efficiency and effectiveness of the four wheel drive mechanism, and also served the purpose of decreasing the number of driver controls to the same level as conventional rear drive vehicles." Roller bearings on the axle steering pivots improved the steering mechanism. Research for World War II developed into four-wheel-drive Oshkosh trucks for specialized use throughout the world. The postwar era brought Oshkosh new markets with six-wheel-drive, specially designed heavy-duty trucks for adverse conditions. Today's all-wheel-drive Oshkosh products include concrete carriers, aircraft crash-rescue vehicles, desert oil field trucks, snow removal vehicles, fire truck chassis, and heavy-duty transporters.

Roll Call

It is doubtful that a complete roll call of all motor trucks built in the United States could ever be published. The criteria for such historical listings varies among historians. Some regard any truck built worthy of inclusion on such lists, while others prefer to restrict entries to bona fide truck manufacturers.

This roll call, hopefully, will not compound that timeless argument. It is derived from association records and automotive trade directories and periodicals, and does not profess to be authoritative. It serves only as a cornerstone upon which future entries will improve, develop, and record most of the motor trucks, or commercial vehicles if you prefer, which have served our nation so well.

We invite your participation in adding makes of motor trucks and complete dates to the list.

A.A. 1920–27
A&B 1906–19
A&B 1914–22
A&R 1913–15
Abbot-Downing 1916–32
ABC 1908–11
Abendroth 1907–16
Abresch-Cremer 1910–12
Acason 1915–25
Ace 1920–28
Ace 1923
A.C.F. 1926–53
ACF-Brill 1946
Acme 1903
Acme 1905–11
Acme 1917–32
Acme Det. 1915–18
Acme 1918–21
Acme Wagon 1916
Acorn 1923–30
Acorn 1910–12
Adams 1911–16
Adams Express 1901–2
Admiral 1914
Advance 1918
Aerocoach 1949
Aerotype Four 1922

Aetna 1914–16
AFA, A.F.N.
AGV Electric
Ahrens-Fox 1913–36
A.I.C. 1913–14
Airoflex 1919–20
Ajax 1911
Ajax 1920–22
Akron 1913
Akron Multi 1920–22
Alamo 1912
Albresh-Cramer 1911 or 1912
Alco 1905
Alco 1910–13
Alden-Sampson 1905–13
Alena 1921–22
All American 1918–20
All American 1926–28
Allen & Clark 1908–10
Allen-Kingston 1907–9
All Four 1918–24
Alliance 1917
Alliance Motors 1916
Allied Truck 1920
All Power 1918–24
Alma 1911–14
Alpena 1910–14

Alter 1914–16
Amalgated 1913–17
American 1906–11
American 1918–20
American 1921–24
American 1930–41
American Brass 1907–8
American & Br. 1906
American Bus 1926
American Commercial 1918–23
American Coulthard 1905–6
American Eagle 1911–12
American Electric 1914–16
American Electro 1906–7
American Foundry 1906
American Ice 1913–14
American LaFrance 1910–
American Machine 1916
American Machine 1906–9
American Motor Truck 1916–17
American Ordnance 1902
American Steamer 1903
American Steam 1918–22

357

American Standard 1911, 1918
Ames 1911
AM General 1971 to date
Amoskeag 1897–1906
AMs Sterling 1917
AMTORG 1930–35
Anchor 1911
Anderson 1909–10
Anderson Coupling 1909–12
Andover Electric 1914–17
Anheuser-Busch 1911–12
Ann Arbor 1912
Anthony-Hatcher 1909
Apex 1919–20
Apex 1917–23
Apperson 1905–20
Apperson-Lee 1911
Anderson Electric 1911
Appleton 1922–34
A&R 1915
Arandsee 1920
Arbenz 1911–16
Argo Electric 1911–17
Argo 1916
Aries 1911–12
Armleder 1909–36
Armored 1915
Armstead Snow 1920
Artana 1912–15
Astor 1925
Atco 1920–23
Atlanta 1911
Atlantic 1913–15
Atlantic Electric 1912–16
Atlas 1907–12
Atlas 1917–25
Atterbury 1909–34
Auburn 1912–18
Auburn Wagon & Buggy 1911–12
Auglaize 1911–16
Auglaize 1911–16
Aultman 1894–1906
Austin 1930–36
Autocar 1907 to date
Autocar Equipment 1904–9
Auto-Dynamic 1901
Autohorse 1918
Automatic 1912–22
Automatic Electric 1921–22
Automobile 1900–11
AutoRailer 1946
Auto Tricar 1909

Auto-Truck 1915–16
Autotruck 1916
Available 1910–62
Avery 1910–23
Ayres 1911 or 1912

Babcock 1911–13
Babcock El 1911–12
Backhus 1925–27
Bacon 1901–10
Bailey 1909–10
Bailey 1914
Bailey-Perkins 1919
Baker 1899–1917
Baker 1921–28
Baker-Bell 1912
Baldner 1901–3
Baldwin 1899–1901
Bantam 1938–41
Bantam 1912
Barber 1906
Barber 1912
Barger 1918
Barker 1912–16
Barker 1912–16
Barron 1918
Barrow 1927–28
Bartholemew 1911–12
Bartlett 1921–22
Bartlett 1926–30
Batton 1898–99
Battronic 1962 to date
Bauer 1914–16
Bauer 1925–27
B. B. Commerce 1912
BCK 1911 or 1912
Beardsley 1915–17
Beardsley Electric 1914
Beaver 1911
Beaver 1915–20
Beaver 1920
Beaver Metropolitan 1949
Beck 1913–22
Beck 1947
Beck-Hawkeye 1923–27
Becraft 1911
Beech Creek 1914–19
Beggs 1918–28
Belden 1911
Bell 1913
Bell 1916
Bell 1919–20
Bellmore 1911
Belmont 1920
Belmont 1923–26
Bendix 1908–9
Bergdoll 1908–13
Bessemer 1910–26

Best 1912–15
Best Ever 1917
Best on Earth 1911–12
Bethlehem 1917–27
Betz 1919–29
Beyster-Detroit 1909–11
Biddle-Murray 1906–7
Biehl 1911
Biederman 1915–56
Big Four 1920
Bill Motor 1933
Bimel 1916–17
Bingham 1914–17
Binghamton 1922
Birch 1916–23
Blacker 1910
Black Crow 1910
Black Diamond 1905
Blacker 1911
Blair 1911–17
Blaidsdell 1905–9
Board 1911–13
BobbiWagon 1946
Bobbi-Kar 1946–47
B.O.E. 1911–12
Bollstrom 1916–21
Boney, Victor 1911–12
Borland 1912–16
Bourne Magnetic 1917–18
Bowling Green 1912–16
Bowman 1921–22
Boyd 1912–16
Boyle 1911
Bradfield 1929–30
Bradford 1919–20
Bradley 1920–24
Brandon 1911–12
Brasie 1912–16
Brecht 1901–3
Breze 1903
Brennan 1907–9
Brennan 1912
Bridgeport 1920–29
Brill 1930–46
Brinton 1914–26
Briscoe 1914–22
Bristol 1909
Britton 1911–12
Britton-Stevens 1916
Broc 1909–15
Brockway 1912
Brodesser 1909–14
Bromfield 1930
Bronx 1911
Brooks 1911–12
Brooks-Latta 1912
Brown 1914–17
Brown 1939–53

Brown & Sauter 1912
Brown 1912–14
Brown 1922–24
Browne 1907
Brunn 1907
Brunner 1910
Brush 1907–13
Buck 1926–27
Buckeye 1910–12
Buckeye 1911–16
Bucklen 1913
Buckmobile 1905
Buffalo 1901
Buffalo 1908–10
Buffalo El 1912–15
Buffalo 1923–26
Buffalo 1920
Bugmobile 1907–9
Buggycar 1908–9
Buick 1910–16, 1918
Bull Dog 1924–25
Burford 1916–17
Burlington 1917
Burroughs 1914–16
Burrows 1914
Bushnell 1912
Bussing 1929–30
Butler 1913–14
Byron 1912
Byron 1933

Cadillac 1903–15
Caldwell 1912
Caley & Nash 1912
California 1911
Cameron 1906–12
Cannon 1912
Canada Cycle 1906
Canton Buggy 1912
Canton 1906
Cantono 1904–7
Capital 1912–22
Capitol 1919–22
Capitol El 1912–14
Capitol 1914
Capitol El 1912
Capitol Car 1912
Caravan 1920
Carharrt 1910–12
Carhart 1911
Carl 1914
Carlson 1904–10
Carlson 1911–16
Carolina Truck
Carrol 1912
Carter 1911
Cartercar 1906–12
Casaday 1905
Casco 1924–30

Case 1910–11
Case 1920–23
Casey 1912–14
Cass 1911–15
Catasauqua 1914
C-B 1914–15
CCC 1949
Ceco 1914–15
C & D 1907
C. DE L. 1913
Cedar 1921
Cedar Rapids 1910–14
Century 1915
Chadwick 1905–17
Chalmers 1907–23
Chalmers-Detroit
    1907–10
Champion El 1903–12
Champion 1903–4
Champion 1909–12
Champion 1917–19
Champion 1919–23
Champion 1955
Champion 1918–21
Champion Rotary
    1922–23
Champion Taxi 1916
Chase 1907–20
Chattaqua 1912
Chatauqua 1912
Checker 1923
Chelsea 1914
Chester 1914–16
Chevrolet 1916 to date
Chicago 1899–1905
Chicago 1905–7
Chicago 1907–10
Chicago 1923–30
Chicago El 1912–16
Chicago 1908
Chicago 1911
Chicago Pneumatic 1912
Childs 1909
Christie 1912–18
Christopher Bros
    1911–12
Chrysler 1925–28
Cincinnati 1912
Cino 1912
City Carriage 1910
Clark 1901, 1911–12
Clark 1910–14
Clark 1911–12
Clark-Hatfield 1909
Clarkspeed 1926–31
Classic 1911
Cleburne 1916
Clemick Hirsch 1905–6
Clermont-Steamer 1923

Cleveland 1903–7
Cleveland 1912–13
Cleveland Gallon 1912
Clifford 1905
Climax 1906–7
Climber 1920–23
Clinton 1919
Clinton 1923–32
Club Car 1911
Clyde 1916–17
Clydesdale 1918–37
Coates 1911–13
Cogswell 1912
Cohes 1912
Colby 1911–14
Coleman 1911–16
Coleman 1925–43
Coleridge 1911
Collier 1917
Collier 1918–22
Collins 1901
Colpitts 1911–12
Columbia 1898–13
Columbia 1916–26
Columbus 1902–7
Comet 1916–25
Commando 1959–
Commer 1911–12
Commer 1913
Commer Wood 1905
Commerce 1907–21
Commerce 1912–33
Commercial 1903–5
Commercial 1906,
    1910–11
Commercial 1909–29
Commercial 1912
Compound 1903–7
Concord 1917–28
Concord 1933–38
Condor 1917–18
Condor 1931–33
Conestoga 1917–18
Connersville Buggy 1914
Conrad Steam 1900–03
Consolidated 1904
Consolidated 1934
Continental 1911–18
Continental 1912–18
Continental 1915
Continental Divco
    1932–36
Cook 1920–23
Cook 1950–
Coppock 1907–9
Corbin 1903–12
Corbitt 1911–50
Corliss 1917–18
Corliss Conqueror

Cortland 1911–16
Cortland Cart 1916
Corwin 1905–6
Cottingham Bros.
  1911–12
Couple Gear 1905–20
Courier 1909–12
Covel 1916
Covert 1901–9
C.P.T. 1912
Cram & Sovereign
  1911–12
Cram 1912
Crane 1953 to date
Crane & Breed 1911–19
Crary 1912
Crawford 1909–15
Crescent 1914–15
Crescent 1917
Crest 1904
Crestmobile 1901–5
Creussen
Cricket 1913–15
Croce 1913–19
Crosley 1939–52
Cross 1914
Crow: Crow Elkhart
  1913–18
Crown 1906, 1911,
  1914–15
Crown 1912–15
Crowther 1911–12
Croxton 1913–14
Croxton-Keeton 1909–10
Cruikshank 1896–99
Cruiser 1917–19
C.T. 1909–28
Cub 1950
Cumback 1910
Cunningham 1900–07
Cunningham 1909–36
Curran 1928
Curtis 1913–15
Curtiss 1913–15
Curtis-Bill
Cutting 1909–12
CV Electric 1956–62
Cyclone Motors 1922–23
Cyclone Starter 1920
Cyco-Lectric 1914
Cyphers 1911–12

Dain 1912
Dairy Express 1926–30
Danielson 1914–16
Darby 1910
Dart 1903
Dart 1916–20
Dauch 1916–26

Davenport 1902–3
Davis 1914–16
Davis & Thompson
  1911–12
Day 1902
Daybrook-Ottowa
Day Elder 1916–37
Day Utility 1911–14
Day Utility 1913
Dayton 1911–13
Dayton 1917
D. E. 1917–20
Dearborn 1919–26
Decatur 1911–14
Decatur 1914
Decatur 1909
Decker 1902–3
Deere 1906–7
Defiance 1918–31
De Kalb 1915–20
Delahunty 1913
Delcar 1946–47
Delia 1915
Deliver-All
Delmore 1923
De Loach 1911–12
De Martini 1918–34
De Motte 1904
Denby 1916–31
Denegre 1920–22
Deneen 1916–18
Denison 1899–1903
Denmo 1917
Denniston 1911–12
Dependable 1914–25
Desberon 1900–04
De Shaum 1908–9
De Soto 1950
Detroit 1904–7
Detroit 1907–38
Detroit 1911–13
Detroit-Wyandotte
  1913–16
Devon 1911–16
DeWitt 1911–12
Diamond 1911
Diamond Reo 1967–76
Diamond-T 1911–66
Diehl 1921–27
Differential 1932–35
Dile 1916
Direct Drive 1907
Dispatch 1911–12
Dispatch 1921
Divco 1927
Divco 1932–36
Dixon 1924–33
Doane 1916–33
Doble 1914

Doble 1930
Dodge 1918 to date
Dodge Brothers
Dolfini 1900
Doe-Wa-Jack 1908–11
D'Olt 1927
Dominion 1911–12
Dornfield 1911–12
Dorris 1906–27
Dort 1915–24
Double Drive 1918–30
Douglas 1918–31
Dover 1929–30
Dowagiac 1908–12
Downe 1911
Downing 1914
Downing 1915
Downs 1911–12
Doyle 1911–15
Drake 1921–22
Draymaster 1931–33
Drier 1929
Driggs-Seabury 1916
Dudly 1914–15
Duer 1926–28
Duerr 1911–12
Dufaux 1903–10
Duhamel & Bruechner
  1911
Dumore 1920
Dumptor 1907–12
Dunlap El 1915
Duntley 1910
Duplex 1908–56
Duplex 1908 to date
Durable Dayton 1913–17
Durant 1928–32
Durant-Dort 1912–13
Duro 1914
Durocar 1907–09
Duryea 1900–16
Dusseau 1912
Duty 1909–27
Duty 1920
Dyke 1900–04
Dynamic 1916–17
Dynamic 1920

Eagle 1920–32
Eagle-Macomber
  1917–18
Earl 1921–24
East Davenport 1912
Eastern Dairies 1925
Easter Power 1909–12
Easton 1912
Eckhard 1917
Eclipse 1911–12
Economy 1906–10

Economy 1914
Economy 1918–20
Edison 1910–28
Edwards 1912
Edwil 1934–40
Ehrlich 1920
Eight Wheel 1923
Eisenhauer 1946–48
Eisenhuth 1904–6
Elbert 1914–15
Elburt 1915
Elburto 1920
Elcar 1920–30
Eldridge 1913
Electra 1913–15
Electric 1911–12
Electrocar 1922
Electro-Coach 1917
Electruck El 1914–23
Electruck El 1925–28
Elgin 1916–24
Elk 1912–14
Elkhart 1917–20
Ellsworth 1917–20
Elmira 1917–21
Elmore 1901–12
Electruck 1916–24
Elwell-Parker 1909–10
Elysee 1926–29
Emancipator 1909
Embree McLean 1911
Emery 1950–52
EMF 1912
Empire State 1901
Empire Steam 1901–3
Enger 1909
Enkel 1915
Epperson 1912
Equitable 1901–3
Erie 1914–23
Erie 1914–20
Erskine 1927–30
Esco 1930–40
Essex 1918
Eugol 1921
Eureka 1903
Eureka 1909
Evans 1917
Evans 1941
Evans Limited 1912
Everett-King 1899
Everitt 1910–12
Ewbank 1916–17
Ewing 1908–10
Ewing American 1911
Ex Cell 1912
Exeter 1903–13
Eysinck 1905–25

Fabco 1946–55
Facto 1920–26
Fageol 1916–36
Fageol 1950–54
Fairbanks 1906–11
Fairbanks-Morse 1909–21
Fairfield 1927
Fairman 1915
F.A.L. 1912
Falcon 1915
Famous 1914
Famous 1917–20
Fargo 1913–21
Fargo 1929–37
Fauber Bi 1914–15
Fawick 1912
F.C.S. 1910–11
Federal 1910
Fidelity 1909
Field 1920
Fifth Ave 1914–30
Findlay 1909–13
Finnigan 1913
Firebaugh 1947
Fire King 1901–4
Fisher 1901–5
Fischer 1901–4
Fisher 1924–34
Fitzjohn 1947
Five Boro Cab 1930–31
Flanders 1910–12
Fleckwick 1933
Flint 1924–27
Flint Roadking 1926
Flxible 1931–46
Ford 1904 to date
Forme 1917
Forschler 1916–20
Fort Wayne 1910–12
Fostoria 1915–17
Four Traction 1911
Four-Wheel Drive 1904
Franklin 1907–13, 1921
Fox 1913
Frayer-Miller 1905–10
Freeman 1921
Freeman 1928–31
Freestone 1911
Freightliner 1938 to date
Fremont 1919–25
Fremont-Mais 1914
Frick 1903–10
Frisbee 1922–23
Fritschle 1907–17
Front Drive 1921–29
Frontenac 1908–15
Frontmobile 1918

F. S. 1912–13
F. S. 1922–24
Fuller 1910–12
Fuller Buggy 1909
Fulton 1918–25
Ful-Ton 1937
F.W.D. 1910 to date

Gabriel 1911–20
Gaeth 1902–11
Gale 1912
Galloway 1911
Galloway 1917–18
Garford 1902–33
Garner 1915–39
Gar Wood 1938
Gary 1916–27
Gasmobile 1901
Galion 1902–11
Garrett 1911
Gas Electric
Gay 1915–16
Gaylord 1911–13
Gearless 1921
Gem 1918–19
Gem 1921–22
General 1902–4
General Cab 1936–38
General Motors Cab 1930–36
General Motors Truck 1913–
General Pacific 1948
General Steele
General Vehicle 1906–18
Geneva 1901–13
Geneva 1917–18
Gerlinger 1915–17
Gersix 1916–21
Gersix 1918–20
G. E. Standard
Giant 1915–21
Gibbons
Gibbs 1903–5
Gifford-Pettitt 1906
Gleason 1912–13
Glide 1911–13
Globe 1916–21
Globe 1915–19
Globe 1920–22
Glover 1911–12
G.M.C. 1913 to date
GMC El 1912–16
Goldengate 1927
Golden State 1928–35
Golden West 1914–15
Golden West 1919–20
Goliath 1920
Goodwin 1922–24

Goodyear 1920–26
Gopher 1911–12
Gotfredson 1922–32
Gotfredson & Joyce
  1922–32
Gould El 1954–55
Gove 1921–22
Grabowsky 1908–13
Graham Bros. 1917–32
Graham-Doane 1946
Gramm 1912–33
Gramm 1926–40
Gramm Bernstain
  1913–22
Gramm Kinkaid 1925–26
Gramm-Logan 1908–11
Grand 1912
Grand Rapids 1913
Grant 1913–23
Grant-Ferris 1901
Grass-Premier 1923–33
Gray 1916
Gray 1922–26
Great Eagle 1910–14
Great Eagle 1920
Great Lakes 1949–56
Great Southern 1912–13
Greenville 1926–28
Greyhound 1914
Grinnell 1910–15
Grout 1898–1906
Guilder 1922–35
Gumprice 1912
G.V. 1907–18
G. V. Mercedes 1914–17
G.W.W. 1919–21

H and M 1919
Haberer 1911–12
Hahn 1914–41
Hal-Fur 1919–32
Hall 1901
Hall 1914–15
Hall 1916–18
Haller Bros. 1911
Halsey 1906–7
Hambrick 1906
Hamilton 1917–21
Hampden 1922
Handi-Kar 1914
Handy Wagon 1909–14
Hanger 1916
Hannay 1917
Hannibal 1915–17
Hanover 1922–26
Harder 1909–14
Harmon-Yount 1913
Harrisburg 1920–21
Harrison 1912–14

Hart-Kraft 1908–13
Harvey 1913–33
Harwood & Barley 1911
Hasbrouck 1899–1901
Hasbrouck & Sloan 1912
Haskall 1916
Hatfield 1907–8, 1910
Hatfield 1916–24
Hatfield 1910–14
Hatfield 1916–18
Hathaway-Purinton
  1924–25
Haughton
Havers 1911
Hawkeye 1916–33
Hawkeye Dart
Hayes 1916–18
Hayes-Anderson
  1928–34
Hayes-Lawrence 1948
Haynes 1904–14
Hebb 1918–1920
Henderson 1915–27
Hendrickson 1915 to date
Hendy 1913
Henney 1915 to date
Hennegin 1914
Henry Lee Power
Hercules 1913–14
Hercules 1961
Herreschoff 1911
Herschmann 1903–9
Hertner El 1934–36
Hertz 1925–28
Hewitt 1906–18
Hewitt-Lindstrom
  1900–01
Hewitt-Ludow 1912–21
Hewitt-Talbot 1920
Highway 1965–68
Highway Knight 1920–22
Highway Tractor 1918
Higrade 1918–21
Hilton 1913
Hinde & Dauch 1908
Hoadley 1916
Hoffman 1913
Hohnsbehn 1913
Holland 1901
Holmes 1921
Holsman 1902–9
Holt 1898–1911; p
  1912–25
Homer 1908–16
Hood 1918
Hoosier 1913
Hoover 1916–18
Hopkins 1911–12
Horner 1914–17

Houghton 1916
House Cold Tire Setter
  1919
Howard 1900–01
Howard 1914–16
Howe 1908
H.R.L. 1921
Hub 1916–17
Hudson 1929–47
Huebner 1914
Huffman 1916–28
Hug Speed 1923–40
Hunter-Weckler 1909
Huntingdon 1912
Hupmobile 1920–25
Hupp 1912–19
Hupp-Yeats 1911–12
Hurlburt 1912–27
Huron 1912–22
Huron River 1912
Hurryton 1922–28
Huselton 1913
Hydraulic 1916–17
Hyrade 1916

Ibex
Ice 1913
Ideal 1905–6, 1964
Ideal 1910–14
Ideal 1912
I.H.C. 1907–13
Imboden 1877–78
Immel 1911
IMP 1913–14
Imperial 1904
Improved 1905
Independent 1911
Independent 1915
Independent 1927–34
Independent 1914–21
Independent 1915–18
Independent 1917–22
Indian 1930
Indiana 1911–39
Industrial 1921–22
Interboro 1914
International 1907 to date
Interstate 1908–18
Interstate 1917–18
Iowa 1908
Iowa 1919
Iroquois 1906
Italia 1922–25
Ives 1914
Ivey 1913

Jaccard J. 1911
Jackson 1891
Jackson 1902–29

James 1909–11
Janney-Steinmetz 1901
Jarrett 1923–30
Jarvis 1906
Jarvis-Huntingdon 1912
Jarms Machinery 1911
Jay
Jeep 1963 to date
Jeffery 1914–17
Jenkins 1901–2
J.&H. 1920–21
J&J 1920–21
Joerns-Thien 1911
Johnson 1901–12
Johnson Peter A. 1912
Johnson Service 1909
Joliet 1912
Joly & Lambert 1916
Jones 1918–20
Jonz 1911–12
Jumbo 1920–32
Juno 1913–15

Ka-Dix 1913
Kaiser 1947
Kalamazoo 1914–24
Kanawha 1912
Kankakee 1918–20
Kansas City 1905–9
Karavan 1920–22
Karbach 1908
Kardell 1918–20
Karwisch 1911
Kastory 1924
Kato 1907–9
Kaws Quality 1922–25
Kearns 1908–25
Keeton 1908
Keldon 1919
Kelland 1915–25
Keller 1914–15
Keller 1947–50
Kelley 1903
Kelly-Springfield
   1910–26
Kelly Steam 1902–3
Kelsey 1910–12
Kemp, Chester D. 1912
Kemper 1909
Kenan 1915
Kendall, George M. 1911
Kenen 1913–15
Kenosha-Winther
   1918–28
Kenosha 1918
Kentucky Wagon 1914
Kenworth 1922 to date
Kerber
Keystone 1919–21

Kiblinger 1907–9
Kidder 1900–07
Kimball 1917–18
Kimball 1920–26
King 1912–18
King 1912
King-Zeitler 1919–30
Kinnear 1911–13
Kissel 1908–30
Kisselkar 1916–19
Klag, John 1912
Kleeber
Kleiber 1914–38
Klemm 1915–20
Kline Kar 1911–14
Klondike 1918–20
Klockner
Knapp 1911–12
Knelly's 1911–12
Knickerbocker 1912–16
Knightstown 1933
Knox 1900–1919
Knox 1904–7
Knuckey 1943–55
Koehler 1910–28
Koehler 1912
Koenig & Luhrs 1916–17
Kopf, Fred 1911
Kopp 1911–14
Kosmath 1913–16
Koterba 1912
Kranz 1911
Kratzner 1912
Krebs 1912–26
Kress & Son 1911–12
Krickwell 1912–17
Krickworth 1912–17
K.R.I.T. 1909–26
Kuehne 1911–12
Kuhn 1918–20
Kunkel 1911
K.W. Dart 1923–25
K. Z. 1919–24

La Crosse 1914
Laderer, W. C. 1911
La France 1910–20
La France-Republic
   1929–43
Lambert 1905–19
Lambert Morin 1912
Lammert & Mann 1922
Lamson 1916–17
Landschaft 1917–20
Lane 1902
Lane 1916–19
Lang 1912–31
Lang & Button
   1890–1900

Lange 1912–31
Langerquist 1911
Lanpher 1909–12
Lansden 1904–28
Lapeer 1919–20
Larrabee 1916–19
Larrabee-Deyo 1915–33
Laurel 1916–21
Lauth Auto & Engine
   1906
Lauth-Juergens 1907–17
Lavigne 1914–15
Lawson 1916
L.A.W. 1912
L.C.E. 1914–16
Lea 1908
Leach 1899–1901
Leach 1920–23
Lear 1909
Lease 1921–22
Le Blond Schacht
   1927–38
Lee Power Lehigh
Lehigh 1925–27
Lehne & Son 1911
Le Moon 1903
Lende 1909
Lenox 1911–18
Leslie 1916–18
Letourneau 1950 to
   date
Leuschner 1911
Lewis 1912–15
Lewis-Hall 1916–30
Liberty 1917–30
Liedtke & Munger
Light 1913–14
Lima 1915
Lincoln 1912–14
Lincoln 1921–30
Lincoln 1916–17
Lindsey 1909
Lindsley 1908
Linn 1916–40
Linn 1946–52
Lion 1907/–12
Lion 1921
Lippard-Stewart
   1912
Lite Way 1953–55
Little Giant 1910–25
L.M.C. 1919–20
Locomobile s1899–03
Logan 1903–7
Lomax 1913
Lombard 1916–21
Lone Star 1920–22
Longest 1913–15
Loomis 1901–4

Lorain 1901
Lord Baltimore 1911–12
Lorraine 1919–22
Los Angeles Creamery
 1913–14
Lo Truk 1940
Louisiana 1919
Low Bed 1926–27
Lowell 1917–18
Loyal 1920
Lozier 1912–17
Luck Truck 1912–14
·Luck Utility 1913
Ludlow 1914
Ludwig, Theodore
Luedinghaus 1919–31
Luitweiler 1912
Lumb 1918
Luverne 1916–21
Luxor 1924–27
L.W.C. 1916
Lynch, Francis T.
Lyon 1911
Lyons 1919–21

Maccar 1904–33
Maccarr 1912–13
Maccar 1914
MacDonald 1924–26
MacInnis Bros. 1911
Mack 1902 to date
Mack Jr. 1936–37
Madsen 1958
Maibohm 1916–22
Mais 1910–14
Majestic 1925–27
Manahan 1911
Manhattan 1907–10
Manly 1917–18
Manly 1919–20
Mansur 1912–44
Mansur 1912–14
Maple Bay 1911–12
Marathon 1905–14
Maremont 1916
Marinette 1909
Marion 1904–16
Markert 1911
Markey 1912
Marks 1901
Marmon 1912–14
Marmon 1964 to date
Marmon-Herrington
 1931–64
Marquette 1910–12
Marshall 1919
Marshall 1920–21
Martin 1914–17
Martin 1929–32

Martin-Parry 1920–21
Marvel 1912
Marwin 1918
Marx, George 1911–12
Maryland 1900–01
Mason 1913–14
Mason Road King
 1922–24
Massachusetts 1900–01
Master 1907–20
Master 1917–29
Matheson 1906–7
Maumee 1906
Maxfer 1916
Maxim 1912–16
Maxim 1915–27
Maxim Tricar 1911–14
Maxwell 1913–25
Maxwell-Briscoe
 1904–13
Maybrath 1949
Maytag-Mason 1910–15
McBright
McCarron 1927–29
McCullough 1899
McCrea 1906–8
McFarlan 1911–18
McIntyre 1909–14
McKay Steam 1901
McKeen 1912
M.D. 1908
M & E.
Mechanics 1926–28
Meech-Stoddard 1922–27
Megow 1909–11
Meir & Son
Meiselbach 1904–9
Menges 1921
Menominee 1911–37
Merchant 1910–14
Merchant & Evans 1914
Merchants 1912
Mercury 1911–16
Mercury 1913–14
Merit 1911
Meserve 1902–3
Meserve Steam 1901–2
Messinger 1913
Metens, Leary 1911–12
Meteor 1917–25
Metro; Metropolitan
 1926–27
Metz 1909
Metz 1916–17
Metzger 1911–12
M.G.T. 1947–50
MH
M.H.C. 1915
Micampbell 1909–11

Michigan Hearse
 1909–11
Michigan 1907–8
Michigan Steam 1907,
 1910
Middleboro 1913–14
Middletown 1911
Midland 1918–19
Mid West 1925
Milburn 1915–22
Milburn El 1915–17
Milburn El 1922–26
Militor 1918
Milford 1946
Miller 1907–8
Miller 1914
Miller Meteor 1949
Miller-Quincy 1924–25
Mills-Ellsworth 1918–19
Milwaukee 1900–02
Milwaukee 1951
Minneapolis 1911–14
Minneapolis 1914
Minneapolis Steel
 1910–28
Mission 1914
Mitchell 1903–22
Mitchell-Lewis 1910–16
Mobile 1899–1902
Mobile Steam 1901–3
Model 1906
Modern 1912
Modern 1913–15
Moeller 1914–17
Mogul 1912–16
Mohawk 1914–16
Mohican 1920–21
Mohler 1901
Moldenhauer 1911
Moline 1920–22
Moller 1919–37
Molzen, Peter 1916
Monarch 1909
Monarch 1916
Monitor 1908–14
Montpelier 1958–59
Moon 1905–18
Moore 1913–17
Moore 1916–21
Mora 1910–14
Moreland 1912–41
Morgan 1903–12
Morgan Steam 1902–3
Morris 1899–1909
Morris & Salom 1896–97
Morrisey
Morse 1909–15
Morton 1917–20
Morton 1929

Moschera
Moseley 1919
Moses & Marris 1920
Mosler 1913
Motokart 1913–17
Motor Buggy 1908–10
Motor Car 1909
Motor Conveyance 1911
Motorette 1913
Motor Products 1914
Motor Storage 1905–8
Motor Truck 1902
Motor Wagon 1910–11
Motox 1921
Moyea 1904
M. & P. 1912–15
M. & P. El 1912
M.P.C. 1925–28
M.T.N.
Muelhauser 1912–14
Muir 1903
Muller & Sons 1911
Muller, John 1912
Muncey 1911
Muncie 1906–9
Munsing 1913
Munson 1899
Murphy 1914
Murty 1949
Muskegon 1917–20
Mutual 1919–26
Myers 1916–18

Napoleon 1917–23
Nash 1918–30, 1947–49
Nason 1912
Natco 1912–16
National 1899
National 1948
National-Kissel 1927–30
Nebraska Auto & Truck
Neilson 1906–07
Nelson 1919
Nelson-Le Moon
   1912–27
Nestor 1911–12
Netco 1914–27
Neumeister 1912
Neustadt 1905
Nevada 1914–16
Neverslip
Nevin 1927–34
Neville 1909
Newark 1911–12
New Champion
Newcomer 1926–30
New England 1898–1900
New England 1915
New Era 1911

New Era 1917
New Haven 1911–14
New Orleans
New York 1900
New York 1914–17
New York 1920–21
Nielson 1906
Niles 1916–26
Nilson 1921
Nilson-Miller 1909
Noble 1918–22
Noller, Samuel
NonParell 1913
Nordyke & Marmon
   1913
Northern 1902–9
North Pacific 1911
Northway 1919–25
Northwestern 1915–30
Norwald 1911–22
Norwalk 1918–20
Nott 1912
Nucar 1930
Nusco 1916
Nyberg 1912–14

Oak Tree
Oakland 1909
O.B. 1923–33
O.B. El 1921–31
O'Brien & O'Connell
O'Connell 1928–30
Ofeldt 1900
Ogden 1919–27
Ogren 1921–23
Ohio 1892–1898
Ohio 1909
Ohio 1911
Ohio Elect 1910–18
Ohio Fall 1913
O.K. 1920–29
O.K. 1917–28
Oklahoma 1917–23
Okodyne
Old Hickory 1915–24
Old Reliable 1910–27
Oldsmobile 1904–39
Oldsmobile 1904–7
Oldsmobile 1919–23
Old Universal
Oliver 1910–13
Olney 1911
Olsen 1921
Olympian 1918–19
Olympic 1922–28
Omaska 1911
Omort 1927–32
Oneida 1917–31
Oneida El

Only 1912
One Wheel 1918
Oren 1932
Orient Buckboard
   1900–1909
Orleans 1920–22
O.S. 1914
Oshkosh 1919 to date
Osmers
Osmers 1911–12
Ottawa 1960
Overland 1908–29
Overtime 1915–24
Owen 1912
Owen-Schoeneck 1914
Owosso 1909–10

Pacific 1942–45
Pacific Metal 1915
Packard 1903–25
Packers 1910–13
Packet 1910
Packett 1916–17
Paco 1905–10
Page 1916
Paige 1908–27
Paige 1918–23
Paige 1930–31
Pak-Age-Kar 1927–41
Palmer 1913–18
Palmer-Meyer 1914–18
Palmer-Moore 1915–17
Pan 1920
Pan American 1919–22
Panhard 1917–19
Panther 1920
Paramount 1927–31
Parcel, Parcel Post
Parker 1918–32
Parr 1911
Parry 1910–11
Parsons 1913
Patent Holding 1911
Paterson 1908–24
Pathfinder 1913–15
Patrick 1916
Patriot 1920–26
Patterson-Greenfield
   1917
Patterson-Olsen 1912
Patton 1899
Paulding 1914–15
Pease & Sons
Peerless 1905–32
Peet 1923–26
Pendell Low Bed
   1925–28
Penn 1911
Penn 1923–27

Pennford 1924
Penn-Unit 1910–14
Pennant
Pennsy 1916–18
Pennsylvania 1909
Penton Cantilever 1928
People's 1901–2
Perfection 1924–26
Perfex 1914–17
Perkins 1909
Peterbilt 1947 to date
Peters 1924
Petrel 1911–12
P. & H.
Philadelphia 1911–14
Phillips-Grinnell 1911
Phoenix 1900–01
Phoenix 1909–11
P.H.P. 1912
Pickard 1912
Pickwick 1920–33
Piedmont 1917–20
Pierce 1955
Pierce-Arrow 1911–34
Piercy 1916
Pierson 1912–18
Piggins 1912
Pilgrim 1912–14
Pilot 1910–14
Pilot 1922
Pioneer 1909–11
Pioneer 1920–25
Pirsch 1936 to date
Pitt 1913
Pittsburgh 1896–1912
Pittsburgh 1908–10
Pittsburgh el 1919–25
Plains 1923
Plymouth 1905–15
Plymouth 1939–42
Pneumatic 1918
Pole 1913–20
Pontiac 1906
Pontiac 1926–27
Pontiac 1949–54
Pontiac 1930–53
Pony 1920
Pony·Cruiser 1948
Pope 1905
Pope-Hartford 1906–14
Pope-Toledo 1904–9
Pope-Waverly 1903–7
Port Albany 1929
Poss 1912–13
Powell 1912
Power Car 1912
Power Truck 1919–25
Power Vehicle
Poyer 1911–15

Pratt, Carter, Sigsbee
    1911
Premier 1903–25
Premier 1906
Premocar 1920–23
Preston
Price 1909
Progress 1912
Progress 1933–34
P.R.T. 1927
Prudence 1902–6
Public 1914
Pullman 1916–17
Pull More 1917
Pungs-Finch 1911–12
Puritan 1914
Purity Electric 1914

Quadray 1904–5

Racine 1917
Rae 1909
Rainier 1905–27
Ralston 1918
Rambler 1904–13
Randolph 1909–10
Ranger 1907–11
Ranger 1920–22
Rapid 1899–1908
Rassel 1911–12
Rauch & Lang 1905–23
Raulang 1922–28
Ravena 1913
Raya
Read 1913–14
Reading 1920
Real 1915
R & B 1929–41
R.C.H. 1913
Rech-Marbaker 1911
Red Arrow 1914
Red Ball 1924–27
Red Shield-Hustler 1911
Red Star 1912
Red Wing 1912
Reeves 1895–1916
Regal L. B. 1911
Rehberger 1924–34
Reichstelter & Son 1912
Reiland & Bree 1924–31
Relay 1927–34
Reliable 1921
Reliable Dayton 1906–9
Reliance 1903–13
Reliance 1918–20
Remington 1911
Remington Standard
    1912
Rennoc-Leslie 1918–19

Renville 1911
Reo 1908
Republic 1914–29
Republic El 1901
Rex 1914
Rex 1922–23
Rex-Watson 1925
Reya 1920
Reynolds 1920–27
Rhode Island 1900
Richmond 1914
Riddle 1916–26
Riker 1896–1902
Riker 1917–22
Riley 1875–1895
R. & L. 1923–24
Road King 1956–57
Roamer 1927–29
Robinson 1914
Robinson 1917
Robinson, Andrew 1911
Robinson Fire 1911
Robinson, Loomis 1911
Rocco 1917
Rochester Mais 1913
Rocket 1925–26
Rock Falls 1919–25
Rockford 1908–12
Rockliff 1902–6
Rockne 1932–33
Rock-Ola 1938
Rockwell 1909–12
Rodefeld 1916–17
Rogers 1921
Rogers Una-Drive 1919
Roland 1914–15
Romer 1921
Ross 1915–18
Ross Carrier 1933
Roto 1916–17
Roustabout 1961
Rovan 1914
Rowe 1911–27
Royal 1914
Royal 1918
Royal Rex 1922
Royal Tourist 1912
R-S 1916
Rugby 1927–31
Ruggles 1920–29
Ruler 1916
Rumely s1885–1923;
    p1923
Rush 1916–18
Russell, C. W. 1912
Ruzicka 1911

S & L
Safety First 1914–16

Safeway 1924–28
Saf-T-Cab 1926
Saginaw
St. Louis 1900
St. Louis 1912
Salter 1909–12
Salvador 1914–16
Sampson 1908–12
Samson 1920–22
Sanbert 1911–12
Sandow 1912–29
Sandusky 1908–14
Sanford 1912–34
Sann, Gustav 1912
Sauer 1912
Sautter 1910–11
Savage 1912
Saxon 1915–18
Sayers; Sayers & Scovill 1907–32
Schacht 1904–38
Schaefer, Wm. 1912
Scheid Bros & Storch 1911
Schierbaum 1911
Schleicher 1895
Schleicher 1917
Schleicker 1912
Schlosser 1911
Schlotterback 1912–13
Schmidt 1911–14
Schnader, Milton 1911
Schoepflin 1914
Schoonmaker 1921
Schubert James 1911–12
Schurmeier 1910–11
Schurmier 1911
Schwartz 1909–23
Scloto 1911
Scott 1904–5
Scott & Clark 1911–12
Seagrave 1910
Sears 1909–11
Security 1921–23
Seitz 1907–13
Seitz 1911–12
Selden 1908–32
Selden-Hahn 1913
Sellen, Henry 1912
Seneca 1917–20
Sequoia 1914
Service 1911–23
Shady Side 1904
Shafer Decker 1905–16
Sharon 1912–16
Shaw 1912–21
Sheffield 1912
Shelby 1912–23
Sheridan 1916–17

Sherwood 1914
Shetzline, Walter 1911–12
Shillito 1901
Shop of Siebert 1911–14
Sicard 1936
Siebert 1907–16
Siervers & Erdman 1911
Signal 1914–24
Sigmund 1912
Sing Sing 1912
Six Wheel 1922–28
Six Wheeled 1919–23
Skootmobile 1939
Smith Flyer 1917–20
Smith Form-A-Truck 1904
Smith Milwaukee 1911
Smyser, Jacob 1911
Snell, George 1912
Soules, 1905–15
South Bend 1914–17
Southern 1911
Southern 1920–22
Southern 1921
Southern Coach 1948–55
South Main Motor 1922
Sowers 1914
Spacke 1919–20
Spangler 1947–49
Spartan 1950
Spaulding 1912–16
Speedwell 1907–14
Spencer 1922
Sphinx 1916
Spoerer 1911–12
Spokane 1911–15
Springer 1903–4
Springfield 1884
Square Turn 1916
S. & S. 1924–30
Standard 1913–32
Standard 1913–15
Standard 1917–22
Standard El 1911–12
Stanley 1901–18
Stanley Steam 1912–16
Star 1909–13
Star 1922–28
Starbuck 1914
Star-Flee-Truck 1927
Starr 1911–16
Star Six Compound 1917
Star Tribune 1914
States 1916–20
Staver 1911–12
Steammotor 1911–12
Steam-O-Truck 1920
Stearns Steam 1901–3

Stearns; Stearns-Knight 1906
Steck & Sons 1911–12
Steel King 1914
Steel Swallow 1911–12
Steele 1915–19
Stegeman 1911–18
Stehling, George 1911–12
Steinhauer 1911–12
Stein-Koenig 1926–27
Steinmetz 1920–27
Step-N-Drive 1928–29
Stephenson 1911
Stephenson 1930
Sterling 1908
Sterling 1913–58
Sterling-White 1951–53
Sternberg 1909–13
Stevens 1888–1906
Stewart 1912–39
Stewart 1913
Stoddard-Dayton 1905–13
Storms 1915
Stoughton 1919–28
Studebaker 1902–63
Studebaker 1913–18
Studebaker 1927–64
Sturgis 1900
Sturtevant 1906–8
Stutz 1920–30
Stuyvesant 1911
Suburban 1911–12
Success 1906–9
Success 1920
Sullivan 1910–26
Sultan 1911–12
Sunset 1911
Super 1922–34
Super Truck 1920
Superior 1910–11
Superior 1915–22
Superior 1946
Super-Traction 1922–23
Super Truck 1919–36
Swampbuggy Fabco 1946
Swanson 1912
Swift 1911–12
Sydmond 1911
Symonds 1912
Synnestvedt 1904–8

Tait 1914–26
Tarrytown 1914
Taylor 1918–20
Techno 1962
Tec Trailer 1920–21
Teel 1913–14

Teel, Elbredge 1911
Teel-Woodworth 1911
Tegetmeir & Riepe
  1913–15
Terraplane 1934–38
Texan 1918–22
Thanisch, Andrew 1912
Theim 1911
Thill, F. F. 1911
Thomart 1922–23
Thomas 1905–17
Thomas 1907
Thompson 1901; 1906–8
Thompson Steam 1902
Thorne 1929–32
Thorpe 1911–15
Thornycroft 1900–02
Three Point 1919–24
Thrift T 1947
Tiffin 1914–25
Titan 1916–29
Titan Steam 1916–17
Toeppner Bros 1912
Toeppinger 1910
Toledo 1900–03
Toledo 1912
Torbenson 1911
Touraine 1914–15
Tourist 1903–7
Tower 1918–25
Townsend 1912
Town Taxi 1933–35
Trabold 1912–29
Traction 1901
Traffic 1912–28
Transit 1912–20
Transit 1947–55
Transport 1919–27
Transport 1918–25
Traveler 1925
Traverse City
Traylor 1924–31
Triangle 1918–20
Tri-Car 1955
Triple 1916
Triumph 1908–14
Triumph 1919–23
Tri-Van 1963
Tri-Wheel 1950
Trojan 1914–19
Troy 1914–16
Truckstell 1937
Tructor 1917–18
Trumbull 1914–15
Tucker 1947
Tulsa 1912–13
Tulsa 1921–22
Turbine 1904
Turnbull 1918–19

Tuttle 1913
Twin City 1919–21
Twin City 1914–15
Twin City 1915–19
Twin City 1920–28
Twin Coach 1927
Twin Parts 1921
Twombly 1913–16
Twyford 1902–8

Ultimate 1920–25
Union 1902–4
Union 1915–26
Union 1916–26
Union Construction 1923
United 1914
United 1918–30
United Motors 1911
Universal 1911–18
Universal Machinery
  1912–13
Upton 1903–7
Urban 1912–17
Ursus 1920–21
United States 1910–30
United States Carriage
  1911
U.S. 1910–25
U.S. Long Distance
  1900–04
Utility 1911–12
Utility 1916–17
Utility Supply

Vacuum and Compressor
  1909
Valley 1927–29
Van 1909–13
Van Auken 1914
Van Auken Electric 1914
Vandewater 1911
Van Dyke 1910–11
Van L. 1911–12
Van Wambeke & Son
  1911
Van Winkle 1913–19
V. C. 1912–13
V.E.C. 1901–7
V. E. Electric 1901
Veerac 1910–15
Velie 1908–28
Velie 1911–15
Velie 1927–30
Versare 1926–30
Viall 1913–26
Victor 1910–29
Victor Electric 1913
Victor City 1922–25
Victor 1920

Victor 1923–28
Videx 1903
Vim 1914–26
Virginia 1932–34
Vitch 1910–13
Vixen 1914
Vogel 1911
Voltz 1914–17
Vreeland
Vulcan 1915
Vulcan 1920–22

Wachusetts 1922–29
Waco 1915–17
Wade 1913–15
Wadsworth 1860
Wagenhals 1910–15
Waldron 1909–10
Walker 1907–37
Walker-Johnson 1920
Wall 1912–15
Wallof 1912
Walter 1910 to date
Walter Electric 1921
Waltham 1921
Waltham-Orient 1900
Ward 1912
Ward Electric 1911–18
Ward Electric 1912–34
Ward Electric 1918–35
Ward La France
  1918 to date
Ware 1913–20
Ware 1912–15
Ware 1918–20
Warford 1937–40
Warner-Swasey 1955–77
Warren 1911–12
Warwick 1913
Washington 1908–10
Waltham 1920–21
Waterville 1911
Watrous 1907–17
Watson 1916–26
Waukesha 1915–22
Waverly 1898–1917
Webb 1908–12
Webberville
Webster 1910–12
Weeden, Havens &
  Kleeden 1911
Weeks 1908
Weier-Smith 1915–19
Werner, Louis 1912
West Coast 1916
Western 1907
Western 1911–28
Western Carriage 1912
Western Star 1967 to date

Western Tool 1901–7
Westfield 1911
Westinghouse 1901
Westinghouse 1905–12
Westman 1911–13
Westrak 1950
Weyher 1910
Wharton 1921–22
Whatoff 1960
Whippet 1929
Whitcomb 1927–35
White 1900 to date
White Steam 1900–09
White Hichory 1916–21
Whitesides 1911–12
White Star 1911–21
Whiting 1905–7
Whiting 1910–11
Whitwood 1914
Whichita 1913–32
Wiggers 1912
Wilcox 1907–28
Wilcox Trux 1911
Wilken Burg Carriage 1911
Wilkey & Son 1911
Will 1928–31
Willet 1913–14

Willett 1909–13
Willingham 1915–16
Wills (C.H.) Motor 1927
Willys 1929
Willys 1930–62
Willys Knight 1928–29
Willys Utility 1913–14
Wilson 1915–20
Winchester 1909
Winkler 1911–12
Winslow 1919
Winter & Hirsch 1922–23
Winter-Marwin 1915–21
Winther 1917–22
Winther-Kenosha 1923–27
Winton 1899–1915
Wisconsin 1914
Wisconsin 1921
Wittenberg 1966
Witt-Will 1916–32
W. J. 1921–24
W.M.C. 1927–28
Wolber Carriage 1911–12
Wolf 1902–7
Wolfe 1909
Wolfwagon 1956–64
Wolverine 1912–18

Wolverine-Detroit 1911–20
Wonder 1917
Wood 1905
Wood Steam 1903–5
Woodburn 1912
Woodknight 1911
Wood-Loco 1901–3
Woods 1927–30
Woods Mobilette 1915
Woolston 1913
World 1927–31
Worlds 1927–30
Worth 1911
W-S 1911
Wijckoff, Church & Partridge 1912
Wyndmoor 1909

Yale 1921
Yellocab Truck 1923–27
Yellow Cab 1915–30
Yellow Coach 1922–42
Yellow Knight 1926 27
Young 1920–23

Zeitler & Lamson 1914–16
Zimmerman 1908–16

Highlights

The story of highway transportation in America and its influence on the American people and their way of life can sometimes be most succinctly told in terms of pure facts and figures. These cold numbers in the following tables actually are the highlights of that story. (Historical Motor Vehicle Statistics)

United States Total Factory Sales of Trucks and Buses

Year	Unit Sales	Year	Unit Sales	Year	Unit Sales
1904	700	1929	881,909	1954	1,042,174
1905	750	1930	575,364	1955	1,249,106
1906	800	1931	432,262	1956	1,104,481
1907	1,000	1932	228,303	1957	1,107,176
1908	1,500	1933	329,218	1958	877,294
1909	3,297	1934	576,205	1959	1,137,386
1910	6,000	1935	697,367	1960	1,194,475
1911	10,681	1936	782,220	1961	1,133,804
1912	22,000	1937	891,016	1962	1,240,168
1913	23,500	1938	488,841	1963	1,462,708
1914	24,900	1939	700,377	1964	1,540,453
1915	74,000	1940	754,901	1965	1,751,805
1916	92,130	1941	1,060,820	1966	1,731,084
1917	128,157	1942	818,662	1967	1,539,462
1918	227,250	1943	699,689	1968	1,896,078
1919	224,731	1944	737,524	1969	1,923,179
1920	321,789	1945	655,683	1970	1,692,440
1921	148,052	1946	940,963	1971	2,053,146
1922	269,991	1947	1,239,443	1972	2,446,807
1923	409,295	1948	1,376,274	1973	2,979,688
1924	416,659	1949	1,134,185	1974	2,727,313
1925	530,659	1950	1,337,193	1975	2,272,160
1926	608,617	1951	1,426,828	1976	2,979,476
1927	464,793	1952	1,218,165	1977	3,441,521
1928	583,342	1953	1,206,266	1978	3,706,239

NOTE: Prior to July 1, 1964, some firms included tactical vehicles in factory sales. After July 1, 1964, all tactical vehicles are excluded.

SOURCE: Motor Vehicle Manufacturers Association of the United States, Incorporated.

Registrations and Vehicle Miles Traveled

Year	Registrations (Thousands)		Vehicle Miles Traveled (Millions)	
	Trucks	Buses[1]	Trucks	Buses
1905	1	*	*	*
1906	2	*	*	*
1907	3	*	*	*
1908	4	*	*	*
1909	6	*	*	*
1910	10	*	*	*
1911	21	*	*	*
1912	42	*	*	*
1913	68	*	*	*
1914	99	*	*	*
1915	159	*	*	*
1916	250	*	*	*
1917	391	*	*	*
1918	605	*	*	*
1919	898	*	*	*
1920	1,108	*	*	*
1921	1,282	*	*	*
1922	1,570	*	*	*
1923	1,849	*	*	*
1924	2,177	*	*	*
1925	2,570	18	*	*
1926	2,908	24	*	*
1927	3,082	28	*	*
1928	3,294	32	*	*
1929	3,550	34	*	*
1930	3,675	41	*	*
1931	3,656	42	*	*
1932	3,446	43	*	*
1933	3,457	45	*	*
1934	3,665	52	*	*
1935	3,919	59	*	*
1936	4,262	63	41,107	2,367
1937	4,509	83	44,151	2,492
1938	4,476	88	44,495	2,508
1939	4,691	92	47,219	2,554
1940	4,886	101	49,931	2,657
1941	5,150	120	54,953	2,820
1942	4,895	136	45,791	3,130
1943	4,727	152	41,658	3,365
1944	4,760	153	41,770	3,799
1945	5,076	162	45,941	3,834
1946	5,982	174	56,230	4,053

—Continued	Registrations (Thousands)		Vehicle Miles Traveled (Millions)	
Year	Trucks	Buses[1]	Trucks	Buses
1947	6,805	187	66,203	4,251
1948	7,534	197	74,009	4,283
1949	8,023	209	77,731	4,252
1950	8,599	224	90,552	4,081
1951	8,994	230	94,844	4,118
1952	9,199	240	99,060	4,334
1953	9,544	244	104,633	4,449
1954	9,789	248	104,559	4,252
1955	10,289	255	108,817	4,194
1956	10,679	259	112,245	4,135
1957	10,943	264	113,206	4,393
1958	11,136	270	115,470	4,310
1959[2]	11,635	265	123,154	4,348
1960	11,914	272	126,409	4,353
1961	12,261	280	128,582	4,396
1962	12,780	285	133,289	4,466
1963	13,360	298	155,569	4,483
1964	14,013	305	164,271	4,616
1965	14,786	314	171,436	4,782
1966	15,503	322	173,905	4,852
1967	16,169	338	182,456	4,894
1968	16,942	352	196,651	4,968
1969	17,874	364	206,680	5,037
1970	18,797	378	214,670	5 043
1971	19,871	397	227,037	5,097
1972	21,308	407	259,735	5,109
1973	23,244	425	267,147	4,960
1974	24,630	447	267,519	5,060
1975	25,781	462	274,454	5,148
1976	27,779	478	306,950	5,761
1977	29,562	492	329,465	5,887

*Not available.
1. Incomplete. Buses are not segregated from passenger cars or trucks in earlier years. Also included are municipally owned buses engaged in public transit. Due to a new method of counting buses in 1959, the bus data for earlier years are not strictly comparable.
2. Alaska and Hawaii data included since 1959.
SOURCE: United States Federal Highway Administration.

Special State and Federal Truck Taxes (Millions)

Year	State Registration Receipts	State Motor Carrier & Misc. Fees	State Motor Fuel Tax	Total State Taxes	Federal Excise Taxes	State and Federal Special Taxes
1977 est	$1,900	$750	$2,950	$5,600	$2,800	$8,400
1976	1,882	706	2,868	5,456	2,523	7,979
1975	1,529	591	2,699	4,819	2,351	7,170
1974	1,521	572	2,534	4,627	2,518	7,145
1973	1,385	572	2,606	4,563	2,533	7,096
1972	1,266	497	2,280	4,043	2,093	6,136
1971	1,172	430	2,066	3,668	2,299	5,967
1970	1,116	377	1,936	3,429	2,203	5,632
1969	1,021	354	1,770	3,145	2,109	5,254
1968	930	307	1,593	2,830	1,822	4,652
1967	878	268	1,453	2,599	1,682	4,281
1966	838	256	1,372	2,466	1,707	4,173
1965	779	240	1,277	2,296	1,548	3,844
1964	735	223	1,192	2,150	1,510	3,660
1963	679	206	1,106	1,991	1,400	3,391
1962	654	191	1,054	1,899	1,267	3,166
1961	628	175	969	1,772	1,124	2,896
1960	616	170	923	1,709	1,121	2,830
1955	470	124	717	1,311	555	1,866
1950	283	69	430	782	345	1,127
1945	129	40	243	412	187	599
1940	112	27	224	363	102	465
1935	84	16	135	235	57	292
1930	79	2	99	180	0	180

NOTE: Excludes tolls, special city and county taxes, and personal property taxes on trucks in operation, income and property taxes on trucking companies, terminals, etc.

SOURCE: 1930 to 1952 estimated by Motor Vehicle Manufacturers Association of the United States, Incorporated, from Bureau of Public Roads data and from other sources. 1953 to 1976 compiled by the American Trucking Association; 1977 estimated by Motor Vehicle Manufacturers Association of the United States, Incorporated.

Index

References to photographs are printed in boldface type

ISBN 0-472-06313-8

The amazing success story of America's trucking industry from its modest beginning in the early 1890s to its present-day impact. Each year's major milestones capture the industry's color, excitement, and accomplishments. Biographical sketches of the most notable pioneers present the human side of the industry. Facts and figures and a listing of hundreds of American trucks that have appeared over the years complement the industry's story. Nearly 200 photographs highlight the nine-decade evolution of the contemporary truck.

The trucking industry–meeting America's needs.

muma

Cover design by Don Ross